THE APPOINTED
TIME

A Commentary on
Daniel
with a Supplemental Narrative of the Olivet Discourse

ZACHARY D. BALL

authorHOUSE®

AuthorHouse™
1663 Liberty Drive
Bloomington, IN 47403
www.authorhouse.com
Phone: 833-262-8899

Published by AuthorHouse 04/10/2023

ISBN: 979-8-8230-0490-9 (sc)
ISBN: 979-8-8230-0488-6 (hc)
ISBN: 979-8-8230-0489-3 (e)

Library of Congress Control Number: 2023906286

Print information available on the last page.

CONTENTS

SPECIAL THANKS

From the depths of my heart come thanks for my wife. Her love and commitment, always being willing to listen to my orations and enduring my late nights of research come from a place of grace and understanding with which I cannot contend. Likewise, to my children who tolerated frequent breaks in the day so that I could write down a thought before forgetting it. I am indebted to "CAZ" who offered his time and expertise in composition to proofread the manuscript and his many other contributions. My thanks to Jordan and Jasmine who read the manuscript in its opening stages, for their initiation of eschatological interest, and for true friendship. To the family and friends who engaged my thoughts to intentionally provide feedback and resistance, thereby exhibiting the biblical mandate of sharpening one another – you have my appreciation.

THE APPOINTED TIME

As God's elect, Israel's purpose was to demonstrate what a true relationship with the Creator of the universe looked like. Indeed, they were the light to the world: "For you are a holy people to the Lord your God; the Lord your God has chosen you to be a people for His own possession out of all the peoples who are on the face of the earth" (Deut. 7:6). This was not because of their own merit, rather His own graciousness. Indeed, God extends faithfulness to countless generations and upholds His covenant oaths. When man sins, God desires to redeem. And He would, unhesitatingly, bestow blessings upon "those who love Him and keep His commandments" (Duet. 7:9). Such was His plan for beloved Israel, "I have loved you with an everlasting love; therefore I have drawn you with lovingkindness" (Jer. 31:3). When Israel first accepted God's proposal for their mutual affection (Exo. 19:8), so began a love story that would show the world Who He is.

The promised rewards for their obedience were incomparable: "He will love you and bless you and multiply you; He will also bless the fruit of your womb and the fruit of your ground, your grain and your new wine and your oil, the increase of your herd and the young of your flock...you shall be blessed above all peoples...the Lord will remove from you all sickness; and He will not put on you any of the harmful diseases...you shall consume all the peoples whom the Lord your God will deliver to you...you shall not be afraid of them" (Deut. 7:13-18). The assurance of abundant gifts continued in His incentive for their perpetual compliance: "...the Lord your God will set you high above the nations...these blessings will overtake you if you obey the Lord your God...blessed shall be the offspring of your body...the produce of your ground...your basket and kneading bowl...your barns and in all that you put your hand to...the Lord will establish you as a holy people to Himself if you keep His commandments...make you abound in prosperity...open for you His good storehouse, the heavens to give rain to your land...the Lord will make you head and not the tail ..." (Deut. 28:1-14).

What can compare to God's favor?

However, He pierced their soul with a double-edged sword: "But it shall come about, if you do not obey the Lord your God...that all these curses will overtake you...Cursed shall you be in the city...in the country...the offspring of your body...when you come in...when you go out...the Lord will send upon you curses, confusion, and rebuke, in all you undertake to do, until you are destroyed and until you perish quickly, on account of the evil of your deeds...the pestilence cling to you... consumption and with fever and with inflammation and with fiery heat and with sword and with blight" (Deut. 28:15-22). This does not match the guitar-playing hippie – envisioned by the contemporary church – that roamed Judea in the first century claiming to be God incarnate: "The Lord shall cause you to be defeated before your enemies...you will be an example of terror to all the kingdoms of the earth...your carcasses will be food to all birds of the sky...smite you with boils...with madness and with blindness...you shall only be oppressed and robbed continually... your sons and daughters shall be given to another people...they will go into captivity...all these curses shall come on you and pursue you and overtake you until you are destroyed..." (Deut. 28:25-45).

What can compare to God's wrath?

And what God can be called just if He breaks His promises? As it were, the pages of Old Testament (OT) literature attest to Israel's spiritual fornication, adultery, and disobedience that would follow their oath of obedience and fidelity. In the book of I Kings, the people worshipped false idols and committed heinous sins against God and one another, quickly exhibiting little faithfulness to the One who had rescued them from Egypt. So vile had their acts become that their covenant Author had identified them as a "harlot" (Is. 1:21). Their city was corrupted, filled with the wicked who were given to shameful lusts.

They abused the land, relentlessly taking from it without giving it rest as they were required to do (Lev. 25:2-4). And so, God would flatten His own vineyard: "I will remove its hedge and it will be consumed; I will break down its wall and it will become trampled ground. I will lay it waste; It will not be pruned or hoed, but briars and thorns will come up" (Is. 5:5-6). The inevitable result would be that His "people would go into exile for their lack of knowledge" (Is. 5:13). The land He had granted them after their deliverance from slavery and oppression – that they had tainted, neglected, and harmed – would be taken away.

So it was that God ordained King Nebuchadnezzar II and the mighty Babylonian Empire to conquer and take captive His cherished people, an exile promised to endure for seven decades as punishment for their iniquities. But this reprimand was not limited only to their excursion. The prophet Ezekiel prophesied that, just a few years into their captivity, Israel's pride and glory – the temple in Jerusalem – would also be abandoned by God's Spirit and, thus, ordained for destruction (Ezk. 10). Within twenty years of Babylon's initial incursion, the Jewish temple – the intersection of heaven and earth – was laid to ruin.

But while the book of Jeremiah had also prophesied these disastrous consequences, it assured that God promised to restore Israel (Jer. 29:11) and grant a blessed future because they were His chosen people. He would not abandon them, though the nation had tallied enough historical transgressions over the centuries to have received a bill of divorcement from Him (Jer. 3:8). When Babylon fell in 539 BC, God made good on His oath to remember Israel. Within a year the Jews had been decreed a return to Jerusalem through an edict by Cyrus the Great of the Persian Empire (538 BC) and, twenty-two years later, rebuilt the temple.

God had restored them.

Why, then, did a prophecy written by Malachi within the century following their return promise further trial that would culminate in a great and terrible day of the Lord for Israel?

Even after their experience in captivity, it took little time for Israel's regression into their previous wrongdoings. A laundry list summarizing the nation's perpetual lapses after their redemption litters the pages of Malachi – ingratitude, thoughtless complaints of the people, polluted offerings, corrupt priestly leadership, spiritual infidelity, all sufferings which continued to profane the name of the Lord. Malachi warned the leadership, "If you do not take it to heart to give honor to My name,' says the Lord of hosts, 'then I will send the curse upon you and I will curse your blessings, and indeed, I have cursed them already because you are not taking it to heart,'" (Mal. 2:2) and, "You have wearied the Lord with your words" (Mal. 2:17). Nineteenth century theologian J. Stuart Russell succinctly described, "The Book of Malachi is one long and terrible impeachment of the nation (Israel). The Lord Himself is the accuser, and sustains every charge against the guilty people by the clearest proof."[1] Such is the gravity of this prophecy against God's chosen people that the book introduces it as a burden (Mal. 1:1).

Similar behavior to that which had previously ruined Israel would, undoubtedly, result in similar consequences, especially with precedent for how God delivered their punishment. And Malachi entered into record that such a pattern, concluding in a great day of the Lord, would befall them: "'For behold the day is coming, burning like a furnace; and all the arrogant and every evildoer will be chaff; and the day that is coming will set them ablaze,' says the Lord of Hosts, 'so that it will leave them neither root nor branch. But for you who fear My name, the sun of righteousness will rise with healing in its wings; and you will go forth and skip about like calves from the stall. You will tread down the wicked, for they will be ashes under the soles of your feet on the day which I am preparing,' says the Lord of Hosts. 'Remember the Law of Moses, My servant, even the statutes and ordinances which I commanded him in Horeb for all Israel'" (Mal. 4:1-4). This is a clear forecast of total destruction against apostate Israel, signified by the axiomatic "day of the Lord," a Hebrew phrase consistently promised as an event in which God executed long-suffering vengeance and justice through judgment upon a rebellious people. But despite the severity of this rebuke, His remnant would be simultaneously redeemed. This was the promise of consummation for Israel.

Malachi was the final word from the Lord prior to the Gospel of Matthew in biblical chronology. Its prediction set into motion a 400-year period between the Testaments when Israel suffered no more prophecy. It was a time of unsettled waiting for a consummation when

---

[1] J. Stuart Russell, *The Parousia*, (Pantianos Classics, 1878), p. 5.

the righteous would shine like the sun and the wicked would be trampled underfoot. An event of such peril that would bring Israel to its knees, yet usher in a new age in which the righteous elect would rule over the nations with the long-awaited Messiah. The arrival of the great day of judgment for Israel would be the event to bring salvation and judgment ordained and executed by the Most High: "He will sit as a smelter and purifier of silver, and He will purify the sons of Levi and refine them like gold and silver, so that they may present to the Lord offerings in righteousness...then I will draw near to you for judgment; and I will be a swift witness against the sorcerers and against the adulterers and against those who swear falsely...from the days of your fathers you have turned aside from My statutes and have not kept them" (Mal. 3:3-7).

To herald this event's imminence, Malachi predicted that the Lord would send a purposeful spirit to prepare Israel's hearts amid a plea for repentance: "Behold, I am going to send My messenger, and he will clear the way before Me...I am going to send you Elijah the prophet before the coming of the great and terrible day of the Lord" (Mal. 3:1, 4:5). This messenger to "prepare the way" is linked to the prophetic Isaiah who foretold that "a voice is calling, 'clear the way for the Lord in the wilderness; make smooth in the desert a highway for our God'" (Is. 40:3).

After this courier of God's warning clears the path, Malachi warns, "'The Lord, whom you seek, will suddenly come to His temple; and the messenger of the covenant, in whom you delight, behold He is coming,' says the Lord of hosts, 'But who can endure the day of His coming? And who can stand when He appears'" (Mal. 3:2), an ominous foreshadow immediately paralleling Revelation 6:17, "For the great day of their wrath has come, and who is able to stand?" The Lord – the messenger of the Covenant – would unexpectedly come to His temple to enshrine the righteous during a time of fierce judgment on His adversaries, a coming against which they would have no hope of opposing.

Israelites familiar with the scriptures, who appreciated the prophecy's sternness, should have been wise to the signs of such an advent when, four centuries later, John the Baptist began incessantly pleading for Israel's repentance (Matt. 3). This wild nomad cared little when the Pharisees mocked his efforts as he confronted their sin without care for reproof. After extensive and painstaking research, Luke confirmed that an angel had promised John's father, Zacharias, that he "will go as a forerunner before Him in the spirit and power of Elijah to turn the hearts of their fathers back to the children" (Luke 1:17). Matthew recorded the confirmation of Isaiah's forecast (Matt. 3:3) when the Lord Jesus, Himself gave praise and affirmation of John's ministry, while the Baptist sat in prison, confirming "for all the prophets and the law prophesied until John. And if you are willing to accept it, he is Elijah who is to come" (Matt. 11:14). Later when the disciples called for knowledge of Elijah's arrival, as Malachi had foretold, Jesus reminded them that "Elijah already came and [the scribes] did not recognize him'…then the disciples understood that He had spoken to them about John the Baptist" (Matt 17:12-13).

This identity is further expounded by Mark's correlation of John's physical appearance – camel's hair with a leather belt around his waist – with the OT description of Elijah as being a "hairy man with a leather girdle bound about his loins" (II Kings 1:8). If John the Baptist had the spirit of Elijah prophesied in Malachi, then Israel's "day of the Lord" was not far behind. So, too, was the "messenger of the covenant" who would administer Malachi's prophesied harvest. Indeed, God's wrath was directed against His chosen people, and John would bring a message that urged their repentance before the punishment took full effect.

The Baptist wasted little time manifesting his purpose. To the Pharisees he shouted, "You brood of vipers, who warned you to flee from the wrath to come?" (Matt. 3:7, Luke 3:7), cautioning them that "the axe is already laid at the root of the trees" (Matt. 3:10), and the One to come after him would carry judgment: "His winnowing fork is in His hand, and He will thoroughly clear His threshing floor, and He will gather His wheat into the barn, but He will burn up the chaff with unquenchable fire" (Matt. 3:12).

Christian, you know to whom John was speaking – apostate Israel. And you know the man about whom he was speaking – Jesus the Messiah. As J. Stuart Russell summarized, "These warnings of John the Baptist are not vague and indefinite exhortations to repentance, addressed to men in all ages, which they are sometimes assumed to be; they are urgent, burning words, having a specific and present bearing upon the then existing generation, the living men to whom he brought the message of God. The Jewish nation was now upon its last trial."[2]

The One who came after him, who John promised would carry the "winnowing fork" for reaping would, likewise, execute a public ministry devoted to restoring the Jews to their place with God to save them from what was destined to come upon them. Predictably, Jesus pronounced that He "was sent only to the house of Israel" (Matt 15:24) and commanded that His disciples "not go in the way of the Gentiles, and do not enter any city of the Samaritans; but rather go to the lost sheep of the house of Israel" (Matt. 10:5-6). Indeed, in all regards, the Jews held priority over the Gentiles (John 4:22, Rom. 3:1-2, 9:5) and even Paul, God's eventual ambassador to the Gentiles, emphasized the Jews' precedence in that "it was necessary that the Word of God be spoken to [them] first" (Acts 13:46) before their judgment arrived.

After 3½ years of ministry, at the week of His death, Jesus came to the temple one final time. When He arrived, "He saw the city and wept over it, saying 'if you had known in this day, even you, the things which make for peace! But now they have been hidden from your eyes. For the days will come upon you when your enemies will throw up a barricade against you, and surround you and hem you in on every side, and they will level you to the ground and your children within you, and they will not leave one stone upon another, because you did not recognize the time of your visitations'" (Luke 19:41-44). He articulated fierce judgment against the nation, physically removing the wicked from the temple grounds and issuing parables that promised destruction because of their treachery, after which he summarized the consequences: "Upon you may fall all the guilt of all the righteous blood of righteous Abel to the blood of Zechariah, the son of Berechiah whom you murdered between the temple and the alter. Truly I say to you, all these things will come upon this generation" (Matt. 23:35-36).

And putting God's simultaneous mercy on full display, Jesus offered them one final prophecy to save them from what was coming. In what is known as the Olivet Discourse (Matt. 24, Mark 13, Luke 21), Jesus told His disciples that the temple would again be destroyed, this time it would be at the hands of the Romans. When these armies arrived at

---

[2] Russell, *The Parousia*, p. 8.

the gates of Jerusalem, it would signal that the time of judgment was upon the nation (Matt. 24:15, Luke 21:20). This was the warning for God's remnant to escape the city and not give one look back because the calamity to take place would produce a critically defining moment in Jewish history – and they need not waste a moment in avoiding it. As it were, countless citizens were murdered, hundreds of thousands more taken into captivity, the city toppled, temple destroyed, and the entire Jewish institution collapsed. This event would be so profound that it would shake the heavens. And Jesus said that this affair was an appointed time, confirming it as the "days of vengeance, so that all things which are written will be fulfilled" (Luke 21:22).

But, things written where? About 600 years before, an extensive OT prophecy composed by a Jewish sage had been given for Israel that also forecasted this hope and destruction – salvation and judgment. But the angel who gave it had ordered it sealed because the narrative described would transpire after several centuries, culminating in some divinely inspired event that required concealment until the appointed time. By shutting it, the angel had no more to say, and until that time there would be nothing more to contribute. The book could suffer only speculation from the mouths of scribes and priests as they awaited its manifestation.

From the Mount of Olives, days before His death, Jesus suddenly began calling upon direct references from this prophecy – that had been ordered closed – to illustrate the temple's destruction soon to take place: the "abomination of desolation" (Matt. 24:15) that would be responsible for destroying the city, the "great tribulation" (Matt. 24:21) upon the people that would fulfill the promised curses of Old Covenant neglect, and the "Son of Man coming on the clouds" (Matthew 24:30) that would bring judgment and usher in the promised kingdom. What was He doing? In the same manner that Jesus was the Lamb Who could open the seals of Revelation (5:2-9), so He must have been the One to reveal this OT prophecy's fulfillment because it could not be endured but at its appointed time – which must have arrived. Assuredly, within that generation – forty years after Jesus delivered the prophecy – Jerusalem was demolished.

What was this source from which the Olivet Discourse found its legs? The book of Daniel.

Jesus used Daniel's prophecies to illuminate the destruction of Jerusalem because the narrative that had been told by the prophet's sixth century revelation described the culmination of Israel's future redemption and judgment. The remnant would finally find rest, but all that represented the Jewish institution, that which established their unique identity, would be thrown down. The old temple would be destroyed to make way for the new. The Old Jerusalem would be swapped with the New Jerusalem. The Old Covenant power of the Holy people about which Daniel had forewarned (Dan. 12:7) would be shattered in their rejection of the Redeemer to pave the way for the New Covenant power – the gospel of God's salvation to everyone who believes (Rom. 1:16). It changed everything.

Daniel is not a book concerned with detailing events surrounding the trials of the twenty-first century Christian church. But because the church has become obsessed with finding answers to its own existence as it wades through a seemingly irredeemable world, it reads the Bible from the lens of its own heritage. This is a major interpretive weakness when attempting to understand a primarily Jewish narrative. Because Christians want to know how the human story ends with their promised glorification, evangelical scholars have pieced together an eschatological chronicle that outlines how the church – God's contemporary spiritual 1% - will finally be rid of all this wickedness that surrounds them.

Thus, they have assembled a futurist tale of rapture, tribulation, Antichrist, Armageddon – even the computer chips with the moniker "666" that will be embedded into our bodies so that citizens can buy and sell – that is constructed from an amalgamation of random bible verses, which have been "raptured" from their context, in Daniel, Joel, Ezekiel, Isaiah, Hosea, Zechariah, Jeremiah, Micah, the Gospels, Paul's letters to the Thessalonians, Revelation, and Peter's epistles. Never mind that such a piecemeal story of the end of the world is placed in juxtaposition with other biblical truths such as the notion that the kingdom that was prophesied by Daniel and was been established by God in the first century – in which we currently exist – has no end (Dan. 2:44, 7:27).

It is difficult for the average Christian to accept that the kingdom of God is already present, because the world is still full of sin. They read the daily headlines and see little except for widespread iniquity.

They see Christians as the target of cultural oppression and believe that their saving grace must be that God will extract them. They know that evil cannot be present in God's sanctuary and wonder how this could, possibly, be the promised kingdom. But that is exactly the problem – they keep looking at the world. Indeed, preaching with God's Word in one hand and the morning newspaper in the other is risky business.

The evangelical church presently waits for their physical Messiah to come destroy her enemies and establish an earthly, millennial kingdom (Rev. 20). Does that sound familiar? It should, because that is exactly what the first century Pharisees expected, too. But Jesus rebuked such a mindset. Recall His clarification that "the kingdom of God is not coming with signs to be observed, nor will they say, 'Look, here it is!' or 'There it is!' (Luke 17:20-21). Indeed, He hoped that they would understand that "My kingdom is not of this world. If My kingdom were of this world, then My servants would be fighting so that I would not be handed over to the Jews; but as it is, My kingdom is not of this realm" (John 18:36). Instead, Paul affirmed, we should "look not at the things which are seen, but at the things which are not seen; for the things which are seen are temporal, but the things which are not seen are eternal" (II Corinthians 4:17-18).

What you are about to engage is a study of Daniel that will demonstrate the book's past fulfillment of prophesied events leading up to the destruction of Jerusalem in AD 70; an event at which the future of the Jewish and Christian faiths – that of the entire world – was forever altered. It tells the account of God's plans for Israel up to their appointed time of reckoning when He would bring everything down to establish a new order. This was a campaign that would produce the chance for true redemption as had been promised, but if refused, would lead to irrevocable consequences.

One scholar notes that even though God destroyed Jerusalem, "annihilating every last vestige of the Old Covenant world-order and system of worship, Israel endures. The Covenant promises to Abraham, Isaac, and Jacob are not jeopardized in the slightest. In fact, the outpouring of God's wrath in the destruction of Jerusalem will only serve to reveal the true Israel in greater glory than ever before. Jerusalem is sacked and burned, its inhabitants killed and scattered; but Israel – all of her people, in all of her tribes – is sealed and saved."[3]

While this project is not devoted to a meticulous deconstruction of futurist eschatology, a significant level of dismantling is inevitable since much of its foundation is derived from Daniel. The objective is to demonstrate that because Daniel was written by a Jew, for the Jews, and about the Jews, its primary message of salvation and judgment found fulfillment in the events of Jewish history. And through Israel "all the nations of the earth shall be blessed." After the book's truth had been ordered sealed, a controversial first-century Jewish carpenter opened it up, six centuries later, when promising judgment upon the people in His generation.

The destruction of Jerusalem was the appointed time of Daniel.

The book is past to us; but was future to those readers. It is complex, trying, and controversial. It is underrated. It is repetitive. It is ambiguous, yet extremely targeted. It is figurative and literal. It is fluid with breaks. It will wear the Bible student down.

This should be fun.

---

[3] David Chilton, *The Days of Vengeance*, (Dallas: Dominion Press, [1987] 2011), p. 207.

THE BOOK OF DANIEL

For the evangelical Christian, there is little question about the authenticity and infallibility of scriptural canon. To such a church congregant, all information presented within the 66-book binding, as established by the early fourth-century Church Council in Nicaea, is without error. Indeed, protestant and catholic denominations must believe in the Bible's inerrancy, for if even one element is found to be incorrect, its credibility as the answer to our most burning questions about human existence, purpose, and life after death are effectively dismantled. While the belief in some form of divine inspiration holds true for most adherents that comprise the Body of Christ, the world of academic scholars, with advanced degrees in theology and ancient languages, typically draw more diverse conclusions about so-called biblical truth. This is not always based on natural skepticism, rather the linguistic or contextual characteristics found within the text itself. Take, for example, the sought-after narrative of the world's most perceived representative of evil – the Devil. Dating back to the first century, much of the evangelical church has looked to advance their understanding of God's foremost adversary by searching for biblical passages that tell his story.

As the bible student begins searching for scriptural clues, there is an important element for consideration when examining the concept of the biblical figure known as "Satan." How did the Jews understand him? As antithetical as it might sound to traditional Christian theology regarding the cosmic battle between good and evil, the Hebrew Bible portrayed "Satan as not necessarily evil, much less opposed to God. On the contrary...as one of God's obedient servants."[4] In Hebrew literature, the Satan character was a faithful employee who served as a member of God's divine counsel (Psalm 82) with the unique responsibility of roaming the Earth (Job 1:7) to help maintain order as the prosecutor of men (Zech. 3:1). His role is that of an "adversary" who "tests human virtue by disrupting normal life through physical ailments, betrayal of friends, floods or drought."[5]

In Jewish theology Satan served God by placing stumbling blocks in front of people that were intended to produce fruits of dependence and loyalty to Yahweh, in that by overcoming such adversity they would draw closer to Him and exhibit the devotion of a true follower. The rabbis taught that Satan's true resolve in torturing Job, for example, was not to turn him away from God, but to weed out false piety, thereby proving Job's righteousness and fidelity to Him. In their own way, Jews view Satan as a blessing to creation rather than a curse, because his purpose is to implement trials that should improve the human relationship with God, not tear it down. Such a concept should not be foreign to the Christian believer, as James reminded his first-century readers to "consider it joy, my brethren, when you encounter various trials, knowing that the testing of your faith produces endurance" (James 1:2-3).

During His first-century ministry, Jesus brought to life the battle between spiritual forces through His exorcisms and healings, which contrasted the kingdom of heaven with that of the world. As the Jewish leaders progressively mocked Him in these circumstances, He regularly and unapologetically identified his religious opponents with the Satan character, even labeling them as children "of their father, the devil" (John 8:44). After Jesus' death, the developing church started to associate Satan exclusively with the apostate Jewish people who had killed their Savior. Such an evil force that would slay the Redeemer of mankind must be isolated and, as Elaine Pagels notes, "in the process, they turned this rather unpleasant angel into a far grander – and far

---

[4] Elaine Pagels, *The Origin of Satan*, (New York: Vintage Book (Random House), [1995], 1996), p. 39.

[5] Judith Lee, "Lucifer a Fantastic Figure," *Journal of the Fantastic in Arts*, Vol. 8, no. 2 (30), Special Issue: Fantasy and The Bible (1997), pp. 218-234. p. 221.

more malevolent – figure…[God's] enemy, even His rival."[6] As the Christian dispositions began slowly separating from their Jewish roots, especially with the grafting of non-Jews into the spiritual fold, the demonization of those outside the assembled church became highly pronounced. As one scholar has noted, it can, thus, be easily maintained that "devils, hell, and the end of the world are New Testament rather than Old Testament realities."[7]

The church has since sought scriptural connections with its growing perception of the struggle between heaven and hell that would provide clarity on the character of this foe who now defines the evangelical theology of sin and transgression. One such section Christian apologists fell upon is found in Isaiah: "How you have fallen from heaven, O star of the morning, son of the dawn! You have been cut down to the earth, you who have weakened the nations! But you said in your heart, "I will ascend to heaven; I will raise my throne above the stars of God, And I will sit on the mount of assembly in the recesses of the north; I will ascend above the heights of the clouds; I will make myself like the Most High'" (Is. 14:12-14). Today the common fundamentalist understanding is that Isaiah was describing the root of Satan's condition from eternity past when, in an instance of pride and reckless ambition, he attempted to supplant God as sovereign over all things. Because of his rebellion, he was cast down from heaven to represent the world's wickedness and presently stands in total opposition to God's plans for redeeming the human race within his perpetual craving for universal dominion.

A closer look at context is most significant for understanding this OT passage, which, dare it be said, reasonably demonstrates that such an interpretation is precarious at best. It is also important to recognize that because Jewish heritage did not perceive Satan in the same way as the modern church this explanation of Isaiah's passage would have been abhorrent to the Rabbis. In Isaiah's previous passage (13), the prophet predicted the fall of Babylon because of their national worship of false gods. Then God had instructed him to "take up this taunt (Hebrew: "mashal") against the king of Babylon" (Is. 14:4). The Hebrew term

---

[6] Pagels, *The Origin of Satan*, p. 47.

[7] James Barr, *Old and New in Interpretation: A Study of the Two Testaments*, (London: SCM, 1966), p. 149.

"mashal" is properly understood as a parable, which used allegory to draw a comparison. Isaiah was, thus, charged to use figurative contrast to mock the Babylonian ruler for thinking that his position as sovereign over the greatest empire in the world had elevated him to some position of divine status. In doing so, he used Hebrew terms for "morning star" and "son of dawn" – descriptive references to the false gods of ancient pagan civilizations – to draw a sarcastic comparison about his self-perceived status.

According to OT scholar Dr. Michael Heiser, "morning star, 'son of dawn,' is an English rendering of the Hebrew "Helel ben Shahar" which literally means 'shining one, son of the dawn....' 'Morning stars' were the visible bright stars seen on the horizon as the sun rose. Astronomers, ancient and modern, knew another celestial object that behaved the same way; an object so bright, it could still be seen as the sun rose. That object was Venus. And so, Venus, although a planet, became known to the ancients as the bright morning star."[8] The Assyrians believed Venus to be "especially under the rule of the goddess Ishtar, or Istar, with whom she is often identified, the sixth month *Elul* being dedicated to her. Ishtar, called Nana by the Babylonians, was their 'queen of love and beauty.'"[9]

Babylonian tablets even left inscriptions that detailed the ancient view, which was that the position or appearance of Venus in the sky could determine everything from crop production to the stately positions of kings.[10] The term for "morning star," thus, had deep roots in ancient astrology and literature that figuratively tied together the unlimited vastness of the cosmos under the direction of the divine with the supreme power of rulers over the nations of the Earth. The term was simply a metaphorical description of earthly kings. The historical context of Isaiah's passage suggests that the prophet used this terminology sarcastically to liken the king to such deities, confirming

---

[8] Dr. Michael S. Heiser, *The Unseen Realm*, narrated by Gordon Greenhill, Audible, 2015. Audiobook.

[9] Irene B. Toye Warner, "Ancient History and Worship of the Planet Venus." *Popular Astronomy*, Vol. 17, p 80-84. p. 80.

[10] Joseph Offord, "The Deity of the Crescent Venus in Ancient Western Asia." *Journal of the Royal Asiatic Society of Great Britain and Ireland*, Cambridge University Press. Apr., 1915, pp. 197-203. 197.

that despite his arrogant, idolatrous self-worship, he was not divine, but would be cast into Hades as other men for the same offense.

When the early church father St. Jerome Hieronymus translated the Greek Bible into Latin (AD 382), he used the word "Lucifer," which meant "light-bearer," to correspond with the Hebrew term for "morning star." Over time, the church connected passages such as Paul's accusation that "Satan disguises himself as an angel of light" (II Cor. 11:14) or Jesus' own description that Satan fell "from heaven like lightning" (Luke 10:18) and established a tale of the Devil's path to destruction. In the evangelical church's joining of scriptures that depicted a predominant representation of the antithetical embodiment of all that is good, they understand Isaiah's passage to be describing how God's nemesis got his start, borne out of man's greatest weakness – pride.

It is well established, however, among language experts that "Lucifer" is not an individual pronoun, but a mere descriptor. Consider, also, that the New Testament (NT) references to the "morning star" are eagerly classified by the church as referring to Jesus. The apostle Peter stated, "We have the prophetic word made more sure, to which you do well to pay attention as a lamp shining in a dark place, until the day dawns and the morning star arises in your hearts" (II Peter 1:19), while John's Revelation explicitly notes that Jesus claimed to be "the descendant of David, the bright morning star" (Rev. 22:16). The context supports Jesus as the subject in these verses, while the Satan figure has been inserted into the passage in Isaiah.

Based on the contextual understanding of the prophet's message, it seems most reasonable to assume that Isaiah 14 is not chronicling Satan's personal history; rather it is narrating the historical downfall of Babylon and its king because of the people's idolatry.

This is merely one example of how a traditional biblical interpretation, based on the unique linguistic tendencies of translators, has become responsible for major, yet uncertain, foundations of evangelical doctrine. And when questions are posed that challenge such established assumptions, the evangelical response is frequently a knee-jerk accusation of heresy against the inquisitor. However, biblical criticism should not be unexpected, especially as anthropologists continue to uncover archaeological artifacts that produce an ever-changing analysis of previously attested conclusions. Scholars do their best to disseminate data in hopes of illuminating biblical understanding for the average person because they know an intensive scriptural examination requires expertise in numerous areas of research. Most people, including this author, lack even a cursory knowledge of ancient Hebrew and Greek, the study of which many scholars dedicate an entire lifetime.

Since many Bible translations continue to adapt to cultural shifts, bringing new perspectives and changing ideas, the meanings of many terms are suffering alterations to accommodate a contemporary understanding. A probing language analysis helps the dedicated Bible student develop a sound grasp of any biblical author's intent and message, thereby revealing the book's truth. In other words, one cannot simply read any translation and assume that all comprehension has been achieved; it requires a habit of study. Unfortunately, however, only 11% of Americans even open their Bible on a daily basis. The servant of the God of Israel shows love to Him through obedience (John 14:15, I John 1:6, Luke 11:28); but what does it mean to obey? If you neglect scripture; you might never know.

Peter also reminded the believer of the importance of "always being ready to make a defense to everyone who asks you to give an account for the hope that is in you, yet with gentleness and reverence" (I Peter 3:15). A thorough examination of God's Word will solidify one's spiritual foundation, especially when opposing arguments are presented that seem to disassemble the Bible's credibility. Indeed, it is easy for the church to recall Paul's explication to Timothy that "all scripture is inspired by God and profitable for teaching, for reproof, for correction, for training in righteousness" (II Tim. 3:16).

But often in the minds of evangelicals, the notion of divine inspiration is equivalent to textual inerrancy since the sovereign God who guided the hands of the writers is incapable of error. And yet, there is a stark reality facing the Christian student regarding biblical canon: there are somewhere between 300,000 and 400,000 variances between all available New Testament manuscripts preserved from antiquity. What does that mean? There is an enormous number of differences in the ancient biblical documents that modern translators use to present you with the Bible that you read, today. This cannot be denied.

Archaeologists have discovered nearly 6,000 preserved NT manuscripts with between 120-130 copies from the first three centuries after Jesus' death. This means that some of these documents that circulated in the ancient world are the closest to the original gospels that humans have uncovered. With these artifacts in hand, scholars and historians employ a process called textual criticism, a method that involves translating and cataloguing them to determine both their evolution and a path back to the autograph (original copy). For example, the oldest manuscript found of John's Gospel is a fragment (known as P52) recovered from the early second century AD. This is within decades of John's autograph. Doing so allows them to cross reference each manuscript to verify its authenticity through a meticulous analysis of textual discrepancies to filter dependable data from its context and language. The reliability of any historical document from antiquity is ascertained by comparing and contrasting these ancient texts.

Within this sound method of analysis, however, skeptics pose the inevitable question of whether anyone can be truly confident in the credibility of biblical texts with the existence of so many variants. Could the realization of so many inconsistencies between ancient manuscripts create such a doubt of the Bible's infallibility that someone previously solid in the faith could fall out of belief? One of the most respected NT scholars in the world has suffered such internal frustrations. A renowned professor at the University of North Carolina, Bart Ehrman, was a Christian in his youth who eventually shifted to agnosticism. He admits that during his more religious days at seminary, the intensive study of ancient languages introduced him to unsettling concepts about the Bible's dictation history, after which he "started realizing that my earlier belief that the Bible was without any mistakes in it was just wrong. There are mistakes....It changed my understanding of the Bible."[11]

His discovery ignited a personal struggle to qualify the NT as reliable for historical information and produced a belief that the variations found over centuries of transcribing and translating permanently affects our ability to ascertain what the original authors truly wrote. Mistakes upon

---

[11] Premier Unbelievable?, "Peter J. Williams and Bart Ehrman – The Story of Jesus: Are the Gospels Historically Reliable?" *YouTube*, Uploaded October 25, 2019, https://youtu.be/ZuZPPGvF_2I.

mistakes were committed as the centuries passed which is especially true, he postulates, since copying texts occurred among early groups who were not highly educated or trained, a fact borne out in that at least 90% of ancient populations were probably illiterate. How can we know what the original text stated? According to Ehrman – we cannot.

However, such wealth of manuscripts is a good thing. Indeed, Christian scholars consider themselves spoiled with such an accumulation of documentation, says Daniel Wallace, Executive Director at the Center for the Study of New Testament Manuscripts, Professor at Dallas Theological Seminary, and one of world's foremost and trusted textual scholars. He has confidently asserted that the NT has more manuscripts from the first three centuries than most authors of antiquity have after 2,000 years, making it "far and away, the best attested work of the ancient world."[12] And discovering excessive variants is simply part of the process since the number of manuscripts at our fingertips will inevitably uncover a high number of realized alterations; the more one must look through, the more one will find.

Additionally, NT experts of both a secular and apologist orientation concede that 99% of these variances are entirely insignificant, comprised of spelling mistakes, questionable grammar, punctuation differences, and numerous inflections in the Greek language subject to fallible interpretation. Professor Wallace points out, for example, that one can use the phrase "Jesus loves Paul," hundreds of different ways in Greek while being translated one way in English. And unfortunately, each translation of the phrase counts as a single variant, inflating the overall number. In other words, scribes committed countless literary errors with such little significance that the theological implications of the faith were never compromised.

Despite this optimism, there are more significant variances than grammatical errors that trouble critics and thus require reconciliation. For example, Mark 16 concludes with the description of how Jesus conferred supernatural abilities to His disciples for casting out demons, handling snakes, speaking in new tongues, and drinking poison as they began their evangelistic commission. This section has helped

---

[12] Bart D. Ehrman, "Ehrman vs Wallace - Can We Trust the Text of the NT?" *YouTube*, Uploaded February 3, 2020, https://youtu.be/WRHjZCKRlu4.

formulate the cornerstone of some Pentecostal church practices where the passage is interpreted as a list of signs and wonders that believers must perform to demonstrate their faith. While this is not only an incorrect understanding of Jesus' purported instruction, scholars have introduced a more interesting component to Mark's conclusion – verses 9-20 were not present in the earliest and what are considered to be the best ancient manuscripts that have been unearthed of this Gospel.

This has led some to question whether it should even be considered scriptural canon, for if this section was absent in the earliest documents, how does one know when it was officially added? Conversely, if it was present in the original, when and why would it have been removed from copies between centuries up to the assembly of biblical canon? Other Gospel passages present similar issues in modern translations, leading scholars to raise questions as they wrestle with how such inconsistencies can synchronize with the notion of divine inspiration.

This is but an example of the intellectual battles that rage in the halls of academe surrounding every facet of the Bible's trustworthiness; a war that will not end until the truth is revealed to each person in God's time. So it should not be surprising that nearly all corners of scripture will receive similarly relentless critical examination. Few suffer as much scholarly criticism as the book of Daniel, primarily because of its symbolic and ambiguous complexities. Fortunately, Daniel's primary critiques focus little on textual variances between the manuscripts. However, the internal information provided within the book challenges scholars because it is saturated with apocalyptic tones and predictive prophecy offering dates and characters that require much work to identify, at times offering vague estimates, while at others presenting an astoundingly accurate historical narrative. And as liberal scholars desire to undermine the Bible's credibility, such a job of proving its unreliability, indeed, rests on their shoulders.

The book was written from a first-person perspective describing events during the dominion of the Babylonian Empire under the reign of King Nebuchadnezzar II which extended from his appointment in 605 BC until his death in 562 BC. The setting, therefore, is sixth-century Babylon, composed by a Jewish exile named Daniel, proclaimed by the book to be in the service of Nebuchadnezzar's court writing about the future of Israel. Such an opinion is shared by both Jewish and Christian scholarship. Written at an early date, around 535 BC, certainly means that if its forecasted future events – described in the book as the subsequent 500 years of world history – came true, it would lend nearly incontestable proof of the Bible's divine authorship. This is something that modern intelligentsia refuses to concede.

As such, liberal scholars have determined that the theological power of predictive prophecy must be weakened. Indeed, the more prophecies that come true, the more it proves the Bible's reliability. Therefore, the most effective method for compromising Daniel's credibility would be to push the date of composition forward. If it was written much later, then his prophecies would be considered ex eventu, that is, written after the fact, thereby casting doubt that the book gave any prophecies at all. Efforts have thus been conducted in contemporary circles of critical scholarship to revive such a narrative that was suggested by the ancient Roman philosopher, Porphyry of Tyre (AD 234-305), who first questioned Daniel's authenticity. In his ancient and famous work "Against the Christians," he asserted that the book of Daniel was composed in the mid-second century BC, around 165, nearly 400 years following the original mid-sixth century dating that had traditionally been accepted.

During that time in history (167-164 BC), Israel had experienced the invasion of Greek King Antiochus Epiphanes IV and his contemptable desecration of the temple in Jerusalem. Widely understood to be one of the greatest villains in Jewish history, Antiochus' oppression and introduction of Hellenistic (Greek) influence onto Jewish culture was fiercely repelled by a group of Jewish patriots called the Maccabees. The book of Daniel records a nearly play-by-play of many of these Periodic details in Chapter 11. This transformed Porphyry's skepticism about prophecy into full-blown distrust, surmising that the only possibility for such an accurate description was for the book to have been written after the events took place. Modern scholars have seized on such a theory and expanded its concept in the contemporary renaissance against religious piety. The prevailing assumption, then, has become that the book of Daniel was primarily fiction, concocted by a Jewish rebel, writing under a pseudonym with the intent of encouraging the Jewish people in the midst of second-century Greek oppression. The remaining implication of this illusory book would be that its primary character – and "author" – was also imaginary. For these scholars, Daniel may never have existed. All of this was based on a single ancient Roman historian's doubt that prophecy is at all possible.

This view stands as today's scholarly consensus. While Wikipedia is not a credible historical source, it has become the most convenient content provider for most people seeking quick information. As such it is telling to read Wikipedia's description of the book of Daniel. The first line of the article wastes no time in declaring the book to be "a second-century BC biblical apocalypse with a sixth-century BC setting."[13] In the section dedicated to analyzing its composition, the webpage states that "it is generally accepted that Daniel originated as a collection of Aramaic court tales later expanded by the Hebrew revelations. The court tales may have originally circulated independently, but the edited collection was probably composed in the third or early second century BC." Later in the section, "It is one of a large number of Jewish apocalypses, all of them pseudonymous [under an alias]. The stories of the first half are legendary in origin, and the visions of the second the product of anonymous authors in the Maccabean period (second century BC)."

In Wikipedia's system of rapid reference, the book is described as having been written in the mid-second century by someone using a fake name and writing fictitious stories based on mere legend. The idea of later dating has gained such enormous traction that even some corners of Christian scholarship have accepted it as truth. Christian scholars, though, have a much greater problem in accepting this hypothesis than those in secular circles. The reason for this will be clarified later.

There is, however, convincing evidence to demonstrate that Daniel was written in the sixth century – as orthodoxy avows. In 1947-48, a number of ancient documents were discovered in a group of caves in Qumran, an archaeological site in the West Bank near the northwestern shore of the Dead Sea. No fewer than eight manuscripts of Daniel were uncovered among the documents and were fully authenticated. Scholars

---

[13] "Book of Daniel." "Wikipedia," Last updated December 2, 2022. https://en.wikipedia.org/Book_of_Daniel.

have come to an accord that these manuscripts are dated to around 125 BC. If true, then the difference between the book's purported composition (165 BC) and these early manuscripts is only forty years. This generates a legitimate question about the second century scribe's ability to create, multiply and canonize the book of Daniel in such a condensed timeframe. According to Gerhard Hasel, Professor of Old Testament and Biblical Theology, this would have been nearly impossible:

> It seems difficult to believe that such a significant number of Daniel manuscripts would have been preserved in a single desert community, if the book had really been produced at so late a date. The large number of manuscripts can be much better explained if we conclude that the book of Daniel had a much earlier origin.... Scholars who theorize that the book of Daniel wasn't written until the Maccabean crisis (around 165 BC) are being compelled to admit that 4QDane [ca. 125 BC] come from 'only a half century later than the composition of the book of Daniel.' This means that these scholars will now have to demonstrate that a mere forty or fifty years was sufficient time for all the editorial and other processes needed – according to their traditio-historical and redaction-critical theories – for the book to be developed into its present form and become canonical![14]

Hasel postulates that such a large number of manuscripts having been preserved in one place better proves the likelihood of sixth-century dating than second-century as such a late date would make such exponential production unlikely. The entire process for canonizing the book of Daniel – including vetting, organizing, consecrating, and circulating – would simply not have been feasible in just forty years of antiquity. And the question of whether the book of Daniel had been canonized can be answered by its preservation among other manuscripts

---

[14] Gerhard F. Hasel, "The Book of Daniel Confirmed by the Dead Sea Scrolls." *Journal of the Adventist Theological Society*: Vol. 1, no. 2, art. 4., 1990. p. 40-41.

found in the same collection of Dead Sea Scrolls, such as Deuteronomy, Kings, and Isaiah, which were unquestionably holy Jewish texts. In addition, Hasel concluded that the high number of manuscripts, which exceeded that of the other books in this archaeological find, indicates that the book must have been "a favorite among the Qumran covenanters."[15]

Internal evidence also demonstrates the book's early dating in the sixth-century BC. Most notably, Daniel provided unique and exclusive historical details only confirmed through later, contemporary archaeological discoveries. For example, Babylon had been in existence prior to King Nebuchadnezzar (605 BC); however, Daniel recorded Nebuchadnezzar's belief that he was solely responsible for its growth as a world empire, as he chronicled the king's declaration, "Is this not Babylon the great, which I myself have built as a royal residence by the might of my power and for the glory of my majesty?" (Dan. 4:30). According to Daniel, Nebuchadnezzar's pride regarding Babylon's rise as a global dominion formulated the king's view that the kingdom had achieved its greatness from his massive physical contributions, a fact about which he boasted incessantly throughout the biblical account.

Daniel, thus, described exceptional information about not only Nebuchadnezzar's benefactions, but his arrogant character. As it happens, evidence uncovered from East India House Inscriptions (604-562 BC) – an extra-biblical source – paints a mirror image of Daniel's assessment recording both Nebuchadnezzar's influence on the immense building and public works projects in sixth-century Babylon and his subsequent boasting – verifying Daniel's witness. If the book were written by a second-century writer, then, as Robert Pfeiffer admitted in his *Introduction to the Old Testament*, "We shall probably never know how our author learned that the new Babylon was the creation of Nebuchadnezzar (4:30), as excavations have proved..."[16]

Likewise, Daniel documented that Belshazzar was the last king of Babylon, in power when it fell to the Persians (539 BC). For millennia, this was feverishly disputed because no secular, historical list of

---

[15] Ibid., p. 40.

[16] Robert H. Pfeiffer, *Introduction to the Old Testament*, (New York: Harper & Row, 1948), p. 758-759.

Babylonian rulers contained the name Belshazzar. Even Jewish historian Josephus seemed unaware of Belshazzar's place in the kingly line, while the "the father of history," Greek historian Herodotus (450 BC), did not list him in his documented line of succession. This certainly did not help the case for Daniel's legitimacy among academic circles.

However, in the mid-nineteenth century, an ancient collection of documents was discovered known as the Nabonidus Cylinder. Nabonidus assumed the throne within a decade of Nebuchadnezzar's death, reigning from around 556 BC until the fall of Babylon's capital. Inside these manuscripts was discovered the existence of the Babylonian ruler Belshazzar. He was identified as the crown prince, Nabonidus' son, to whom was "entrusted the army...the troops in the country he ordered under his command. [Nabonidus] let everything go, entrusted the kingship to him, and himself."[17] The description provided by this documentation not only verified Belshazzar's existence, but that during his father's reign, he was made a co-regent of the empire, sharing kingly duties and title. One scholar has promoted the great worth of this discovery in that "Daniel's knowledge, then, of Belshazzar is quite surprising on the Maccabean dating of Daniel, but not at all on the traditional dating of Daniel. It is therefore of significant evidential value in confirming the authenticity of the book."[18]

As expert in Hebraic and Judaic studies, Dr. Justin Rogers, notes the critical scholar cannot answer how the "authors" of Daniel, if writing in the second-century, could have demonstrated advanced knowledge of sixth-century events such as Nebuchadnezzar's role in the creation of the New Babylon or Belshazzar's role as "king" when Babylon fell and surmises the obvious conclusion that Daniel must have been present to provide such accurate descriptions. This poses a dilemma of contradiction for the critic: "Daniel knows too much about sixth century

---

[17] William Shea, "Nabonidus, Belshazzar, and the Book of Daniel: An Update." *Andrews University Seminary Studies*, Summer 1982, Vol. 20, no. 2, pp 133-149. p. 134. This is taken from Sidney Smith, *Babylonian Historical Texts, Relating to the Capture and Downfall of Babylon*, (London, 1924), pp. 83-91.

[18] Jonathan McLatchie, "The Authenticity of the Book of Daniel." July 14, 2021, https://jonathanmclathie.com/the-authenticity-of-the-book-of-daniel-a-survey-of-the-evidence/.

BC to be writing 350 years after the event but he knows too much about late third century and early second century BC to be writing 350 years before the event."[19] The logical conclusion for such detail must be that it was provided by an eyewitness of sixth-century events.

Among other arguments for Daniel's later dating (165 BC) is the book's unique linguistic characteristics. First is the division of the book into two separate languages. Verses 1:1-2:4 are composed in Hebrew, Verses 2:5-7:28 in Aramaic, and Hebrew again finishes the book in Chapters 8-12. Hebrew and Aramaic are both part of Jewish heritage and are considered "sister" languages, but with clear distinctions. Differing languages might, therefore, suggest differing authors to modern scholars. Additionally, there are traces of late Aramaic in the book that some scholars have identified as typical of the Maccabean period (167-164 BC). Since languages go through developmental stages during which they evolve, scholars can identify transitions that mark their progress, thereby drawing distinctions between time periods. How could Daniel have traces of Aramaic distinctive to second century BC if it were written 400 years before?

These skeptical thoughts are legitimate and have been considered by proponents of the early dating theory. First, the use of different languages should not greatly contribute to a discussion about the book's legitimacy as this approach can be found in other books in the Bible whose authenticity scholars do not question. For example, the book of Ezra retained sections which were also written in Aramaic (4:8-6:18, 7:12-26) while the majority of the book was composed in ancient Hebrew. One answer to Daniel's linguistic hopscotch is found in the context of each respective section. One scholar has proposed that "it should be carefully observed that in the Babylon of the late sixth century, in which Daniel purportedly lived, the predominant language spoken by the heterogenous population of this metropolis was Aramaic. It is not surprising that an inhabitant of that city should have resorted to Aramaic in composing a portion of his memoirs."[20]

---

[19] Justin Rogers, "The Date of Daniel: Does it Matter?" *Reason and Revelation.* Vol. 36, no. 12. December 2016. p. 142.

[20] C. Hassell Bullock, *An Introduction to the Old Testament Prophetic Books,* (Chicago: Moody, 1986), p. 287.

Why, then, use Aramaic for only half the book? Dwight J. Pentecost has suggested, in his commentary of Daniel, that chapters two through seven comprise a historical narrative that applied predominantly to the Gentile nations rather than Israel. Daniel thus ensured their comprehension of a passage that pertained to their future by implementing their principal language. In contrast, the chapters written in Hebrew had clear implications for the nation of Israel, which would have been more effectively expressed in the Hebrew dialect.[21]

But why is there second-century Aramaic present in a sixth-century narrative? The greatest likelihood is that as translations proceeded through the centuries, scribes updated linguistic usage based on the development of the culture. One scholar, Siegfried Horn (1950), endeavored to demonstrate that the Aramaic problem in Daniel is "reconciled by the assumption that the wording of [Daniel and Ezra] had been modernized by some centuries after they had been written, and put into up-to-date language in the same way as the English Authorized Version has been brought into agreement with current usage...."[22]

Within the two decades after Horn, British linguist K.A. Kitchen also examined a separate group of ancient Aramaic texts, primarily business documents, and found this also to be the case. After an invasive investigation, Kitchen concluded that since these biblical canons were "scribally transmitted literary texts, the phonetic changes have shown themselves in modernization of spelling, probably in or after the third century BC. A second-century date could be [better] held by proving that no modernization had occurred...."[23] This, Kitchen concluded, was "the common fate of all such transmitted literature in times of linguistic change," and therefore, "we have no inherent right to assume the present orthography of the Aramaic of Daniel requires a second century date for the original composition of that Aramaic text"[24] This conclusion

---

[21] Dwight J. Pentecost, *The Bible Knowledge Commentary*, (Chicago: Moody, 1987), p. 1324.

[22] Siegfried H. Horn, "The Aramaic Problem of the Book of Daniel - No. 1." *The Ministry*, (May 1950), p. 6.

[23] K.A. Kitchen, "The Aramaic of Daniel," D.J. Wiseman, ed., *Notes on Some Problems in the Book of Daniel*, (London: The Tyndale Press, 1965), p. 78.

[24] Ibid., p. 67.

is compounded by the fact that scholars verify traces of explicitly early Aramaic in these same manuscripts.

However, while the liberal scholar can attempt to discredit the predictive prophecy of Daniel by shifting its time of authorship, there are predictions in the book that are not subject to the dating question because they were, indeed, fulfilled in the first century, around 250 years after the Maccabean period (165 BC). For example, Daniel 9:24-27 gives details about the lengthy process for Israel's redemption from their national transgressions. This passage is commonly referenced by evangelical scholars in their eschatological theories because of its messianic implications, an interpretation disputed by Jewish rabbis.

However, whether this passage receives a Jewish or Christian interpretation, Verse 26 predicted that Jerusalem and the second Jewish temple would eventually both be destroyed: "The people of the prince who was to come will destroy the city and sanctuary. And its end will come with a flood, even to the end there will be war, desolations are determined." This could not be referencing Antiochus Epiphanes IV because he did not destroy the city or the temple; rather he desecrated the latter's sanctity. This destruction occurred in AD 70 at the siege of Jerusalem by the Roman armies. It also happens to be the primary message of Jesus' Olivet Discourse (Matthew 24) when he warned the disciples of the signs that would indicate when Daniel's prophecy would be fulfilled. Additionally, Daniel's prediction would have been even more astonishing had it truly been given in 535 BC since the second temple was not rebuilt until 516 BC.

Likewise, Chapter 12 provides extensive foreshadowing of unforeseeable events that would ultimately find their fulfillment at the destruction of Jerusalem. In Verse 1 Daniel warns, "There will be a time of distress such as never occurred since there was a nation until that time," a promise whose corroboration has only one other similar event in Jewish history, the destruction of the first temple (Eze. 5:9). This very phrase is repeated by Jesus of Nazareth in the Olivet Discourse when predicting what will happen to the people who remain in Jerusalem when the Roman armies began their assault (Matt. 24:21). Also, in Verse 7, the man in linen answers the question of when the judgments described in Daniel will come to an end with the reply that "as soon as they finish shattering the power of the holy people, all these events will be completed."

As will be shown in this book's commentary on Chapter 12, Dr. Don Preston has convincingly argued that the "holy people" can be none other than the Jews. Their true "power" – the one element that separated them from the nations, the authority with which they defeated their enemies, their identity as a people – was their exclusive relationship with the one true God. It was their Old Covenant. This institution was made obsolete at Jerusalem's destruction. Over one million people were viciously slaughtered, hundreds of thousands taken into captivity, and the survivors unceremoniously and helplessly dispersed as the Jewish polity, economy, social structure, and religious system were devastated, heralding the official end of the Judaic age. Since these descriptions received first-century fulfillment, Daniel's predictive prophecies effectively render the dating question moot.

There is not enough room here to examine the breadth of arguments for dating Daniel. Rather the intent is both to inform the reader that such debate is extensive and worthy of great interest for the Bible believer and to equip them for answering possible objections to Daniel's authenticity, since the Bible will serve as an infinite target of skepticism. This book's abridged explanation of evidence for earlier dating should give the reader enough to come alongside and work under the distinct position of its sixth-century dating, written not only during the dominion of the Babylonian Empire but by a man present for its current events and so far ahead of its fulfilled prophecies that they not only contribute to both the book's general reliability as history but provide unassailable proof of the divine influence of the God of Israel.

However, for the liberal scholar who advocates a second-century composition date, the remaining implication about the book is that its primary subject, and author, must be fictitious. One influential atheist scholar Richard Carrier, for example, has stated that "all evidence points to there never even having been such a Jewish prophet before the book of Daniel was fabricated in the 160's BC. Legends of such a prophet may have circulated in previous centuries...."[25] In his view, Daniel was

---

[25] Richard Carrier, "How We Know Daniel is a Forgery." May 9, 2021, https://www.richardcarrier.info/archives/18242.

merely a character invented to produce hope and encouragement for Jewish readers struggling under the weight of second-century Gentile oppression.

Though scant, there does exist internal and external evidence for Daniel, the man. The book of Ezekiel, about which scholars are unanimous in their acceptance as authentic, produced three references corroborating Daniel's existence. Ezekiel was a prophet among the exiled Jewish captives in Babylon who wrote from around 593-571 BC, a few years following Nebuchadnezzar's attack on Jerusalem (597 BC). Thus, Ezekiel was present in the kingdom at the same time as Daniel. In his initial call to prophecy, Ezekiel was divinely instructed to convey God's pronouncement of judgment against Israel.

In distinguishing the remnant from the transgressors, God referenced three men as an example of righteousness surrounded by a nation in sin: "'Even though these three men, Noah, Daniel, and Job, were in its midst, by their own righteousness they could only deliver themselves,' declares the Lord God. 'If I were to cause wild beasts to pass through the land, and they depopulated it, and it became desolate so that no one would pass through it because of the beasts: though these three men were in its midst, as I live,' declares the Lord God, 'they could not deliver either their sons or their daughters. They alone would be delivered, but the country would be desolate. Or if I should bring a sword on that country and say, 'let the sword pass through the country and cut off man and beast from it, even though these three men were in its midst, as I live,' declares the Lord God, 'they could not deliver either their sons or their daughters, but they alone would be delivered. Or if I should send a plague against that country and pour out My wrath in blood on it to cut off man and beast from it, even though Noah, Daniel, and Job were in its midst, as I live,' declares the Lord God, 'they could not deliver either their son or their daughter. They would deliver only themselves by their righteousness" (Ezk. 14:14-20).

Ezekiel is later commanded to speak to the king of Tyre about the haughty spirit of his kingdom and gives an ironic allusion to how the ruler's own wisdom compared to that of the famed Jewish exile who had gained renown in the Babylonian Empire: "Son of man, say to the leader of Tyre, 'thus says the Lord God, 'Because your heart is lifted up and you have said, 'I am a god, I sit in the seat of the gods in the heart of the seas,' yet you are a man and not God, Although you make your heart like the heart of God - behold you are wiser than Daniel; there is no secret that is a match for you" (Ezk. 28:2-3).

Ezekiel's reference to Daniel without any further elaboration can only be explained by the fact that the king must have been aware of Daniel's prominence. It is safe to assume that word of the young sage's assistance to King Nebuchadnezzar and his subsequent elevation to leadership positions within the Babylonian government had reached Tyre and the surrounding regions. Ezekiel, then, mocked the king for his own perceived wisdom against the man who was considered to be one of the wisest in the known world in Daniel. As critical scholars maintain the authentic nature of the book of Ezekiel, the prophet's reference to Daniel as a man presently alive within the same kingdom should suffice as reliable corroboration.

External Jewish literature likewise speaks of Daniel. Commentaries, which clarify tradition, note that among the intelligentsia exiled to Babylon during Nebuchadnezzar's reign, Daniel was the only one from the tribe of Judah.[26] Furthermore, the book of Maccabees, written in the mid-second century, recalls Daniel's unquestionable incident in the lion's den, encouraging readers to remember "from generation to generation, that none of those who put their trust in [God] will lack strength." The latter work was composed around 100 BC, which makes it odd that these writings would invoke the piety of a fictitious character created just sixty-five years prior, especially considering Jewish appreciation for the sanctity of tradition. If Daniel had been formed in the mind of a faceless, second-century Jewish scribe, it seems improbable that such a condensed timeframe would have established his legend as useful for religious teaching in the midst of subjugation. In other words, calling upon Jews to find encouragement in an event that they knew never occurred would seem ineffectual.

First-century Jewish historian Flavius Josephus recorded, in *Antiquities of the Jews*, a description of Daniel's endeavors as a leader in the Persian ranks. For example, Josephus preserved the tradition

---

[26] *Talmud*, Commentary by Rabbi Adin Even-Israel Steinsaltz, English from the William Davidson Edition, Koren Publishers, "Sanhedrin 93b."

that, while Daniel served in his position of authority, he constructed a massive tower that served as a burial location for Persian royalty in a town called Ecbatana in Media.[27] Josephus also told the story of Alexander the Great's entrance into Jerusalem and the Holy Temple (332 BC) where he paid appropriate homage and was shown the book of Daniel. In it he read that "one of the Greeks should destroy the empire of the Persians" and "he supposed that himself was the person intended."[28] Josephus believed that this favorable prophecy for military conquest so pleased Alexander that the young, Greek leader granted the priests their continued rituals and customs and allowed Israel's laws and customs to continue unhindered within his realm. In other words, Alexander the Great read about himself in the book of Daniel, which, if true, further supports its sixth-century composition.

Though the Christian church labels Daniel a prophet, the majority of rabbinical Jewish scholarship believed that Daniel did not meet the qualifications for this office because he did not experience direct communication from the God of Israel. Indeed, the Talmud, Judaism's definitive collection of Jewish commentaries on the Hebrew Bible, explicitly states that he was not a prophet, and therefore, the book is not included with the other "prophets" in Judaism's division of the Hebrew Bible. (Torah, Prophets, Writings). Rather, Daniel is placed among the Writings with Esther, Psalms, Proverbs, etc.

Daniel was blessed with divine inspiration from the angel Gabriel or the Holy Spirit to interpret visions and dreams, but these were experiences that were absent a live, personal interaction with God. Since he did not achieve this qualification for being called a prophet, he is considered a sage. However, the Talmud also states that "a sage is superior to a prophet,"[29] meaning that despite not receiving the traditionally esteemed designation, Daniel was yet recognized for the unique blessings and gifts that God had bestowed upon him. Not only

---

[27] Flavius Josephus, *Antiquities of the Jews*, William Whiston, A.M. ed., Perseus Digital Library, Tufts University: Gregory R. Crane Editor-in-Chief. Book 10, Chapter, 11, Section 7, hereafter cited as 10.11.7.

[28] Ibid., 11.8.5.

[29] *Talmud*, Davidson, Bava Batra 12a.

is his place in Judaism preeminent, but the book remains an integral element of Jewish theological, historical, and apocalyptic thought.

In addition to the arguments mentioned, this author would contend that the primary evidence for the historicity of Daniel is found in its explicit affirmation by Jesus of Nazareth in Matthew's gospel: "Therefore when you see the abomination of desolation which was spoken of through Daniel the prophet, standing in the holy place (let the reader understand), then those who are in Judea must flee to the mountains" (Matt. 24:15-16). In this discourse, Jesus called upon Daniel's predictions to verify forthcoming historical events.

Jesus validated the Old Testament scriptures by demonstrating the satisfaction of God's long-awaited promises: "Do not think that I came to abolish the Law of the Prophets; I did not come to abolish but to fulfill," (Matt. 5:17), "You search the scriptures because you think that in them you have eternal life; it is these that testify about Me" (John 5:39), and "These are My words which I spoke to you while I was still with you, that all things which are written about Me in the Law of Moses and the Prophets and the Psalms must be fulfilled" (Luke 24:44). His own dependence and belief in the scriptures was paramount as they were essential for revealing God's truth to man. When Satan tempted Jesus in the wilderness to defy God's provision in favor of autonomy, each offer was abruptly refuted with scripture rather than reason. How a "Christian" scholar can call into question the historicity of the book of Daniel – knowing that the namesake of the very faith to which they claim allegiance verified its authenticity – is quite baffling.

Jesus cited God's established order of creation from Genesis (Mark 10:6-8), promoted the Ten Commandments as the foundation of morality but being brought to fullness in Himself (Luke 18:20), authorized the teachings and edicts of Moses (Luke 10:26-28, John 7:22), and confirmed the histories provided therein such as the judgments upon Tyre and Sidon, the trials of David, and the narrative of I Kings (Mark 2:25, Matt 12:42, Luke 11:50-52, Matt. 11:21-22). He verified the Psalms (Mark 12:10), affirmed the prophecies of Isaiah (Matthew 13:13-14), and directed his listeners to study Hosea (Matt. 9:13), Jonah (Matt. 12:40), and Malachi (Matt. 11:10) further. Jesus reminded the Israelites of God's provision as they wandered through the wilderness following their exodus out of Egypt (John 6). He also admonished the Pharisees for not knowing the scriptures better themselves: "You are mistaken, not understanding the Scriptures nor the power of God"(Matt. 22:29), and He established its everlasting inspiration by confirming that it cannot be annulled (John 10:35).

Not only did Jesus reference Daniel in His prophetic warning about the destruction of the Jewish temple in the Olivet Discourse, but His prediction to the Jewish leaders about His kingly status over Israel (Matthew 26:64, Mark 14:62) and preferred self-identification – "Son of Man" – throughout his public ministry has roots in Daniel. Matthew 24's dialogue lists at least three separate references to Daniel in Jesus' prophetic revelation about the temple's destruction (24:1). The first was His call out by name: "When you see the abomination of desolation which was spoken of through Daniel the prophet, standing in the holy place" (Matthew 24:15), aligning with the prediction of Daniel 9:27. The second was His allusion to the unparalleled suffering that the people in the city would endure: "For then there will be a great tribulation, such as has not occurred since the beginning of the world until now, nor ever will" (Matt 24:21), corresponding to Daniel 12:1. The third mention was a confirmation of the eventual establishment of His position of King and Judge over Israel: "And they will see the Son of Man coming on the clouds of the sky with power and great glory" (Matt. 24:30), a direct quote from Daniel 7:13-14.

There is enormous significance to Jesus' purposeful references to Daniel. In this discourse, the Savior plotted the signs that would indicate the imminence of the temple's destruction for the disciples as time elapsed. In other words, the more predictions that came to fruition, the closer the time for its demise approached. In doing so, Jesus was not only confirming its reliability but establishing the context of Daniel's many prophecies as having impending first century fulfillments.

If a scholar identifies oneself as a "Christian," then by questioning the authenticity of Daniel, one is denying the very claims that Jesus and scripture make in confirming His identity as God in the flesh. If Jesus of Nazareth were lying or mistaken about the book of Daniel and its application, He could not be who He claimed because the one true God cannot lie or suffer error (Numbers 23:19, Titus 1:2, Psalm 147:5).

There was no flaw in Him, or He could not be the Savior of the world. If Jesus affirmed the authorship of these Old Testament canons, the Christian scholar is obligated to do the same, regardless of how such a belief could jeopardize their status in the world of secular academia.

The book of Daniel does appear to produce historical inquiries when juxtaposed with secular documents from antiquity, but not to the extent of forfeiting credibility. In response, the Christian scholar must honestly seek reconciliation of the texts based on a further study of ancient language and literary methods. It is surprising that Christian scholarship freely ignores the authenticity attributed to the Hebrew Bible by their very Savior in favor of the perceived enlightenment of accepting that it is more reasonable to conclude that such accurate predictions found in Daniel could only be the result of authorship ex eventu (after the fact). In denying the power of these prophecies, these scholars inadvertently deny the power of prophecy as a biblical concept, a spiritual gift promised and confirmed throughout the Old and New Testaments and utilized to verify Jesus' own Messiahship.

In truth, the sum of scholarly arguments put forward against the authenticity of the book of Daniel amounts to manipulating the distinction between the apparent vagueness of the book's descriptions pertaining to sixth-century characters (Babylonians, Persians, etc) against the manifest accuracy of the second-century narrative surrounding Greece. In other words, academics are attempting to delegitimize the notion of predictive prophecy by showing the improbability of such targeted accuracy. Doing so, they believe, should cast enough doubt on Daniel to achieve widespread skepticism.

Their questions and arguments regarding Daniel's information are not illegitimate, but also not so profound that its authenticity can be disproven; a job that lies squarely on them to accomplish. In the end, if Jesus verified its genuineness, then the Christian is obliged to do the same; otherwise, one purports Him to be a liar. This book will, therefore, proceed from the premise that the Jewish sage, prophet, and noble – Daniel – authored the book's contents during the dominion of the Babylonian, Mede, and Persian kingdoms in the sixth-century BC. And as will be demonstrated, these promised events were future to those readers – but past to us.

THE FUTURE ACCORDING
TO THE FUTURIST

Daniel's apocalyptic aura and prophetic nature have generated a flurry of "end-times" predictions by both Jewish and Christian theologians. Many different images and phrases from Daniel have piqued the interest of readers and generated rampant speculation about the future of God's followers. What is the meaning of the "seventy weeks" (Dan. 9:24)? Does Nebuchadnezzar's statue represent nations with implications for the past or future (Dan. 2)? Who was the "little [horn]" (Dan. 7:8)? Why are the calculations of days in Chapter 12, predicting future events, different by 45 days, and what did they represent (Dan. 12:11-12)? Indeed, numerous American churches have become more fascinated with "end-times" gossip than any other theological topic in the Bible.

Many believers read Daniel with a historicist intrigue in which they believe the book describes a continuous flow of world events that begin with Daniel's time in sixth-century Babylon and extend to the consummation of all things at Jesus' future, second advent. Others apply a more localized approach by which Daniel is largely concentrating on the immediate future of Israel as they suffer under the dominion of pagan rulers. Some more eccentric thinkers interweave elements of the past and future into simultaneous portions of the narrative to make sense of modern-day, one-world-order conspiracy theories. For example, they concede that while the first four metallic elements of Nebuchadnezzar's statue (Dan. 2) represent past empires before the common era (BC), the statue's ten toes made of iron and clay represent a yet future (twenty-first century) confederacy of religions or nations that will form a one-world government under the final Antichrist. Indeed, one of the great philosophical hypocrisies from which the modern church suffers is its proclivity for internal division based on this diversity of interpretations.

However, the most popular contemporary eschatology held by the evangelical church is known as premillennial Futurism. This Christian "end-times" perspective interprets the prophetic portions of the Bible's most apocalyptic books like Revelation, Ezekiel, and Daniel as describing exclusively future events. Such an understanding holds that major predictions regarding wars, catastrophes, and perpetually declining morality are indicators of the forthcoming consummation of all things at which point the world will experience the Second Coming of Jesus Christ. And the eschatological blueprint that has gained the fiercest momentum in recent decades has been that which was put forth by the release of the fictional *Left Behind* Christian book series from the mid-1990's by Tim LaHaye and Jerry B. Jenkins. It goes something like this (along with the scriptures used to support it)….

Sometime in the very near future, a rapture of the Christian church will occur at an unexpected moment (Matt. 24:42). This event, some evangelicals believe, is the sudden and privileged removal of all Christ-followers from the earth for transportation to heaven that will leave the rest of an unbelieving world behind in its transgressions (I Thes. 4:15-17). This mysterious departure of multitudes of people will confuse those remaining into unprecedented chaos, paving the way for the commencement of the "last days" and the coming Great Tribulation (Matthew 24:21) that futurists believe is prescribed upon the earth by God and executed by His archenemy – the Antichrist (II Thes. 2:3, Matt. 24:15, II John 1:7). Immediately after the rapture, this Antichrist will catapult into global power through deception, masquerading as the earth's white knight, ushering in peace and unity.

In a display of unparalleled diplomatic expertise, the Antichrist will make a peace treaty with Israel for seven years (Dan. 9:27), deceiving the Jews into a sense of false security as the world recovers from the rapture event. During this time, Israel will be permitted to rebuild its temple and re-implement its Old Covenant sacrificial system of national atonement. He will break this covenant at its mid-point (3½ years). At that moment, this man's Satanic influence will become evident and he will trigger a time of extraordinary global persecution of God's remaining followers, especially the Jewish people. At some point God's appointed wrath will intervene and destroy not only the Antichrist, but all remaining earthy people who declared allegiance to his rulership (Rev. 4-19). Once God's judgment has been completed, Jesus will return and reign over an earthly kingdom for 1,000 years (Rev. 20:2) after which Satan will be given one more chance to rebel (20:7) and suffer an eternal defeat (Rev. 20:10). Finally, the culmination of all things arrives with the long-awaited New Heaven and New Earth (Rev. 21) where all manner of pain, suffering, and death have been vanquished and eternal life with the Creator achieves its fullness.

I pray that I have conveyed this narrative clearly to those not already familiar with it, because it dominates modern evangelical eschatology. One can see, by the references provided, that this evangelical tale is derived from three primary apocalyptic, biblical sources – Matthew, Revelation, and Daniel. The more one studies Christian eschatology, one will find additional support for this theory in books like Isaiah, Ezekiel, Zechariah, and Joel; however, Daniel's portion in this narrative is what concerns our study. From the book, futurists derive two main concepts. Both come from Daniel's ninth chapter.

As the book's narrative describes, Daniel's interpretive abilities and wise counsel had earned him a trusted status before Babylonian King Nebuchadnezzar, who had conquered and ruled over Israel in the sixth century. Daniel displayed unique spiritual resilience despite the darkness that surrounded him, structuring his character and virtue into a fortress of fidelity and humility. As Chapter 9 begins, Daniel is engaged in solemn prayer over the self-inflicted punishment his people have incurred through their national sin. However, his manner is not one of making demands from God, but of reverence to His character and glory, praising His loyalty despite the transgressions committed against Him.

Daniel's confession on behalf of his people is humble, thorough, and intense, remembering that it would not be their own righteousness from which mercy was produced, but God's holiness. He knew there was no question about the justification of God's chastisement of the Jewish people, yet he anticipated the eventual restoration of Israel's status. And his desperate and repentant appeal to the Almighty produced a divine reply from an angelic messenger. This angel, Gabriel, would outline an exact timeline leading to Israel's redemption that, to Daniel's chagrin, prophesied further desolation, but was yet veiled in a messianic promise that assured the answer to ultimate salvation.

Gabriel foretold that Israel's process for redemption would last seventy prophetic weeks (Dan. 9:24). All commentators agree that one week is equivalent to a seven-year period according to standard rules of linguistic interpretation, meaning that seventy weeks would translate to 490 years. Once completed the Jews would see their opportunity for restoration reach its fulfillment. In accordance with the timeline provided by the next two verses (Dan. 9:25-26), Christian commentators believe that sixty-nine of these weeks have been completed. However, the futurist believes that the seventieth week is yet unaccounted for, meaning that there has been a 2,000-year gap since the sixty-ninth week lapsed in the early first century. The inevitable futurist conclusion is that the earth presently awaits this final seven-year period during which it will experience unparalleled global calamities as it barrels toward the consummation of all things, most of which they believe are outlined by the book of Revelation.

This leads to the second futurist perception from Daniel which provides their description of this final period. Daniel 9:27 states, "And he will make a firm covenant will the many for one week, but in the middle of the week, he will put a stop to sacrifice and grain offering." One should see the connections: "he" (Antichrist) "will make a firm covenant" (peace treaty) "with the many" (Israel) "for one week" (seven years), "but in the middle of the week" (halfway through), "he will put a stop to sacrifice" (end the re-implementation of the Jewish system of atonement). Thus, the futurist believes the last seven years of Daniel's prophecy will be the Antichrist's peace treaty with Israel – sometime in our future.

Though fairly straightforward in its basic explanation, this in no way fits the true meaning of Daniel's passages – which you will see in this commentary. I would encourage you to return to this portion of the book upon arrival to the section analyzing Daniel 9:24-27 to compare the true meaning of the verses against what this narrative teaches. This chronicle of rapture, tribulation, and the Antichrist is given to much of the church by its favorite, time-tested pastors like David Jeremiah, John MacArthur, Charles Stanley, and John Hagee. And who is to question them? Indeed, they have decades of experience backed by secondary theology degrees and ministries supported by thousands of followers. The confidence with which their answers to congregant's questions are conveyed builds people's assurance in their expertise. However, human conceit, combined with the church's emphasis on pastoral authority, has often led many church leaders to proclaim superior knowledge which congregants are expected to absorb with minimal inquiry. And though these men might be considered effective, expositional teachers – they are not infallible.

If one performs even a cursory examination of this futurist theory against scripture, the holes become big enough to fall through. The simplest examples include the absence of textual evidence that a 2,000-year gap exists between Daniel's sixty-ninth and seventieth weeks, the concept of a pre-tribulational "rapture" appears nowhere in the biblical manuscripts, and the term "Antichrist" never describes a singular, eschatological enemy who personifies all evil by wreaking havoc throughout the earth under the control of Satan himself. These themes have been interpreted into scripture by the evangelical church.

This author would wish to present a commentary on Daniel to the reader with a "fresh slate," one on which there are minimal "end-times" preconceptions for the Bible student; however, evangelical culture has been so saturated with wild eschatological interpretations that there can be little hope that the ear of the average local congregant has been left unbiased. While this aforementioned futurist narrative is quite intriguing, it has a major flaw – it is not biblical. This account is not explicitly described anywhere within the Bible's pages; it is the product of a merger of selective verses from different corners of scripture that formulate a proposal to fulfill the Christian desire for avoiding tough times. In surmising that God would never let the church go through such travesty as a "Great Tribulation," it has concocted a narrative that provides an outline for such a belief, then subjectively chosen to provide scriptural support.

Futurism's leading interpretive methodology is known as Dispensationalism, a hermeneutic that argues for a strictly literal interpretation of biblical prophecy and, more importantly, advocates for a sharp theological distinction between Israel and the Christian Church. Within these two concepts, its readers contemplate scripture as it develops the hope of future glory through a melodramatic end to all things. But the problem with this theory is not that it provides hope to the average Christian that God can and does save His remnant from suffering, but rather the hope itself has generated the hermeneutic.

There is great danger in a decidedly literal interpretation of the Bible. But it is especially perilous when considering the numerous writing styles with which the Bible is composed. One example can be found in the Matthew 24 narrative, which will be evaluated later in this book. When describing the calamitous fall of a powerful nation, Old Testament prophets would use figurative language to describe the consequences that it would have on the geopolitical landscape at that time. Isaiah described the profound effects of Babylon's collapse in such language: "For the stars of heaven and their constellations will not flash forth their light; the sun will be dark when it rises and the moon will not shed its light" (Is. 13:10). And about Israel, Joel said: "The sun will be turned into darkness, and the moon into blood before the great and awesome day of the Lord comes" (Joel 2:30-31).

The moon did not literally become as organic blood nor was the sun's fire literally extinguished when it rose from the east as these empires collapsed. These are figurative images intended to describe the impact of a significant historical event. However, futurists await earth's complete physical destruction when the weight of God's cosmos falls directly onto our planet as stars literally come crashing through the atmosphere, sending everything we see before us into interstellar oblivion. Because this will all be destroyed, there is little reason to oversee it properly.

Consider when biblical phrases are used simply as rhetoric to establish emphasis. One such instance is in Ezekiel when the prophet predicted the destruction of the first temple (Solomon's) under the Babylonians in 586 BC: "And because of all your abominations, I will do among you what I have not done, and the likes of which I will never do again" (Ezk. 5:9). Taken literally, what happened at that time would have no parallel in the course of human history or else God would be a liar. And yet six and one-half centuries later, a greater destruction indeed occurred when the Roman armies destroyed the second temple. Even still, futurists hold that the seven-year Great Tribulation for which the world presently awaits will also be the worst time ever recorded.

Clearly, such a phrase should not be taken literally. As accomplished author Gary DeMar notes, "The language of Ezekiel 5:9 and Matthew 24:21 is obviously a proverbial rhetorical hyperbole."[30] Likewise, if Christians treated Mark 9:47 as literal, the Christian church would experience a difficult existence: "If your eye causes you to stumble, throw it out; it is better for you to enter the kingdom of God with one eye, than, having two eyes, to be cast into hell." One would struggle to find a Christian who has followed through with such a command. In such hidden allegory, Jesus gave revealing truth that affected the heart. It is not possible, therefore, to interpret all scripture literally.

The preconception about a sharp distinction between Israel and the church has also guided biblical interpretation down a questionable path. Within this understanding there are two peoples of God, the Jews descended from Abraham, Isaac, and Jacob juxtaposed against the Church, those saved from the Day of Pentecost until the future rapture of the church. Indeed, this is the primary root of rapture theology, a theological innovation purported by a nineteenth century Irish minister named John Nelson Darby (1800-1882). It began with his belief in different historical time periods; not an innovative concept. Darby referred to these ages as "dispensations." A "dispensation," he stipulated, is a historical era defined by God's dealings with mankind in which He offers progressive revelation based on how humans respond to His will. Darby understood that the age of the Mosaic Law had been in effect upon the arrival of Jesus Christ. However, when Israel rejected her Messiah, it triggered a new "dispensation" that interrupted God's

---

[30] Gary DeMar, *Last Days Madness*, (Powder Springs, GA: American Vision, [1999] 2019), 120. Demar attributes his claim to William Greenhill's *An Exposition of Ezekiel* (Carlisle, PA: banner of Truth Trust, [1647-1667], 1994), pp. 145-146.

timeline for redeeming them; out of their rejection of Christ was borne the Christian Church.

However, Darby held that this was unforeseen by the Old Testament, which caused a break in history in which God's promises to Israel could not be immediately fulfilled. The Church is, therefore, a parenthesis in history which has no place in the fulfillment of Israel's promises. This understanding produced the distinguishing philosophy of Dispensationalism: Israel and the Church are completely distinct entities, with separate purposes, in God's divine redemption plans. Indeed, properly understanding this theological separation was, as Darby noted, "the hinge upon which the subject and the understanding of scripture turns."[31]

Since the Church was an accident, it had no prescribed portion in Israel's redemption and consequently required a different purpose. It could not be earthly like the Jews; rather a transcendent, heavenly body that should be purified of the world's ruin. Because of this heavenly status, Darby believed that anything God arranged for earth could not apply to Christians because "[their] calling is on high. Events are on earth. Prophecy does not relate to heaven."[32] Christians were, therefore, exempt from all biblical prophecy. His literal interpretation postulated that Israel was an ethnic people awaiting a salvific, earthly reign wrought through God's physical judgment. And in order for them to pass through to righteousness and fulfill God's promises, they must yet endure the prophesied Great Tribulation (Matt. 24:21, Jer. 30:7) which, Darby believed, will occur in the "seventieth week" of Daniel's prophecy (Dan. 9:24-27) – sometime in the future. For this final stage of God's redemption plan to get back on track, the church – this addition in history – must be removed. Cue the rapture.

One will not find this teaching in the theological literature of church history because historic Christian theology understood the Church to be the continuation of God's singular program of redemption that began with Israel. The Church was "grafted" into the root of Israel;

---

[31] John Nelson Darby, "Reflections Upon the Prophetic Inquiry And The Views Advanced In It." Dublin 1829. https://plymouthbrethren.org.

[32] John Nelson Darby, "The Rapture Of The Saints And The Character Of The Jewish Remnant." https://plymouthbrethren.org.

not replacing or separating from them but becoming one people of the Living God (Romans 10-11, Eph. 2, Gal. 3) because of the promised blessing through the Messiah (Heb. 11:39). Romans 11 undoubtedly describes the two growing together on the same tree, one having been grafted in after previous branches were broken off. This tree came from Old Testament Israel.

Likewise, Paul explained in Ephesians 2:11-22 that Gentiles had become partakers of God's covenant promises. Dispensationalism's distinction between the two is intensified because of its firm view that Israel is the literal seed, or physical offspring, of Abraham, making the church is own separate entity. However, Paul stated in Galatians that "the promises were spoken to Abraham and to his seed…that is Christ" (Gal. 3:16) and clarified that "if you belong to Christ, then you are Abraham's descendants, heirs according to promise" (Gal. 3:29). This interpretative system is founded upon faulty theology and, therefore, is not a recommended method for understanding scripture.

If Dispensationalism is so flawed, then what is an alternative understanding for biblical prophecy?

BIBLICAL PRETERISM

The term "preterism" is derived from the Latin word "preter," meaning "past" or "gone by." Simply understood, preterism interprets most or all biblical prophecies as having already been fulfilled. Such a view is obviously contrary to "futurism," which believes that nearly all "last days" prophecies listed in biblical canon have not yet been completed. The latter is the overwhelmingly favored interpretation for the evangelical church. There are two principal groups that comprise preterist thought. The first is comprised of "partial" preterists, who believe that the vast majority of biblical prophecies have experienced fulfillment, such as those from the most popular eschatological biblical sources – Daniel 9, Matthew 24, and Revelation 1-19. These need no further interpretation because they have come and gone having been confidently harmonized with historical events. However, partial preterists also believe in Jesus' future return, a conclusion supported by verses like I Corinthians 15:23-26, Hebrews 9:28, and Revelation 20-22.

The second and much smaller group is made up of "full" preterists, who assert that every prophecy in scripture has been fulfilled – with no exceptions. This includes Jesus' Second Advent, as they believe the Bible teaches that Jesus already returned to destroy the city of Jerusalem in the first century. They are, therefore, not awaiting a physical reappearance of Jesus Christ. Unsurprisingly, modern evangelicals who eagerly await events hereafter generally abhor preterism because it challenges popular church suppositions that teach hope found in future events. Indeed, an important religious element for futurists is that they find little optimism in previously fulfilled prophecy, i.e., "What do we have to look forward to if it has already happened?" As such, there exists a nearly irreconcilable chasm between preterism and futurism.

All Christians must concede that even a small level of preterist understanding is unavoidable. Numerous Old Testament biblical prophecies foretold events that occurred in the first century, even the arrival of the Messiah. As Gary Demar points out, if a Christian accepts the reality that *any* prophecy stated in the Bible has already been fulfilled (which they must), then they are preterist in some form. Even for the futurist, it is impossible to deny this as a basic, yet integral part of the Christian method for understanding God's Word. And yet it is frequently dismissed, primarily because it challenges popular eschatological assumptions about an established supposition upon which the entire institutional church is built.

To challenge the idea of Jesus' future return would be to uproot settled doctrine that has provided the church with unified creed for nearly two millennia (Apostle's, Nicene, etc). What internal struggles would erupt for Christians who believe something their entire lives, only to be told they might have had it wrong all along. Especially with how engrained an eschatological tale that promotes a rapture, an Antichrist, and a Great Tribulation has become in people's minds thanks to numerous Christian authors. Make no mistake that futurist eschatological literature is a multi-million-dollar industry for Christian authors, and to undo their blueprint for the future would discredit the majority of interpretive work produced by evangelical scholarship in the last half century. For example, the popular Christian Book Series *Left Behind*, first published in 1995, has sold around eighty million copies.

The preterist view is derived from the belief that each book of the NT was written prior to AD 70, the year Jerusalem was destroyed by the Romans. As such, it describes a fluid narrative of Jewish struggle and Church progress from Jesus' arrival to the city's destruction. However, much of the evangelical church undervalues the impact of this past event on the course of Judaism and Christianity after the first century, but even more are unfamiliar with its basic history. In conversation with pastoral leadership, this author has heard the event described as a "blip on the radar" of human history. There are millions of Jews who might disagree with such a characterization.

In the year 63 BC, the Roman General Pompey captured Jerusalem. Rather than implementing tyrannical colonization, the Romans installed a local sovereign and permitted the continuation of traditional Jewish religious practices. Though this was loosely acceptable for Jewish leaders, in that national customs were largely unhindered and priests personally benefitted from helping maintain local stability, many of Israel's most zealous patriots were uneasy with the growing influence of Roman religion in Jewish culture. Roman administrative requirements produced such frustration in Jewish society that by late AD 66, revolution was fomented.

Jewish zealots began severely punishing priests allied with Roman leadership and ousting the Roman forces present within Jerusalem. To quell the rebellion, the emperor Nero (AD 54-68) sent his armies to the city. The consequential event that would proceed fulfilled exactly what Jesus had prophesied in His Olivet Discourse as recorded in the Gospels of Matthew and Luke: "Truly I say to you, not one stone here will be left upon another, which will not be torn down," (Matt. 24:2) and "When you see Jerusalem surrounded by armies, then recognize that her desolation is near" (Luke 21:20). Jesus gave this warning in AD 30, just prior to His crucifixion, and it occurred within the generation to whom He had spoken (Matt. 24:34).

For the following 3½ years, Jerusalem was under siege as the Romans cut off supplies to the city that resulted in rampant famine and pestilence for its inhabitants, while slaughtering any civilians who attempted to flee. By AD 70, total desperation had affected all social, economic, and religious elements of the Jewish establishments, and factions inside Jerusalem were competing for leadership, creating further division against the city's defensive efforts. Within the city's walls were outsiders who had arrived to participate in Jewish celebrations of worship, strategically allowed in by Roman forces to aid in depleting Jerusalem's resources, and subsequently prevented from leaving. It was during this timeframe that Roman General Titus Vespasian, who had assumed command of Nero's original mission, conducted a final assault.

Jewish historian Flavius Josephus, a former officer in the Jewish army, testified that blood ran like water during Jerusalem's siege, burial was forbidden, leaving rotting bodies in the streets to spread incurable disease, and mothers were forced into cannibalizing their children to avoid starvation. By August AD 70, the objective was complete. The Romans sacked Jerusalem and destroyed the Jewish temple (Dan. 9:26), slaughtering over one million people, taking hundreds of thousands into captivity, and forcing remaining survivors to be unceremoniously dispersed among the surrounding nations. The entire Jewish institution and identity were shattered. For the preterist, this event was the fulfillment of God's Old Covenant promises of punishment against His chosen people for their covenantal adultery (Deut. 28) and rejection of His redemption offer through the Messiah – who had come forty years earlier in Jesus of Nazareth.

Rome's desolation of the city officially ended the Judaic age, bringing the Old Covenant to its sanctioned end, an event predicted in Jeremiah: "'Behold days are coming,' declares the Lord, 'when I will make a new covenant with the house of Israel and with the house of Judah, not like the covenant which I made with their fathers in the day I took them by the hand to bring them out of the land of Egypt, My covenant which they broke, although I was a husband to them,' declares the Lord" (Jer. 31:31-32). When Jerusalem was destroyed it officially heralded the changeover of world epochs from an age in which temporary atonement was offered exclusively through a Jewish covenant of lawful obedience, to one in which a new agreement established redemption free from legality – to all people. Indeed, what more demonstrative action could be taken to ensure the elimination of recurring physical sacrifices than to destroy the place where they were offered?

The Judaic age, governed by the administration of Mosaic Law where ritual and sacrifice provided temporary atonement, succumbed to a Church age governed by a gospel that taught the whole world a forgiveness of sin through faith that brought settlement with its Creator. An Old Covenant kingdom spread by war through generations of Jewish kings became a New Covenant kingdom that established peace through spiritual reconciliation. This is the kingdom that God promised to set up, according to Daniel 2 & 7, during the Roman Empire, over which the promised Messiah, Jesus of Nazareth, currently exercises "all authority...in heaven and on earth" (Matt. 28:18). The very same kingdom preached at the onset of Jesus' public ministry when both He and John the Baptist advised that Israel "repent, for the kingdom of heaven is at hand" (Matt. 3:2, Mark 1:15). Thus, the biblical prophecies surrounding the Messiah and His kingdom have been fulfilled – the nutshell perspective of the average preterist.

Many prominent evangelical futurists consider preterism a profane method of interpretation. As such, it is often labeled as "unbiblical" or even, heretical. Thomas Ice, executive director of the Pre-trib Research Center at Liberty University has described the preterist view as "destructive," Mark Hitchcock, pastor of Faith Bible Church and author, regularly writes articles and holds public debates that promote scathing critiques of its perspectives, and renowned minister of Grace Community Church, John MacArthur, believes preterist views are egregiously mistaken representing "heresy of the worst stripe" such that individual faith is endangered.[33] Because full preterists, for example, believe the promise of Jesus' Second Advent to have already occurred, they are typically labeled as apostates and not fit to be considered, by some, as "brothers and sisters" in Christ.

I would desperately challenge the church on this condemnation. The gospel message, the "good news" that the church perpetually professes, is directly given by Paul to the Corinthians: "…that Christ died for our sins according to the Scriptures, and that He was buried, and that He was raised on the third day according to the Scriptures" (I Cor. 15:3-4). This is confirmed in his letter to the Romans: "If you confess with your mouth Jesus as Lord, and believe in your heart that God raised him from the dead, you will be saved" (Rom. 10:9). The honest reader should note that Paul did not list anything else, traditionally stipulated in the statement of faith for most denominations, as a contingency for salvation. This includes many treasured concepts in church theology. And though much of the church-at-large might

---

[33] See Thomas Ice's article "The Destructive View of Preterism" in the Conservative Theological Journal (Dec 1999), Mark Hitchcock's article series critiquing the preterist views of Revelation in Bibliotheca Sacra (2007), and John MacArthur's "Quick Reference Guide to the Bible (181) and *The Second Coming* (13). See John Noe's *Unraveling the End* for an extensive survey of evangelical criticism of the preterist view (94-99) including MacArthur's "heresy" articulation.

find preterism detestable – evidenced by the intense criticism levied by evangelicalism's most popular leaders – author John Noe has discovered that "the Evangelical Theological Society does not consider preterism to be heretical. For more than twelve years, it has allowed the International Preterist Association to exhibit its books and materials at its annual meeting and both preterists and anti-preterists to present theological papers...."[34]

Something imperative to understand about the term heresy is that it does not mean an opinion contrary to God's Word. Heresy, by definition, is a belief that conflicts with generally accepted, orthodox religious doctrine, the principles of which are established by an ecclesiastical organization. The church, therefore, labels someone a heretic based on one's opposition to recognized creed – dogmatic statements which can differ drastically between groups. Consider the countless protestant divisions: Lutheran, Baptist, Anglican, Presbyterian, Methodist, Assemblies of God, Nazarene, Reformed, etc. Each provides a statement of faith that diverges from another in some facet; for otherwise, there would be no purpose for internal division. It is no secret that even the early church fathers, upon whom much of our biblical understanding rests today, had several differing perspectives on interpretation. And though futurism has captured the hearts of most contemporary evangelicals, preterism has deep roots in the historic Christian church.

Indeed, first-century believers were convinced that Jesus would return in their lifetime. It was part of their fervent passion for gathering together to anticipate what they understood to be the hope promised them that His return would complete the process of simultaneous salvation and judgment. Some had heard the words Jesus spoke in Matt 10:23, "For truly I say to you, you will not finish going through the cities of Israel until the Son of Man comes," or Matt 16:27-28, "For the Son of Man is going to come in the glory of His Father with His angels and will then repay every man according to his deeds. Truly I say to you, there are some of those who are *standing here* [emphasis mine] who will not taste death until they see the Son of Man coming in His kingdom."

Peter and the disciples must have had little doubt when Jesus told them that John would still be alive at His coming. After being warned

---

[34] John Noe, *Unraveling the End*, (Indianapolis: East2West Press, 2014), p. 99.

about the manner of his death, Peter asked about John, to which Jesus scolded with "'If I want him to remain until I come, what is that to you?'...Jesus did not say to him that he would not die, but only, 'If I want him to remain until I come, what is that to you?'" (John 21:22-23. Numerous church fathers from antiquity believe that John was the last disciple, tasting death during the reign of Trajan (AD 98). Likewise, what did Paul anticipate about the arrival of this kingdom? He reminded Timothy of this temporal expectation that Christ Jesus would "judge the living and the dead, and by His appearance and His kingdom" (II Tim. 4:1), clearly predicting that of those to whom he wrote, some would be alive to see it and others would have passed (I Cor. 15:52, I Thes. 4:15).

The notion that the coming of the kingdom would initiate the judgment against the wicked and salvation of God's faithful was at the forefront of Paul's mind. And the New Testament authors, likewise, confirmed their belief in its imminence. James' letter conveyed the sentiment encouraging believers to "be patient; strengthen your hearts, for the coming of the Lord is near" (James 5:8-9), while Peter's epistle also stated that "the end of all things is near; therefore, be of sound judgment and sober spirit for the purpose of prayer" (I Peter 4:7). Indeed, some of the very same church fathers from whom the evangelical church will quote on matters of theology expressed preterist understandings of biblical prophecy. The following is a brief sample of ancient, yet recognizable Christian theologians and apologists who believed, for example, that Jesus' Olivet Discourse in Matthew 24 was fulfilled at the destruction of Jerusalem in AD 70; not in some distant event 2,000 years in the future.

Clement of Alexandria

Titus Flavius Clemens (AD 150-218) was an intellectual apologist who specialized in biblical commentaries that focused on ethics and morality. He was renowned within the Christian community for his devout theological opposition to Gnosticism, a pseudo-religious movement with a philosophical emphasis on acquiring hidden spiritual knowledge about the existence of man. Gnostics were considered heretics in the larger Christian community because they held that salvation was achieved through procuring mystical knowledge and that the ultimate human destiny is to realize one's own divinity. Clement was influential in expressing the Christian duty to manifest the gospel through action.

He believed, for example, that wealth was not to be dismissed, but stewarded wisely, which would produce soteriological (salvation theology) fruit. Among his most famous teachings were *A Discourse Concerning the Salvation of Rich Men* and *Exhortation to Patience*, but his *Protreptikos* was a trilogy that attempted to explain the progressive stages of individual Christian knowledge, from the gospel's introduction to an unbeliever to its fullness in a mature believer. He underscored the necessity for illuminating the intellectual aspects of Christianity while acknowledging that personal faith is integral, calling the believer's true devotion a "faith of knowledge."

In one distinct sermon, Clement developed the argument that Jesus stressed the implications of the temple destruction by using the Discourse to expand on its significance: "But, as I have already said, being a prophet by an inborn and ever-flowing Spirit, and knowing all things at all times, He confidently set forth, plainly, as I said before, sufferings, places, appointed times, manners, limits. Accordingly, therefore, prophesying concerning the temple, He said, 'See ye these buildings? Verily I say to you, there shall not be left here one stone upon another which shall not be taken away; and this generation shall not pass until the destruction begin. For they shall come, and shall sit here, and shall besiege it, and shall slay your children here.' And in like manner He spoke in plain words the things that were straightaway to happen, which we can now see with our eyes, in order that the accomplishment might be among those to whom the word was spoken."[35] Indisputably, Clement was describing that the event Jesus was prophesying (Matt. 24:1) and the subsequent "things that were straightaway to happen,"

---

[35] Alexander Roberts and James Donaldson ed., "Ante-Nicene Christian Library: Translations of The Writings of the Fathers Down to AD 325." Vol. XVII, The Clementine Homilies. The Apostolical Constitutions. (Edinburgh: T & T Clark, 1870). Homily III, Chapter XV, "Christ's Prophecies." p. 63.

would occur within the generation to whom He was speaking, thereby invalidating any yet future consequences of the Discourse.

Origen of Alexandria

Oregenes Adamantius (AD 185-254) was a Christian theologian who lived during a time when church persecution was particularly widespread and the Body held little consensus in their doctrinal orthodoxy. It is fair to credit Origen for being the first to develop a systematic theology for the church by examining such concepts as the Trinity, free will, and man's eternal state after death. Regarding soteriology, he struggled to believe that sinners experience eternity in hell, a doubt from which he developed a theology of "universalism" in that all created beings eventually receive salvation, though the process may run an extensive, individual course.

An especially shocking addition was that this salvation opportunity extends to even the devil, himself. Origen arrived at such a conclusion through the logical supposition that if Satan fell from his heavenly post by free will, then by the same free will, he could repent. Origen was summarily condemned for such a view, and today universalism is considered absolute heresy by the church. His most famous work was *The Hexapla*, a 20-year project that contrasted the Hebrew and Greek versions of the OT for purposes of reconciling discrepancies among the manuscripts.

In an exchange with a doubting correspondent, Origen expressed that the Olivet Discourse articulated its first-century fulfillment. Regarding Luke's interpretation of the Discourse, he argued, "But let this Jew of Celsus, who does not believe that [Jesus] foreknew all that happened to Him, consider how, while Jerusalem was still standing and the whole Jewish worship celebrated in it, Jesus foretold what would befall it from the hands of the Romans....Now it is recorded, that 'when ye shall see Jerusalem encompassed about with armies, then shall ye know that the desolation thereof is nigh."[36] Origen marvels at the notion that Jesus successfully predicted the city's demise at a moment when such a thing was inconceivable. And yet the Jews who doubted his prophetic nature ignore such clear evidence of divine foreknowledge.

Origen concluded "And anyone who likes may convict this statement of falsehood, if it be not the case that the whole Jewish nation was overthrown within one single generation after Jesus had undergone these sufferings at their hands. For forty and two years, I think after the date of the crucifixion of Jesus, did the destruction of Jerusalem take place."[37]

This church father can be considered a provocative figure in church history. However, such a designation can be vindicated in that he lived during an uncertain time for the church in which not only was its future in jeopardy, but it lacked doctrinal consensus, thereby allowing for innovative, but experimental, theological thought. How else would the church have identified its future canon and incorporated statements of faith were it not for its most profound thinkers evaluating all religious interpretations of the spiritual concepts put forth by the revolutionary gospels of the apostles and letters of Paul that had been circulating for the previous two centuries?

And yet despite his controversies, such was the Christian community's faith in his theological wisdom and general intellect that he was called to settle disputes in foreign cities. Though he was accused of heresy because of "universalism," his correspondence offers evidence that he eventually realized that not everyone will be saved: "But, we say that the soul of the bad man, and of him who is overwhelmed in wickedness, is abandoned by God."[38] Nonetheless, this author is inclined to consider Origen a source of early preterist leanings by the end of his life.

---

[36] Origen, *Contra Celsum*, Book 2, Chapter 13. Hereafter cited as 2.13. Kevin Knight, ed. http://www.newadvent.org/fathers/0416.htm Source cited is: Translated by Frederick Crombie. "Ante-Nicene Fathers, Vol. 4. Edited by Alexander Roberts, James Donaldson, and A. Cleveland Coxe. (Buffalo, NY: Christian Literature Publishing Co., 1885).

[37] Ibid., 4.22.

[38] Ibid., 4.5.

Eusebius of Caesarea

Eusebius Pamphilus (AD 260-340) is quite possibly the most respected Christian apologist in church history, as his *Ecclesiastical History* was a watershed composition in church historiography. This ten-volume work was the first complete history of Christianity that provided an exhaustive chronicle of events from the time that Jesus' public ministry began to that of his own contemporary church influencers (fourth century). Also known as Eusebius of Caesarea, his *History* also provides modern scholars with a glance into early heresies against which the church had to compete and invaluable information about other theologians and historians for which few records exist.

He did tend to exhibit bias for whom he had favorable relationships and seemed to omit the more uncomplimentary episodes from early church history, but his attention to detail, scholarly penchant for acknowledging and validating his sources, and goal for establishing the preservation of church legacy have earned him the designation "the father of church history." While he is widely recognized by the evangelical church as a precious source for history, he supported Arianism, a theology purporting that Jesus did not eternally coexist with God from eternity past, but rather was a created Being. The church decided that such a Christology was heretical, and he was excommunicated in AD 325.

In books 5 and 6 of *Ecclesiastical History*, Eusebius introduces his readership to "The Last Siege of the Jews After Christ" in which he begins a historical account of the destruction of Jerusalem, corroborating much of his analysis with the chronicle provided by Flavius Josephus, the Jewish historian and officer in first-century Jewish military ranks. Eusebius clearly establishes the context of this portion of history by stating that "Vespasian, who had distinguished himself in the operations against the Jews, was proclaimed Imperator by the army there and appointed Emperor in Judea itself. He at once set off for Rome and entrusted the war against the Jews to his son Titus."[39]

In this preface to the account of Jerusalem's assault, he clarified that

---

[39] Eusebius, *The Ecclesiastical History*. Vol. 1, Translated by Kirsopp Lake, (London: William Heinemann, 1926), Book 3, p. 199.

despite the impending calamity, "the people of the church in Jerusalem had been commanded by an oracle given by revelation before the war, to those in the city who were worthy of it to depart and dwell in one of the cities of Perea which they called Pella"; however, regarding Apostate Israel, "the judgment of God might at last overtake them for all their crimes against the Christ and his Apostles, and all that generation of the wicked be utterly blotted out from among men."[40] He understood that Christians in Jerusalem, by prophetic revelation, knew they had been commanded to flee the city (Matt. 24:16) when the Romans arrived at its boundaries.

Eusebius confirmed that this destruction of Jerusalem was the event described in biblical prophecies: "How many evils at that time overwhelmed the whole nation in every place and especially how the inhabitants of Judea were driven to the last point of suffering, how many thousands of youths, women, and children perished by the sword, by famine, and by countless other forms of death;...how terrors and worse than terrors were seen by those who fled to Jerusalem as if to a mighty capital...the nature of the whole war, all the details of what happened in it, and how at the end the abomination of desolation spoken of by the prophets was set up in the very temple of God, for all its ancient fame, and it perished utterly and passed away in flames."[41]

He verified that the "abomination of desolation" was not a prescribed future event but that of the arrival of the Romans who would desolate the Jewish temple, an event prearranged as devastation at the hands of divine justice. His *History* proceeded to articulate the disturbing calamities endured by those yet within the city upon the commencement of the Roman enclosure of Jerusalem, most represented by an incomparable famine that left citizens mercilessly stealing from each other "while their dearest were wasting away before them there was no scruple in taking away the last drop of life."[42]

Drawing his ultimate conclusion, Eusebius corroborated the suffering of Jerusalem's citizens during the assault with Jesus' words in the Olivet Discourse: "Such was the reward of the iniquity of the

---

[40] Ibid., p. 201.
[41] Ibid.
[42] Ibid., p. 205.

Jews and of their iniquity against the Christ of God, but it is worth appending to it the infallible forecast of our Saviour in which he prophetically expounded these very things, 'woe unto them that are with child and give such in those days, but pray that your flight be not in the winter nor on a Sabbath day, for there shall then be great affliction such as was not from the beginning of the world until now, nor shall be.'"[43] Eusebius expressed astonishment at Jesus' premonition of such judgment against Jerusalem described by the gospel accounts (Luke 19:43, 21:24), noting that "if anyone compares the words of our Saviour with the other narratives of the historian concerning the whole war, how can he avoid surprise and a confession of the truly divine and supernaturally wonderful character both of the foreknowledge and of the foretelling of our Saviour."[44]

Eusebius also verified that the numerous signs foretold by Jesus in Matthew 24 that should lead up to the destruction were unquestionably fulfilled in that "imposters and lying prophets perverted the miserable people" [Matt. 24:5, 12] and "at one time a star stood over the city like a sword, and a comet which lasted for a year...before the revolt and before the disturbances that led to the war" [Matt. 24:29-30], an interpretation of impending judgment.[45] Regarding the destruction of Jerusalem, Eusebius undoubtedly believed the Olivet Discourse to be Jesus' direct appeal to His faithful to save themselves from the unprecedented tribulations inflicted by the first-century Roman armies against the city. It was what the Jews had brought upon themselves.

Athanasius of Alexandria

Saint Athanasius (AD 239-373) was a Christian apologist and bishop known for his extensive theological study of Christ's divine relationship with God the Father, evidenced by even the title one of his principal works, *On the Incarnation*. He ardently opposed the Arianism (Christ was a created being) supported by Eusebius of Caesarea and

---

[43] Ibid., p. 215.
[44] Ibid., p. 219.
[45] Ibid., p. 221.

attended the First Council of Nicaea in AD 325, a conference at which the issue of Christ's divinity was a chief debate topic. Athanasius' emphasis on the significance of the city's fall in AD 70 is without dispute, as he connected it directly to Daniel's prophecy about Israel's opportunity for redemption (Dan. 9:24); "So the Jews are indulging in fiction, and transferring present time to future. When did the prophet and vision cease from Israel? Was it not when Christ came, the Holy One of holies? It is, in fact, a sign and notable proof of the coming of the Word that Jerusalem no longer stands, neither is prophet raised up nor vision revealed among them."[46]

Upon further analysis of the event, he noted, "And shortly after He says, 'when ye therefore shall see the abomination of desolation, spoken of by Daniel the prophet, stand in the holy place; then let them which be in Judea flee into the mountains: let him which is on the housetop not come down to take anything out of his house: neither let him which is in the field return back to his clothes [Matt. 24:15]. Knowing these things, the Saints regulated their conduct accordingly."[47] This is an acknowledgment of the historical actions taken by those present in Jerusalem when the events Jesus described in the Olivet Discourse began to take form. Jesus' scriptural ties to Daniel also verify his belief that a preterist interpretation of that book's eschatological implications is appropriate.

John Chrysostom

Saint John Chrysostom (AD 347-407) was the Archbishop of Constantinople. Though he attained a reputable background in law, he was drawn to theology and became a well-respected teacher and leader who espoused the piety of the true Christian institution – serving those in need. It was less his theological acumen but his eloquence as an orator

---

[46] St. Athanasius, *On the Incarnation of the Word*. Chapter 6, Sec. 40, "Refutation of the Jews." Made available by the Christian Classics Ethereal Library, https://ccel.org/ccel/athansius/incarnation.html.

[47] St. Athanasius, *Apologia de Fuga*, "Examples of Scripture Saints in defense of flight" No. 11. Kevin Knight, ed. http://www.newadvent.org/fathers/2814.htm

that grabbed the attention of the people, especially since he favored their cause by condemning exuberant wealth, a stance that would lead to his removal from office and banishment from Constantinople at the hands of the elite who saw his teaching as a threat to their affluence. He did speak with certain antisemitic undertones but, out of the spirit of preaching a gospel of grace in which ancient customs played no part in salvation. He read the scriptures plainly, interpreted simply, and offered clear application of the scriptures to everyday life. Such a method aided in his understanding of Jesus' Olivet Discourse as prophecy that did not require an eschatological code for interpretation, but rather a simple look at history to verify that it had, indeed, already occurred in the lives of first-century Christians.

For example, Chrysostom said of Jesus' warnings of false prophets, wars and rumors of wars, (Matt. 24:5-6) and their inevitability, "But of wars in Jerusalem is [Jesus] speaking; for it is not surely of those without, and everywhere in the world; for what did [the disciples] care for these? He would thus say nothing new; if He were speaking of the calamities of the world at large, which are happening always...but [Jesus] speaks of the Jewish wars coming upon them at no great distance, for henceforth the Roman arms were a matter of anxiety."[48] Of the additional signs given by Jesus, he wrote, "The famines, the pestilences, the earthquakes, the other calamities, peruse the history about these things composed by Josephus, and you will know all accurately."[49] Indeed, Josephus gave such a detailed first-century history that he unknowingly verified Jesus as the kind of prophet he denies, an account to which Chrysostom gives full credibility.

Speaking on Jesus' advance notice of the coming calamities comprising a great tribulation, Chrysostom said, "Seest thou that His discourse is addressed to the Jews, and that He is speaking of the ills that should overtake them? For the apostles surely were not to keep the Sabbath, day, neither to be there, when Vespasian did those things... neither would the Jews dare to flee on the Sabbath day, because of the

---

[48] Philip Schaff, ed. *Nicene and Post-Nicene Fathers of The Christian Church. Vol. X, St. Chrysostom: Homilies on the Gospel of Saint Matthew.* (New York: The Christian Literature Co., 1888) Homily LXXV, p. 451.

[49] Ibid., p. 453.

law, neither in winter was such a thing easy; therefore, 'pray ye,' saith He; 'for then shall be a tribulation, such as never was, neither shall be.'"[50] He also noted of this tribulation that "the exceeding greatness of the ills, when not only compared with the time before [temple destruction in 587 BC], they appear more grievous, but also with all the time to come. For not in all the world, neither in all time that is past, and that is to come shall any one be able to say such ills have been. And very naturally; for neither had any man perpetrated, not of those that ever have been, nor of those to come hereafter, a deed so wicked and horrible. Therefore, he saith, 'there shall be tribulation such as never was, nor shall be....'"[51] One can see that the preterist understanding of Matthew 24 permeated the revered teaching of John Chrysostom.

The reader might be surprised to discover that some of the more recognizable names in contemporary evangelicalism – Jonathan Edwards (1703-1758), John Wesley (1703-1791), and Charles Spurgeon (1834-1892) – also believed that the Olivet Discourse was a prophecy about the first century destruction of Jerusalem. Furthermore, some early church fathers and theologians also casted doubt on additional futurist concepts. One such example is the appearance of a future Antichrist. In his *Commentary on Daniel*, Saint Jerome (AD 345-440), made famous for his translation of the Greek Bible into Latin, believed that the early church exhibited a logical understanding that the Antichrist figure – made especially well-known to popular culture as a human embodiment of pure evil that will usher in a forthcoming tribulation upon the earth sometime hereafter – was fulfilled in the past: "As for the Antichrist," he noted, "there is no question that he is going to fight against the holy covenant, and that when he first makes war against the king of Egypt, he shall straightaway be frightened off by the assistance of the Romans. But, these events were typically prefigured under Antiochus Epiphanes so that this abominable king who persecuted God's people foreshadowed the Antichrist, who is to persecute the people of Christ.

---

[50] Ibid., Homily LXXVI, p. 457.
[51] Ibid., p. 457.

So, there are many of our viewpoint who think that Nero Caesar was the Antichrist because of his outstanding savagery and depravity."[52]

In Jerome's understanding, not only was the Roman emperor Nero a plausible identification for the character, but such an understanding was accepted by a large portion of ancient Christian populations. The view that this adversarial figure had already appeared in history was also shared by John Chrysostom, when he said that Paul's "man of lawlessness" in the second letter to the Thessalonians – whom the modern evangelical church unequivocally identifies as this final Antichrist – "speaks here of Nero, as if he were the type of Antichrist. For he too wished to be thought a god."[53] Likewise, the seventieth week of Daniel that many contemporary evangelical leaders believe to be a future seven-year tribulation period was believed by numerous church fathers to have found fulfillment in the first-century. Among the more prominent names observing such a supposition included Clement of Alexandria, Origen, Tertullian, and Athanasius.

Renowned church theologian St. Augustine (AD 354-430) affirmed that both a futurist and preterist view can be drawn from the Olivet Discourse, "For who can fail to see that the words, 'but when you see Jerusalem surrounded by an army know that its desolation has then drawn near' (Luke 21:20), pertain to that city? Likewise, who can fail to see that the words, 'when you see these events take place, know that the kingdom of God is near (Luke 21:31), pertain to the last coming of the Lord?' But his words, 'woe to those who are pregnant or nursing in those days. But pray that your flight may not be in winter or on the Sabbath. For then there will be great tribulation such as there has not been from the beginning of the world and will not be afterwards' (Mt. 24:19-21), are written in such a way in Matthew and in Mark that it is uncertain

---

[52] St. Jerome, *Commentary on Daniel.* Translated by Gleason Archer. (Grand Rapids: Baker Book House, 1958), pp. 15-157. Chapter 11:27-30. https://www.ccel.ord/ccel/pearse/morefathers/files/jerome_daniel_02_text.htm.

[53] Philip Schaff, ed. Nicene and Post-Nicene Fathers of The Christian Church. Vol. XIII, St. Chrysostom, (Edinburgh: T&T Clark), Homily IV, 2 Thessalonians 2.6-9.

whether they ought to be understood of the destruction of the city or of the end of the world."[54]

Augustine seems to be sympathetic to an integrated interpretation, one in which, at the very least, the Olivet Discourse could be a dual prophecy of both past events but recapitulated in a future Second Coming. In either case, Augustine submits that, "the one who admits that he does not know which of these is true hopes for the former, endures the latter, and is mistaken in nothing, because he does not either affirm or deny any of them. I beg you not to look down on me for being such a person...."[55] He not only refused to claim infallible wisdom in the interpretation, but he pled with his correspondent not to disparage him for such a stance. In other words, the two interpretations may co-exist without Christians condemning one another.

Please understand that preterist leanings were not only prevalent among many early church theologians but may have been predominant. Modern evangelical scholars often ignore this truth when engaging others in eschatology, instead pinning their futurist hopes on one of the earliest church fathers, Irenaeus of Lyons, who exhibited a shaky, futurist interpretation of many prophetic passages. Irenaeus is also the modern church's primary source for dating the book of Revelation which, thereby, establishes how it should be interpreted. He believed John received and documented his Revelation while exiled to the Isle of Patmos around AD 95, a year with little significance and over two decades after the destruction of Jerusalem. Since this vision, according to Irenaeus, was given to John in the burgeoning church age, when the majority of Christ followers believed that His Second Coming was all that remained, the prevailing assumption is that the information provided in the book pertains to events leading up to that future consummation.

However, if Revelation were not written as Irenaeus postulated, but 30 years prior (AD 65), then the interpretation changes. Suddenly, the events described in the book might be painting a picture, not of a

---

[54] Jay Rogers, "Augustine on Matthew 24 and 'The End of the World." January 7, 2018, "Augustine to Hesychius," Letter 199. https://www.forerunner.com/blog/augustine-on-matthew-24-and-the-end-of-the-world.

[55] Ibid.

future Day of the Lord in the twenty-first century, but an event that was much closer to those receiving John's letter. Could that event have been the destruction of Jerusalem? There are numerous works by more qualified theologians that examine the evidence for dating the book of Revelation (see *Before Jerusalem Fell* by Kenneth L. Gentry, Jr.). This example simply demonstrates the selective habits of modern Christian apologism. Preterism, however, littered the thoughts of the first half century of church theologians and continued up to the Great Awakening of the eighteenth century. But the arrival of Dispensationalism (see **Christian Eschatological Terminology** in the back of this book) to the United States in the mid-nineteenth century triggered a radical shift in evangelical hopes for the future and has since overwhelmed Christian eschatology, leaving no room for an opposite disposition.

NARRATIVE OF MATTHEW 24

There can be little doubt that the Olivet Discourse is among the most significant passages in the NT but one that has also been desensitized by rampant eschatological speculation. For centuries, Christian apologists and commentators have used its contents to assess their contemporary existence, each exhibiting the seeming hopefulness that *their* generation would be the one that sees the consummation of all things. It is reasonable to expect that someone who thinks that the world is presently experiencing the "end-times" – the last days of human existence – would have a worldview shaped by such a belief. This perspective tends to guide such a person to begin associating every global event portrayed in the news media as having some profound contribution to God's eschatological plans. This habit usually stokes fear, anxiety, and produces an "end-times" fever that generates demonization against those who disagree.

Some frantic Christians are stricken with bewilderment and grief that the Savior has not returned to rapture them off this doomed planet. How dare God Almighty ask them to stay among the heathens as representatives of His kingdom? As it were, Jesus scolded His disciples when their frantic eschatological desires, for what they perceived to have been their promised end game, narrowed their focus. Immediately before His ascension, they pleaded, "Lord, is it at this time You are restoring the kingdom to Israel?" To this He replied, "It is not for you to know times or epochs which the Father has fixed by His own authority..." (Acts 1:6-7). And yet many futurist Christians clamor with frustration as they cannot understand why God makes them wait so long. The Savior advised that it is not their concern.

Many influential church pastors have taught that the Olivet Discourse is a prophetic timetable for twenty-first century Christians. They acknowledge that Jesus predicts the destruction of the temple in the first verse, but immediately after the disciples ask Him about the signs of His "coming" (Matt. 24:3), many scholars believe the context shifts to the distant future. This is simply because, for 1,700 years, the church has believed it is still waiting for that event. Thus, much of the Christian world perpetually looks for signs of global pestilence, earthquakes, and persecution – all described in this prophecy – to determine whether Jesus' return is at hand and they might be the lucky ones to experience its consummation. And of course, when Russia invaded Ukraine in 2022, this was seen as *the* fulfillment of Jesus' prediction of "wars and rumors of wars" (Matt. 24:6), thereby igniting a firestorm of predictions from careless evangelical influencers that the end is near.

Unfortunately for these overzealous minds, the context of the Olivet Discourse poses a serious contest to their supposition that Jesus' prophecy is an exclusively future narrative. One could begin by asking a basic question as to why Jesus would initiate his chronicle by promising that *their* temple was going to soon be destroyed but immediately switch to a monologue about events that would not occur for thousands of years into the indefinite future? What concerns would His disciples – the direct recipients of this discourse – have had for issues that would affect Christians in the twenty-first century? They sought information about what was going to happen to the temple that their teacher had just promised would be brought to nothing. Did Jesus ignore their inquiry? Did He respond with, "Never mind about that. I must tell you what will happen to a particular generation of Christians in the indefinite future?" Such a paradigm shift makes no sense.

However, a more significant feature is that the heart of Jesus' discourse is pulled from verses found in Daniel, an exclusively Jewish book written for Israel about *their* contemporary events. Daniel has no knowledge or concern about a future Christian church and his own context must be applied to Jesus' application in His message. This means that the primary subject of His prediction in Matthew 24 was Israel. While the OT origin of Jesus' reference to the "abomination of desolation" (Matt. 24:15) is clear, there are other connections that the Savior makes that breathe life into the prophecies describing the destruction of the Second Jewish temple, which reinforces the topic of His prophecy. This architectural wonder had been constructed in 516 BC, twenty years after Israel's return from Babylonian captivity and stood at the center of Jewish life. Jesus' prediction, therefore, would not have been but a trivial matter to the disciples.

To set the stage for the Olivet Discourse, Matthew 21 placed Jesus in the temple for the final time before His crucifixion, pronouncing judgment against apostate Israel. During his visit, He physically cleared the Temple of those who had corrupted its sanctity, announced woes upon the hypocrite leaders, and foretold covenantal retribution for their rejection of God's salvation. And in closing out Jesus' time within its walls, Matthew's pertinent quote that brings together these judgments was the Savior's warning to the leaders that their "house is being left to [them] desolate" (23:38).

The original manuscripts of Matthew did not have chapter breaks; rather they were separated into larger sections that presented narratives with the express purpose of guiding the reader through the chronicle. The end of Chapter 23 placed Jesus in the temple, while the beginning of 24 shows Him departing – a location change that acts as a convenient breaking point in the narrative. An English version that presents a chapter break should, therefore, not characterize a shift in the topical subject; rather Jesus' discourse in the temple event (Ch. 21-25) should be read as one fluid account.

Following His departure from the temple, Jesus headed east and sat on the Mount of Olives. This is no insignificant point. In fact, this setting provides a subtle, yet momentous contribution to the context within which Jesus is speaking, for His destination to this mountain on the east side of Jerusalem was no accident. As Matthew's primary purpose was to persuade Jews of Jesus' Messiahship, his Gospel is saturated with OT imagery and fulfillment, consistently citing ancient verses to bring the contemporary Jewish thinker to the truth. As passing generations characterize God, they assess His patterns of discourse and action throughout history and determine appropriate parallels for understanding the world around them. Jesus' location was one such instance.

The Babylonian captivity (exile) was a period in Jewish history, beginning around 605 BC, when the first Judean citizens were taken captive to Babylon by Nebuchadnezzar following a siege upon Jerusalem. The city and temple remained intact, but after four years the Jewish king Jehoiakim, who ruled over Israel, angered Nebuchadnezzar, which resulted in Jerusalem's eventual capture and the Judean monarch's death (598/597 BC). Thus began a tenuous Jewish-Babylonian relationship that culminated in 586 BC when Nebuchadnezzar ordered the total destruction of Jerusalem and Solomon's temple (II Kings 25:9).

While history looks upon this event as a dance between dueling armies through the natural course of a powerful force decimating one weaker, the Bible is clear that God ordained and enforced this destruction as punishment upon His covenant people for their spiritual adultery against their Old Covenant. The prophet Ezekiel described the details of Israel's abominations in the holy places of the temple and their rebelliousness against God's sovereignty and prophesied in 592 BC the destruction of His House. However, the precipitous condition that permitted the temple's destruction was that God's spirit had departed from it, thereby forsaking its continued defense.

In showing Ezekiel the numerous violations against His edicts and Israel's covenantal responsibilities, noting their generational transgressions and labelling them insolent and stubborn, God revealed the devastating consequence of their iniquities. His spirit left the inner sanctuary, the holy place in which His presence had always resided (Ezk. 8:6), marking His path as He reached the front door (Ezk. 9:3) and eventually withdrawing to the outer walls (Ezk. 10:8). Finally, God departed the city: "Then the cherubim lifted up their wings with the wheels beside them, and the glory of the God of Israel hovered over them. The glory of the Lord went up from the midst of the city and stood over the mountain which is east of the city" (Ezk. 11:22-23).

The reader is given a chronicle of God's forecast of definitive judgment against His temple, years before its total destruction in 586 BC. In Ezekiel's vision, God moved through the temple, pointing out its sins and corruption, demonstrating the ruins of its leadership, and expressing fury at the sanctioned idolatry occurring within its walls. After promising a heaping judgment with which He "will have no pity nor will [He] spare" (Ezk. 8:18), His Spirit went out, leaving Israel unprotected and vulnerable to hostile forces. Where did He go? East – to the Mount of Olives.

Astonishingly, Matthew described this exact course taken by Jesus during his final visit to the temple prior to His crucifixion. In a mirror narrative of Ezekiel, Jesus Christ, God incarnate, filled with zeal, swept through the temple, flipping tables and identifying corruption, while lamenting over the disloyalty, fraud, and hypocrisy of the apostate leadership (Matt. 21-23). Promising desolation, He left and headed east.[56] The pattern of judgment against Israel, in Ezekiel 8-11, is so definitive that it is reenacted in Matthew 24, as Jesus followed the precise route out of Jerusalem, foreshadowing its destruction. This divine pattern firmly supports the context of what follows in Matthew 24:3-35 as the judgment of the temple in Jerusalem, not a malleable, future "end-times" tribulation for which twenty-first-century Christians should be watching.

As Jesus departed, the disciples "came up to point out the temple buildings to Him" (Matt. 24:1), reminding Him of its status as their nation's pride and glory. Indeed, its inner sanctuary acted as the intersection of heaven and earth yet their Lord showed little restraint in promising its institutional reduction which would leave nearly no trace of its previous existence: "Do you not see all these things? Truly I say to you, not one stone will be left upon another, which will not be torn down" (Matt. 24:2). They must have been befuddled.

Upon Jesus' arrival to respite on the mount, four of His disciples privately asked Him when this desolation and the signs leading up to

---

[56] One particular Christian commentary makes this connection. In their analysis of Ezekiel 11:23, Jamieson-Fausset-Brown acknowledged that "The mount was chosen as being the height when the missiles of the foe were about to descend on the city. So it was from it that Jesus ascended to heaven when about to send His judgments on the Jews; and from it He predicted its overthrow before His crucifixion" (Matt. 24:3). Also see Iain M. Duguid's *The NIV Application Commentary: Ezekiel,* (Grand Rapids, MI: 1999), p. 153.

it would occur (Matthew 24:3). The corresponding Gospel accounts of Mark and Luke reinforce the temple as the targeted subject. When Jesus stated that the "great buildings" would be destroyed, the disciples responded, "Tell us, when will these things be and what will be the sign when all these things are going to be fulfilled?" (Mark 13:4) and, "When therefore will these things happen? And what will be the sign when these things are about to take place?" (Luke 21:7). Mark and Luke described the disciples' direct response to the stunning promise made by the Savior and the manifestation of the preliminary events indicating its imminency.

However, most Bible readers believe that Matthew asserts an additional perspective. The King James Version (KJV) reads that the disciples ask not only when the temple's destruction would occur, but also about the "sign of thy coming, and of the end of the *world* [emphasis mine]" (Matt. 24:3). This has contributed mightily to the evangelical conception that the Olivet Discourse is an entirely futuristic prophecy in which Jesus subsequently relays the "signs" leading up to this distant future event. Even in the last decade, the *King James Bible* of 1611 remains the most popular translation in history. One major study on "The Bible in American Life" has discovered, even in the last decade, that 55% of Bible readers "most often reach for the King James Version."[57] The primary challenge with this reading is the word "world." This is a KJV mistranslation. The Greek word used in this verse is "aionos," meaning "age." The conflation of "world" (Greek: "kosmos") and "age" has caused a grave misinterpretation of the passage causing the "end of the age" to blend into a vision of a future consummation of all things at the "end of the world." The Greek terms are highly distinct and not so easily interchangeable.

One of the foremost anticipations in Jewish eschatology was the future arrival of an earthly kingdom over which the Jews would rule the nations, alongside the Messiah, under a banner of universal peace and prosperity. Since the purpose of Matthew's Gospel was to

---

[57] David Briggs, "The Lord is their shepherd: New Study reveals who reads the Bible – and why." March 7, 2014. *The Association of Religion Data Archives.* Blogs.thearda.com/trend/featured/the-lord-is-their-shepherd-new-study-reveals-who-reads-the-bible---and-why/.

persuade Jewish readers of Jesus' Messiahship, he was required to speak their language. The disciples immediately assumed that the temple destruction would herald the end of the present "age" and transition to this anticipated messianic kingdom; i.e., one "age" to the next. Why would these men have thought that Jesus meant a future generation 2,000 years from that moment? This was not a public statement to the masses intended to warn as many people as possible in a setting that would suggest a large-scale prophecy concerning the world at large. God was not angry at the world; He was angry with Israel. Jesus' upcoming response was given directly to a private group of disciples in answer to their question about the Temple's destruction. Watch carefully, for in the following verses, Jesus unceasingly told these men, "See to it that no one misleads *you*" (Matt. 24:4), "*You* will be hearing of wars and rumors of wars" (Matt 24:6), and "They will deliver *you* to tribulation, and will kill *you*" (Matt. 24:9); (emphasis mine).

Thus begins Jesus' discourse on the impending signals that would lead to this momentous event so He could save as many people as possible. The ensuing grace-filled warnings of misfortunes that would permeate that generation of Israelites began with the promise of false messiahs and the need to be watchful: "For many will come in My name, saying 'I am the Christ,' and will mislead many" (Matt. 24:5). As further evidence of Jesus' focus on His first-century contemporaries, this notice was extremely pertinent to the Jews. Christians are not fooled by men claiming to be the Messiah, precisely because they know Who the Messiah is. Their "Christian" designation depends on that understanding.

Why warn the owner in possession of a genuine article not to be hoodwinked by a counterfeit? This particular exhortation was given to a generation that could yet be deceived by an imitation. One commentary has noted, "In the Epistles, it is never exactly established such a thought as warning persons against false 'Christs,' for the epistles are addressed to Christians; and a Christian could not be deceived by a man's pretensions to be Christ. It is most appropriate, here, because the disciples are viewed in this chapter, not as the representatives of

Christians now, but of future Godly Jews."[58] The Jews had rejected Jesus; therefore, they were the ones still looking for the Messiah. It was the Israelites who needed to be warned of false messiahs as their judgment drew nigh, not future Christians.

Indeed, the following decades witnessed the arrival of those who would fulfill the prediction. One such biblical character sparred with Peter in Acts: "Now there was a man named Simon, who formerly was practicing magic in the city astonishing the people of Samaria, claiming to be someone great; and they all, from smallest to greatest, were giving attention to him, saying, 'This man is what is called the great power of God'" (Acts 8:9-10). Simon's historical verification can be found in Justin Martyr's correspondence with the Roman emperorship, as the church father dated the sorcerer's appearance during the reign of Claudius Caesar (AD 41-54).[59] Also, according to church father Irenaeus, "He was worshipped by many as a god, and seemed to himself to be one; for among the Jews he appears as the Son, in Samaria, and among other peoples as the Holy Ghost."[60] Church tradition accuses Simon of being among the first to exhibit gnostic philosophies.

As explained when discussing Clement of Alexandria, Gnosticism is a spiritual tradition alleging hidden knowledge that supersedes church orthodoxy and leads to the human awareness of its own divine nature. Luke's description in the book of Acts is quite astute in relaying the people's view of Simon as "the great power of God," which described him as the revealed manifestation of God's power. His ability to perform "miracles" served to fool the weak-minded into the notion of his role as a "saving" force, thus qualifying him as a messianic figure. Simon Magus' place in history should not be overstated as his influence was local and his capacity for sorcery proved troubling to the burgeoning

---

[58] William Kelly, "William Kelly Major Works Commentary." From *Kelly Commentary on Books of the Bible*. https://biblehub.com/commentaries/kelly/matthew/24.htm.

[59] Justin Martyr to Emperor Titus Aelius Adrianus Antonius Pius Augustus Caesar, *The First Apology*, Kevin Knight, ed. http://www.newadvent.org/fathers/0416.htm

[60] Ibid., Irenaeus of Lyons, *Against Heresies*. Book I, Chapter 23.

church in those Jewish communities. He nonetheless served as a partial fulfillment of Jesus' warning.

Likewise, a man named Theudas was recognized by Jewish historian Flavius Josephus as having a messianic effect. In his *Jewish Antiquities* he stated, "A certain charlatan, whose name was Theudas, persuaded a great part of the people to take their effects with them, and follow him to the river Jordan; for he told them he was a prophet, and that he would, by his own command, divide the river, and afford them an easy passage over it. Many were deluded by his words."[61] The implications from the passage suggest salvific undertones as the Jewish tradition of parting open waters was a distinct reference to Israel's redemption. Josephus identified the time frame as having occurred during Fadus' appointment as procurator of Judea from 44-46 BC, within two decades after Jesus' prediction.

Unfortunately, Theudas' effect produced a cult-like mentality within his fellowship and resulted in their unceremonious slaughter at the hands of Fadus' militia, who could not afford to allow this group's participation in the slightest insurrection. Theudas himself was captured and decapitated. Josephus, however, expanded on the influence of first-century deceivers like Theudas as the days of Israel's judgment approached: "There were many who deceived and deluded the people under the pretense of Divine inspiration, but were in fact for the procuring of innovations and the changes of government. These men prevailed with the multitudes to act like madmen, and went before them into the wilderness, pretending that God would there show them the signals of liberty."[62]

Jesus' description of "wars and rumors of wars" (Matt. 24:6) may not have turned many heads since the human proclivity for conquest guarantees a generational recurrence of physical combat for land, resources, or simply pride. However, His ministry fell into the heart of a nearly 200-year age of imperial harmony for the Roman Empire called Pax Romana. A term first coined by Roman philosopher Seneca

---

[61] Josephus, *Antiquities*, 20.97-98.

[62] Flavius Josephus, *The Wars of the Jews*, William Whiston, A.M. ed., Perseus Digital Library, Tufts University: Gregory R. Crane Editor-in-Chief. Book 2, Chapter 13, Section 4. Hereafter cited as 2.13.4.

the Younger, this was a time of propagandized peace throughout the kingdom during which imperial Rome established such law and order that societal tranquility rarely wavered and trade increased such that the empire's economy experienced unprecedented expansion.

Rome's efforts to maintain this stability were exemplified by their tolerance for provincial diversity and intentional efforts toward improving the human condition like constructing roads and aqueducts. Likewise, the arts flourished as writers and poets composed literary masterpieces, and engineering improvements produced architectural wonders. This time period solidified Rome's position as the center of the western world. Yet despite the peace and prosperity of this age, Flavius Josephus' most famous historical narrative of first century Judaism under the Roman dictate is entitled *Wars of the Jews*.

Within the first century the Jewish institution experienced visible tension between groups. There existed numerous conflicts between the clerical sects of leadership comprising the Essenes, Pharisees, and Hellenized priests, giving rise to zealots and extremists. Roman influence brought a dichotomy of economic growth to Judea at the expense of societal morality which created political and cultural pressures that produced several internal rebellions up to the approach of the destruction of Jerusalem in AD 70. Roman authorities in Judea frequently exhibited a lack of decorum while overseeing their subjects causing the most trivial circumstances to explode into tragedy.

Josephus conveyed the story of one centurion keeping guard at the feast of unleavened bread who "pulled back his garment, and cowering down after an indecent manner, turned his breech to the Jews, and spake such words as you might expect upon such a posture."[63] For lack of a more appropriate description, it appears this soldier broke wind in the direction of the gatherers during this sacred Jewish ceremony. Such an offense stirred the crowds to assemble with a hostile disposition, demanding the soldier's immediate reprimand. However, upon the arrival of supporting legions to quell the dissent, the Jews dispersed in dread, trampling each other in the confusion and panic. According to Josephus, 10,000 citizens were killed.

Jews in surrounding locales also experienced notable struggles,

---

[63] Ibid., 2.12.1.

such as occurred in Alexandria when they refused emperor worship of Caligula (AD 37-41) by destroying alters erected for such a purpose. Caligula thereby developed skepticism of the Jewish population and responded by ordering a statue of himself erected within the temple in Jerusalem. This undoubtedly would have spawned a massive rebellion and civil war, from which the inevitable result would have been significant regional instability. Caligula was assassinated before the statue could be placed.

Outside of Jewish context, there were numerous Romans conflicts under emperors Caligula, Claudius, and Nero – during this time of perceived Roman peace – that spanned the nearly four decades of Christ's prophecy. Caligula expanded Roman rule into Mauretania and spent much effort squashing rebellions in Rome's eastern territories. Claudius directed expeditions to Britain – which he conquered after the nation had long resisted Roman conquest – as well as North Africa. Nero furthered Roman hold on Britannica and conducted military affairs into the Armenian territories. It was also Nero who instituted the extreme persecution of Christians in Rome (AD 64-68) and ordered the assembly of Roman armies to Jerusalem in latter AD 66.

Jesus' prediction of "wars and rumors of war" is confirmed in Josephus' *Wars*. In one instance, when the Roman army was directed to Jerusalem for the installation of statues in the Jewish temple, the Jewish historian noted, "As to the Jews, some of them could not believe the stories that spake of a war, but those that did believe them were in the utmost distress how to defend themselves, and the terror diffused itself presently through them all."[64] The leader, Petronius, arrived with a show of force to establish imperial authority, against which the Jewish citizens gathered and proclaimed their utter devotion to Yahweh, a commitment they would defend unto death. To these people Petronius expressed pity but maintained a semblance of representing Roman power to ensure their compliance with imperial edicts and to remind them who still exerted control over their earthly affairs.

In addition to nations rising against nations, "in various places there will be famines and earthquakes" (Matt 24:7), marking natural disasters as integral components of Jesus' prophecy. The appearance of famines

---

[64] Ibid., 2.10.

is well attested as taking place in Rome in AD 41, 42, and 51, verified by secular historians of antiquity such as Seneca and Tacitus. But a large number of localized conditions contributed to an empire-wide famine under the reign of Claudius (AD 41-54). For example, Egyptian agriculture was heavily dependent on appropriate water levels in the Nile River such that a significant variation could considerably distress the crop production of any given year. Such a disparity occurred in AD 45. That year the Nile rose to heights not seen in the previous century and produced an exceptionally poor harvest, which historian Kenneth Sperber Gapp noted was felt throughout the Roman world (AD 44-48).[65] Roman historian Suetonius recorded in his *Life of Claudius* that there was "a scarcity of provisions, occasioned by bad crops for several successive years."[66]

This very famine was predicted by Agabus, a relatively unknown NT prophet, on whom Luke shined the spotlight in Acts 11. In the years following Jesus' death, the church began its spread under the evangelical leadership of Peter and the miraculous conversion of Paul (AD 34-35). In Antioch, there had been an uprising of the gospel after which many believed and turned to the Lord such that leaders from Jerusalem came to observe and encourage. Indeed, this was the location, described by Luke, where "the disciples were first called Christians" (Acts 11:26). Among the group of prophets that had arrived was "one of them named Agabus, [who] stood up and began to indicate by the Spirit that there would certainly be a severe famine all over the world" (Acts 11:28-29). Such insight caused those present to commit to preparation for the impending adversity by providing assistance to Christians living in Judea. Within the decade, famine would strike – as prophesied.

Jesus likewise specifically warned of earthquakes. Certainly, there was no shortage in the first century. The Bible records that shortly after Pentecost, the assembled church prayed for the continued spread of the gospel despite reported threats. Following their prayer, "the place where

---

[65] Kenneth Sperber Gapp, "The Universal Famine Under Claudius." The Harvard Theological Review, Vol. 28, No. 4. October 1935. pp. 258-263. This fact is, as Gapp noted, reiterated by Roman historian, Pliny the Elder.

[66] Suetonius, *The Lives of the Twelve Caesars*, Alexander Thomson ed., "Life of Claudius." (Philadelphia: Gebbie & Co., 1889). https://www.perseus.tuft.edu

they had gathered together was shaken" (Acts 4:31). There was a similar event in Philippi as Paul and Silas prayed (Acts 16:25-26). The most famous might be Pompeii's geological catastrophe in AD 62. While Pompeii is most renowned for its complete demolition by the eruption of Mt. Vesuvius in AD 79, it first experienced a severe earthquake, the effects of which spread to surrounding areas. From Roman historian Seneca, Pompeii, "the busy Campanian city, has been ruined by an earthquake, and all the neighboring areas have been badly affected," which included Herculaneum, Nuceria, and Naples.[67]

Tacitus also mentioned that under Claudius in Rome "several prodigies occurred that year. Birds of evil omen perched on the Capitol; houses were thrown down by frequent shocks of earthquake."[68] According to Christian apologist and commentator Henry Alford, "The principal earthquakes occurring between this prophecy and the destruction of Jerusalem were, (1) a great earthquake in Crete AD 46 or 47; (2) one at Rome on the day when Nero assumed the toga virilis AD 51; (3) one at Apamaea in Phrygua, mentioned by Tacitus AD 53; (4) one at Laodicea in Phrygia AD 60; (5) one in Campania, Seneca... in the year AD 58."[69] In addition, Laodicea, Hierapolis, and Colossae were likely also ravaged at the same time.

Jesus' prediction of Christian persecution in the decades following His death and resurrection is also well documented in history: "Then they will deliver you to tribulation, and will kill you..." (Matt. 25:9). The disciples themselves experienced traumatic deaths, such as Peter, who was sentenced to crucifixion under Nero around AD 64-66, the very method of death that Jesus prophesied would overcome him in John's Gospel (21:18-19). James, son of Zebedee, was "put to death with a sword" (Acts 12:1-2) around AD 44. Paul was beheaded and Stephen

---

[67] Lucius Annaeus Seneca, *Natural Questions*. Harry M. Hine, translator. Book 6, "On earthquakes." (Chicago: The University of Chicago Press, 2010), p. 87. Pompeii's destruction is also recorded in *The Annals* of Tacitus (15.22).

[68] Tacitus, *Complete Works of Tacitus*, Alfred John Church, William Jackson Brodribb, Sara Bryant. Edited for Perseus. (New York: Random House, Inc, 1942). *The Annals*. 12.43.

[69] Henry Alford, *The New Testament for English Readers*. Vol. I, Part I – The Three First Gospels. (London: IL: Rivingtons, Waterloo Place; and Deighton Bell and Co. Cambridge, 1863), p. 163.

stoned. Church tradition suggests that other disciples were killed in similar manners, though these are facts that are more difficult to verify: Bartholomew was flogged, Matthew was killed by the sword, and Jude was pierced by arrows.

Nero's unprecedented persecution of Christians in Rome from 64-68 is also notorious. Mark's version of the Olivet Discourse described that they would be brought before "courts," (Mark 13:9) which was fulfilled when Peter and John were brought before the Sanhedrin (Acts 4:5-7). Likewise, Luke mentioned "prisons," (Luke 21:12), which was satisfied when Peter and John were imprisoned (Acts 4:3). Of note are these instances occurring to other disciples like Paul and Silas, though technically outside the immediate context of apostolic reference in Matthew.

Jesus' next explicit promise that "this gospel of the kingdom shall be preached in the whole world as a testimony to all the nations" (Matt. 24:14) has significantly contributed to the perceived necessity of the Olivet Discourse being read with an exclusively futuristic outlook. Today, as the gospel continues to reach places where it is unknown, the logical assumption is that this promise of the Olivet Discourse remains to be fulfilled. However, what does "the whole world" mean?

There were three primary Greek terms that scriptures use to describe "people" in gathered setting. The first was "kosmos," which described an ordered system in a universal context. It most often portrayed "worldly affairs" (Strong's) or the "inhabitants of the world," (Thayer's) even in secular Greek texts. The second was "oikoumene," which referred specifically to "the inhabited earth" (Strong's & Thayer's), giving a portrayal of a regional empire. The final word was "ge," a simpler term with a narrower focus on physical earth like "soil, land, region" or specifically "inhabitants of a region" (Strong's & Thayer's). The word "ge," therefore, described a very targeted area of the earth, which most often contextually described the nation of Israel.

Matthew chose to use "oikoumene" as his "world" in the present verse. And like most Greek words with multiple uses, the context helps reveal the true meaning. According to Strong's concordance, "oikoumene" often meant "the inhabited world, that is, the Roman world, for all outside it was regarded as of no account," while Thayer's

Lexicon stated either "the portion of the earth inhabited by the Greeks," or "the Roman empire." In short, the context put forth by Matthew must have been the Roman world and all those under the empire's dominion. Thus, Jesus did not promise that the gospel would reach the most hidden corners of the globe to trigger His return, but that it would be preached into every corner of the only "world" that people knew – the boundaries of the Roman Empire.

Writers from other cultures, similarly, would have used such terminology to describe that which resided within their territory and subject to the ruling empire. The citizenry had little awareness of a populated world outside the realm and would have had no grasp of continents or ethnic groups from every "nation" under the sun. Their understanding was limited to their local environments. For example, the claim in Acts 2:5 that "there were Jews living in Jerusalem, devout men from every nation under heaven" cannot refer to a globalized outlook, for there certainly were no Jews in Madagascar. The historical context, therefore, must be limited to the perspective of the first-century reader; the "world" that they knew was the empire under which they lived.

According to Paul's letters – the gospel spread was accomplished. To the Romans, between AD 56-58, Paul wrote, "I thank my God through Jesus Christ for you all, because your faith is being proclaimed throughout the whole world," (Rom. 1:8) and, invoking OT prophecy about Israel's rejection of the gospel and the Gentile reception, "Their voice has gone out into all the earth, and their words to the ends of the world" (Rom. 10:18). Likewise, to the Colossians in AD 60-62, Paul confirmed that the "word of truth, the gospel, which has come to you, just as in all the world also it is constantly bearing fruit and increasing" (Col. 1:5-6), reiterating "the gospel that you have heard, which was proclaimed in all creation under heaven, and of which I, Paul, was made a minister" (Col. 1:23).

It is also important to understand what Jesus meant when He stated that, after all these things mentioned, "the end will come" (Matt 24:14). As the evangelical psyche remains preoccupied with eschatological insight, the mainstream presumption is that such a phrase must reference the end of the cosmos. However, Jesus' public ministry had an immediate objective – to deliver the House of Israel. The spirit of Elijah prophesied by the book of Malachi had come in the person of John the Baptist (Matt. 11:13-14), denoting that Israel's definitive judgment was upon them (Mal. 4:5). Likewise, Jesus' message that this was the time of salvation and judgment for Israel was elucidated in that "these are days of vengeance so that all things which are written will be fulfilled" (Luke 21:22). The spiritual adultery, religious idolatry, sexual immorality, and general disregard of God's law had brought the promise of Deuteronomy to their doorstep (Deut. 28). All this would be fulfilled in the very event that Jesus used to open the Discourse – the temple destruction. These signs previously listed by the Savior would indicate the imminence of this consummation so that by God's mercy the Jewish Christians in Judea could flee and escape the tribulation, thereby preserving the remnant.

Thus, all signs foretold by Jesus were fulfilled in the first century as a Messianic prophecy of the destruction of the temple and the end of the Jewish polity; not intended for Christians in present day. Any future interpretation, unfortunately, is susceptible to relativism and can be molded into a prediction of any teacher's partiality or presupposition. This "end" spoken of, therefore, was not 2,000 years in the future; rather the end of the Judaic age in the first century. God would destroy the ways of Old, making a path for the New.

Jesus then intensified the Discourse with the consequences of ignorance to His heeding by entering into an account of the horrors from which people would suffer at Jerusalem's destruction. To introduce this, He cited Daniel's well-known descriptive, the "abomination of desolation" (Matt. 24:15). Regarding Daniel, there are three references to an "abomination of desolation" in the prophecies spoken therein; 9:27, 11:31, and 12:11. Dispensationalism (See **Christian Eschatological Terminology**) interprets "the abomination" as describing Jesus' final archenemy – the Antichrist – in the indefinite future, as he assumes a sacrilegious place in a rebuilt Jewish temple. There is no evidence to support this conclusion. First, there is no text that associates this term with one individual. Second, all of Daniel's references are accounted for in history, a fact that this commentary will verify. But most importantly, Luke's corresponding account of this discourse explicitly identifies the subject: "When you see Jerusalem surrounded by armies, then recognize that her desolation is near" (Luke 21:20). Jewish historian Josephus explained that the Roman ensigns were an abomination to the Jews, so when the armies arrived with their emblems, it meant that the abomination that would make desolate was upon them.

Jesus accordingly warned those who would await the fulfillment of this prophecy at the arrival of the Roman army to the gates of Jerusalem, "Then those who are in Judea must flee to the mountains" (Matt. 24:16), for the subsequent affair to occur would produce unprecedented anguish upon those left behind. And for those who realized the significance of the moment, their departure from the city would require the swiftest of responses: "Whoever is on the housetop must not go down to get the things out that are in his house. Whoever is in the field must not turn back to get his cloak" (Matt. 24:17-18). Why the urgency to drop everything and leave in haste?

On the Sabbath, the gates of the city were closed, which would have prevented anyone from leaving. Winters caused roads to flood, making for difficult, if not impossible, travel. The armies would cut off supply lines to Jerusalem, leaving people to starve. To convey the gravity of this event, Jesus cautioned there would be no shelter given to even a nursing mother. To those who would listen, the exodus should waste no time, and for those who rejected Him, there would be no tomorrow, for He could not cloak the horror of the slaughter with any diplomacy.

This forthcoming event that would soon come upon Jerusalem provides the foundations for the majority of evangelical eschatological preconceptions about the future – The Great Tribulation. Nearly all futurist believers are convinced of an approaching time of unprecedented Tribulation upon the earth, led first by dreadful persecutions at the hands of the final Antichrist and followed up by the bowls of God's wrath (Rev. 16). Of course, that is unsurprising if the Olivet Discourse is interpreted from an exclusively futuristic perspective. However, in the narrative context of the Roman armies laying siege to Jerusalem, this assault would herald the unprecedented first-century Jewish holocaust, "For then there will be great tribulation, such as has not occurred since the beginning of the world until now, nor ever will" (Matt. 24:21).[70] This is another reference from Daniel's last chapter: "And there will be a time of distress such as never occurred since there was a nation until that time; and at that time your people, everyone who is found written in the book, will be rescued" (Dan. 12:1).

Luke gives additional detail here, where Matthew did not: "Because these are days of vengeance so that all things which are written will be fulfilled...for there will be great distress upon the land and wrath to this people; and they will fall by the edge of the sword and will be led captive into all the nations; and Jerusalem will be trampled underfoot by the Gentiles, until the times of the Gentiles are fulfilled" (Luke 21:22-24). Indeed, prominent Jewish historian Flavius Josephus detailed the calamities of this siege, during which the horrors of families and citizens within the walls and those who attempted to escape were extreme. One story, described by Josephus, relays such unbelievable suffering:

> There was a certain woman that dwelt beyond the Jordan, her name was Mary; her father was Eleazar, of the village of Bethezob, which signifies the house of Hyssop. She was eminent for her family and her wealth, and had fled away to Jerusalem with the rest of the multitude, and was with them besieged therein at this time. The other effects of this woman had been already seized upon, such I mean as she had brought with her out of Perea, and removed to the city. What she had treasured up besides, as also what food she had contrived to save, had also been carried off by the rapacious guards, who came every day running into her house for that purpose. This put the poor woman into a very great passion, and by the frequent reproaches and imprecations she cast at these rapacious villains,

---

[70] This is what many Christians believe is coming upon the world – but from which they will be raptured. Indeed, one's theological position on the rapture is, often, identified by its timing within the context of this Tribulation: pre-trib, mid-trib, post-trib, etc. A proper understanding of this event's significance for today's Christian Church cannot be understated.

she had provoked them to anger against her; but one
of them, either out of the indignation she had raised
against herself, or out of commiseration of her case,
would take way her life; and if she found any food,
she perceived her labors were for others, and not for
herself; and it was now become impossible for her any
way to find any more food, while the famine pierced
through her very bowels and marrow, when also her
passion was fired to a degree beyond the famine itself;
nor did she consult with any thing but with her passion
and the necessity she was in. She then attempted the
most unnatural thing; and snatching up her son, who
was a child sucking at her breast, she said, 'O thou
miserable infant! For whom shall I preserve thee in
this war, this famine, and this sedition? As to the war
with the Romans, if they preserve our lives, we must be
slaves. This famine also will destroy us, even before that
slavery comes upon us. Yet are these seditious rogues
more terrible than both the other. Come on; be thou
my food, and be thou a fury to these seditious varlets,
and a by-word to the world, which is all that is now
wanting to complete the calamities of the Jews.' As
soon as she had said this, she slew her son, and then
roasted him, and eat the one half of him, and kept the
other half by her concealed. Upon this the seditious
came in presently, and smelling the horrid scent of this
food, they threatened her that they would cut her throat
immediately if she did not show them what food she
had gotten ready. She replied that she had saved a very
fine portion of it for them, and withal uncovered what
was left of her son. Hereupon they were seized with a
horror and amazement of mind, and stood astonished
at the sight, when she said to them, 'This is mine own
son, and what hath been done was mine own doing!
Come, eat of this food; for I have eaten of it myself! Do
you pretend to be either more tender than a woman,

or more compassionate than a mother; but if you be so scrupulous, and do abominate this my sacrifice, as I have eaten the one half, let the rest be reserved for me also.' After which those men went out trembling, being never so much affrighted at any things as they were at this, and with some difficulty they left the rest of that meat to the mother. Upon which the whole city was full of this horrid action immediately; and while every body laid this miserable case before their own eyes, they trembled, as if this unheard of action had been done by themselves. So those were thus distressed by the famine were very desirous to die, and those already dead were esteemed happy, because they had not lived long enough either to hear or see such miseries.[71]

Even such a horrific description about God's judgment was prophesied upon Israel's first temple in the sixth century BC, only to be recapitulated in this assault: "Therefore, fathers will eat their sons among you, and sons will eat their fathers; for I will execute judgments on you and scatter all your remnant to every wind" (Ezk. 5:10). The effects of their tribulation would yield the complete destruction of the Jewish nation and institution. Even on his path to death, lumbering His cross to Golgotha, among Jesus' final utterances, He tried to warn them, "Daughters of Jerusalem, stop weeping for Me, but weep for yourselves and for your children. For behold the days are coming when they will say, 'blessed are the barren, and the wombs that never bore, and the breasts that never nursed.' Then they will begin to say to the mountains, 'fall on us' and to the hills, 'cover us.' For if they do these things when the tree is green, what will happen when it is dry?" (Luke 23:28-31). The disaster that loomed over Jerusalem would be so terrible that hopeful mothers would appreciate their infertility more than allowing a child to experience what would occur.

In context, however, Jesus yet noted that God's promises to His people would be fulfilled even amid this desolation. God showed extreme mercy to His remnant, the true Israel, who embraced the

---

[71] Josephus, *Wars*, 6.3.4.

gospel, for "unless those days had been cut short, no life would have been saved, but for the sake of the elect those days will be cut short" (Matt. 24:22). As the prevailing historical analysis suggests, the entire Jewish population would have been pursued and wiped out had those days continued without ceasing. Fortunately, God's divine protection for His remnant is a consistent biblical refrain extending from the Israelite experience during the final plague on Egypt in Exodus 12 to the 144,000 sealed from divine judgments in Revelation 7. Despite the nations ruling over them for centuries, suffering exile from their promised land, and enduring predetermined times of captivity – Israel would not be annihilated (Jeremiah 29:11).

It is reported that during the assault of Jerusalem, three factions began to split the citizenry, led by individuals claiming to be messiahs, thereby fulfilling Jesus' timely reiteration that "false Christs and false prophets will arise and will show great signs and wonders, so as to mislead, if possible, even the elect" (Matt 24:24). Seeking to organize resistance against the attacking armies, John of Gischala, Simon Bar-Gioras, and Eleazar (a temple priest) wrestled for leadership control through messianic contention, acting as saviors of the city.[72] Josephus, again, also supplements the narrative with confirmations of Jesus' predictions: "A false prophet was the occasion of these people's destruction, who had made a public proclamation in the city that very day, that God commanded them to get upon the temple, and that there they should receive miraculous signs of their deliverance. Now there was then a great number of false prophets suborned by the tyrants to impose on the people, who denounced this to them, that they should wait from deliverance from God."[73] Jerusalem would experience such devastation of death that Jesus likened it to what would be a great feast for the birds: "Wherever the corpse is there the vultures will gather" (Matt 24:28) in that no location within the walls was absent of dead bodies.[74]

---

[72] Ibid., 5.3.1.

[73] Ibid., 6.5.2.

[74] If this Great Tribulation happened 1,952 years ago, against the Jews at the destruction of Jerusalem as the fulfillment of a prophecy given by Jesus of Nazareth that promised judgment against first century, apostate Israel for their covenantal adultery – then we do not presently await one in the future.

Jesus then began a symbolic depiction of the consequences of this judgment upon Israel utilizing direct OT metaphorical, apocalyptic language to confirm its end: "But immediately after the tribulation of those days, the sun will be darkened, and the moon will not give its light, and the stars will fall from the sky, and the powers of the heavens will be shaken" (Matt. 29:29). This first image is taken from prophetic accounts that figuratively articulated the disastrous fall of a nation or people. For example, Babylon is marked as having been destroyed in this manner: "For the stars of heaven and their constellations will not flash forth their light; the sun will be dark when it rises and the moon will not shed its light" (Is. 13:10). Egypt's role in the biblical narrative yet remains as God promised: "And when I extinguish you, I will cover the heavens and darken their stars; I will cover the sun with a cloud and the moon will not give its light" (Ezk. 32:7).

The fate of Edom was foretold in such representational language, "And all the host of heaven will wear away, and the sky will be rolled up like a scroll; all their hosts with wither away" (Is. 34:4). These allegories are not exclusive to the pagans, as seen in Joel, who prophecies about the time of future judgment against Israel, "The sun will be turned into darkness, and the moon into blood Before the great and awesome day of the Lord comes" (Joel 2:31) and, "the sun and the moon grow dark and the stars lose their brightness" (Joel 3:15). Amos offers a like description: "'It will come about in that day,' declares the Lord God, 'that I will make the sun go down at noon and make the earth dark in broad daylight'" (Amos 8:9).

All instances of this OT language clearly refer to destruction, ruin, or a period of calamity against those in rebellion to God; how great nations are brought to nothing. Matthew 29:29 does not describe a literal, physical collapse of the universe in which the elements of God's cosmos fall directly on this world sometime in the indefinite future. Earth itself would be obliterated should it collide with even a large fragment of any interstellar object. And yet the Bible says, "The earth remains forever," (Ecc. 1:4) and that "He established [it] upon its foundations, so that it will not totter forever and ever" (Ps. 104:5). Thus, within a figurative understanding, this phraseology defines the consequence of this Tribulation episode upon Israel in that the collapse of its religious, economic, and political standing would occur when their greatest spiritual power, their Old Covenant bond with Yahweh, was shattered (Daniel 12:7). Jesus' language emphasized that so impactful would the devastation of their entire institution be that it would shake the powers of heaven.

The metaphorical language continues into a promise that "the sign of the Son of Man will appear in the sky, and then all the tribes of the earth will mourn, and they will see the Son of Man coming on the clouds of the sky with power and great glory" (Matt. 24:30). Jesus' language is a direct quote from OT prophetic imagery in the book of Daniel: "Behold, with the clouds of heaven one like a Son of Man was coming. And He came to the Ancient of Days, and was presented before Him. And to Him was given dominion, glory and a kingdom" (Dan. 7:13-14). Daniel visualized the Messiah approaching God the Father, in heaven, Who would grant Him universal power and authority, as King and Judge, to rule over a coming kingdom.

The careful bible student, then, must interpret the Savior's use of Daniel's phrase by taking its original meaning and applying it to the context described in Matthew – as an answer to His disciple's questions about the temple destruction (Mark 13:3-4, Luke 21:7). If "Son of Man coming on the clouds," therefore, represents a spiritual exaltation – not a physical descent to earth – that would bestow the universal right to save and to judge, to what could Jesus be referring? One must identify the "sign of the Son of Man." What was this sign – and who would see it?

In Matthew 26, Jesus stood before the Sanhedrin, prior to His crucifixion, and promised judgment against apostate Israel. He assured Caiaphas that Israel would, personally, see His heavenly exaltation: "Hereafter, you will see ("harao") the Son of Man sitting at the right hand of power, and coming on the clouds of heaven" (Matt. 26:64). If Daniel's meaning of this phrase guides the interpretation, then, Jesus was not promising that they would see Him physically coming down from the sky, landing on two feet, and leading an army of warriors onto an earthen battlefield. Rather, His position of Lordship over them would be fully established as unmistakable – something they had steadfastly denied to that point. The very thing that Jesus prophesied would happen – the temple destruction – would be the "sign" that

He was in heaven, seated as ruler over the coming kingdom with the absolute power as Israel's Judge.

This corresponds flawlessly with Jesus' description that the "tribes of the earth will mourn" (Matt. 24:30) upon witnessing this event. The Greek word for "tribe" is "phuo," which maintained a persistent scriptural reference to the twelve tribes of Israel. As already discussed, the Greek term for "earth" ("ge"), had particular associations with a specific region of land. Within context, the "earth" spoken of contains the twelve tribes of Israel. According to one scholar then, "upon purely lexical considerations, the term can be understood as designating the Promised Land."[75] Jesus has thus confirmed that Israel will enter into a state of despair and lamentation upon the realization of the truth about the arrival of judgment.

As an added bonus for biblical context, this exact portion of Jesus' Discourse is copied into Revelation's introduction where John quotes nearly word for word, Jesus' prediction: "Behold, He is coming with the clouds, and every eye will see Him, even those who pierced Him; and all the tribes of the earth will mourn over Him" (Rev. 1:7). This helps to establish the subject of John's apocalypse which would be the same as that of Jesus' Olivet Discourse – the destruction of Jerusalem.

This devastation of the entire Jewish institution validated Jesus as the One who sat in judgment having received such authority from the Ancient of Days. Indeed, He was the new temple; the old was destroyed. As John Lightfoot stated in his commentary, "Then shall the Son of man give a proof of Himself, whom they would not before acknowledge: a proof, indeed, not in any visible figure, but in vengeance and judgment so visible, that all the tribes of the earth shall be forced to acknowledge him the avenger....Many times they asked of him a sign; now a sign shall appear, that he is the true messiah...."[76] If understood in context and language, it becomes clear that Jesus promised to *return* in judgment against Israel from on high, and upon its completion, His position would become distinct.

This would be the "coming" that He had promised His listeners

---

[75] Gentry, *Before Jerusalem Fell*, p. 128.

[76] John Lightfoot, *Hebrew and Talmudical Exercitations*, Robert Gandell, ed. Vol. II, (Oxford: Oxford University Press, 1859), p. 320.

would occur before they had finished going through all the towns in Israel (Matt. 10:23) and that those standing before Him would see before they died (Matt. 16:28). This would be the "coming" of which Jesus told Peter that John would be alive to see (John 21:22). This would be the "coming" at the end of the Age, about which the disciples had desperately inquired to open the Olivet Discourse (Matt. 24:3). The harvester would arrive with His "winnowing fork" (Luke 3:17) to administer the only other "coming" He had ever promised. This was indeed the Second Coming. And it occurred at the destruction of Jerusalem.

Wrapping up His symbolic description of the city's fall, Jesus stated that "He will send forth His angels with a great trumpet and they will gather together His elect from the four winds, from one end of the sky to the other" (Matt. 24:31). As this group of verses seem to be alluding to the final consequences of Israel's punishment, the last phase must be the promised harvest consummating their judgment. Jesus applied this same language during His public ministry when He had used parables to describe this forthcoming event: "So just as the tares are gathered up and burned with fire, so shall it be at the end of the age. The Son of Man will send forth His angels and they will gather out of His kingdom all stumbling blocks, and those who commit lawlessness" (Matt. 13:40-41). Likewise, when visualizing the process with a dragnet, He stated, "When it was filled, they drew it up on the beach; and they sat down and gathered the good fish into containers, but the bad they threw away. So it will be at the end of the age; the angels will come forth and take out the wicked from among the righteous" (Matt. 13:48-49).

This section of verses (Matt. 24:29-31) succinctly describes how the destruction of Jerusalem would be Israel's promised consummation event. The tribulation upon the city (Matt. 24:21-28) would cause such destruction to the Jewish polity and identity that it would shake the powers of heaven, ushering in a monumental shift in world affairs (Matt. 24:29), at which point the truth about Jesus' position, power, and authority would become unmistakable as He administers final judgment upon Israel from God's right hand (Matt. 24:30), which was accomplished when His angels spread out to collect "His elect" for the harvest of the just and the unjust (Matt. 24:31), thereby bringing an end to the Judaic Age.

Drawing the discourse to a close, Jesus gave a parable of the "fig tree" (Matt. 24:32), which was known to have lost its leaves in winter to begin blossoming in late spring. They were commonplace on the Mount of Olives, making it easy for Jesus to draw a lesson from something close by. But His description of the tenderness and natural growth indicated a coming season, signaling that as the fresh green of the tree is a sign of summer, so will be signs of everything that He had just pronounced.

Despite the historical information just presented, the vast majority of the evangelical church reads this Discourse with an exclusively futurist lens. Every generation quietly hopes that theirs is the one to see the end of all things, thus, the keen interest in how contemporary events can align with something found in Jesus' prophecy, which intensifies that desire. However, if one reads Matthew 24:1-33 as entirely futuristic, then the next verse poses a substantial textual problem that requires reconciliation. In concluding the heart of this address, Jesus explicitly stated, "Truly I say to you, this generation ("genea") will not pass away until all these things take place" (Matt. 24:34). How does one interpret the Greek word "genea"? By definition, a "generation" is the typical period of time during which a collective group of people live, which scholars agree encompassed an average of 33-40 years in the first century. *Strong's Exhaustive Concordance* defines the word as an "age" or "time" during which a people exist, while Thayer's Lexicon attributed the definition of "the whole multitude of men living at the same time" as pertaining to this verse.

One may also examine its preceding scriptural usage and read it within the proper context. Scholar John Nolland noted in his commentary that "Matthew uses genea here for the tenth time... 'This generation' is the generation of Jesus' contemporaries."[77] Every single time that Matthew utilized the term "this generation," he was describing those to whom Jesus was speaking in that moment; never a "future" generation (See 11:16, 12:41, 42, 45, 23:36). This is supported

---

[77] John Nolland, *The Gospel of Matthew: A Commentary on the Greek Text.* (Grand Rapids: Eerdmans, 2005), pp. 988-989.

by Matthew's grammatical use of a near demonstrative ("this") which emphasizes an unambiguous directive to that present audience.

That Jesus was referring to that climactic generation as His audience is also supported by the surrounding context in the book. In this portion of Matthew's narrative, Jesus had spent the three previous chapters (21-23) pronouncing judgment upon apostate Israel; He physically cleared the temple of its malefactors and cursed the nation for its hypocrisy, prophesied covenantal retribution for their rejection of God's salvation, and pledged perilous afflictions against the priestly leadership for their deceit, all culminating in His prediction that the blood of all God's prophets and saints would be upon *their* heads resulting in "your house is being left to you desolate" (Matt. 23:38). Even as Jesus delivered these warnings, Matthew stated that "the chief priests and Pharisees...understood that He was speaking about *them* [emphasis mine]" (Matt. 21:45).

The definitive answer to the question of the Olivet Discourse's status as a fulfilled prophecy is found in its clarification that "this generation will not pass away until all these things take place" (Matt. 24:34). This has a simple meaning: the events that Jesus had previously indicated must all transpire before that generation expired. Thus, the Olivet Discourse should be not read as describing contemporary affairs for future readers. It was a prophecy given to the disciples as a warning of the trials they would face in the coming years after Jesus' death – during the time of transition between world ages – as the time about which the scriptures had foretold drew near (Luke 21:22). Jesus prophesied the city and temple's destruction as described in Daniel and instructed the remnant to flee upon the arrival of the armies so they would be saved from Israel's Great Tribulation that was promised them but that Jesus would also administer.

The events foretold were fulfilled nearly two millennia ago at the destruction of Jerusalem, as retribution for Israel's covenantal adultery and rejection of God's salvation. If this Discourse has come and gone, then futurist eschatological assumptions about a rapture, Antichrist, and seven-year Great Tribulation meet their immediate theological end, at which point the church can begin to promote a gospel of peace – not of fear.

THE PERILS OF RECKLESS
ESCHATOLOGY

C.S. Lewis was one of Christianity's most ardent apologists who penned several important fiction and non-fiction works to evangelize his proud faith. His contributions to Christianity have guided countless people into its spiritual truths by creatively harmonizing reason and faith. In fact, in 2000 *Christianity Today* named Lewis' *Mere Christianity* the number one religious book of the twentieth century. Millions of Lewis' books are sold every year in America and Britain, cementing his distinction in such a way that the author's prevalence demands a continual stream of updated critical analysis with each new generation.

In the early 1950's, Lewis gathered a collection of his articles that had been published in independent circulations like *The Saturday Evening Post* or *The Atlantic Monthly* (now called *The Atlantic*), and issued a lesser-known book that focused on the challenges of evil in the world called *The World's Last Night and Other Essays*. In it he emphasized how Christians navigate the world's temptations and highlighted the significance of such an awareness in the Christian life as essential for influencing contemporary affairs, even suggesting the future should be of much less concern as dealing rightly with the present. To elaborate on this point, his last essay in the publication dealt directly with the nuances of Jesus' Second Coming, an element that he rightly considered to be "an integral part of the faith."[78]

Lewis did not shy away from the Second Coming's theological

---

[78] C.S. Lewis, *The World's Last Night and Other Essays*, (New York: Harcourt, Brace and Company, 1952), p. 97.

complexities, but drew attention to the Christian propensity for desperately prophesying its imminence. The famed author admitted that the doctrine of the Second Coming "has, in the past, led Christians into very great follies. Apparently many people find it difficult to believe in this great event without trying to guess its date, or even without accepting as a certainty the date that any quack or hysteric offers them. To write a history of all these exploded predictions would need a book, and a sad, sordid, tragi-comical book it would be."[79] Lewis recalled one contemporary prediction in 1843 by William Miller, who believed he had precisely calculated the minute that Jesus would return. Of the alarm generated among local believers, Lewis said, "Thousands waited for the Lord at midnight on 21 March, and went home to a late breakfast on [the next day] followed by the jeers of a drunkard."[80]

Likening this event to a bout of "mass hysteria," Lewis cautioned that Christians should never teach about the day of Jesus' "future" return to an emotional crowd without reminding them that everything related to its timing is merely conjecture on the part of the speaker. Indeed, Lewis captured one of the essential points of the doctrine: when Jesus promised it, no one would know when it would occur because such a crucial element heightened the need for individual urgency. In closing his essay, he stated, "You cannot guess it. If you could, one chief purpose for which it was foretold would be frustrated. And God's purposes are not so easily frustrated. One's ears should be closed against any future William Miller in advance."[81] Read that last sentence carefully. The most respected Christian author of the twentieth century has advised that when a man begins predicting the day of Jesus' return – one is to turn away immediately.

With that in mind, consider the current ministry of famed evangelical pastor John Hagee, a man devoted to offering complete political and theological support to the nation of Israel. Hagee, the Chairman of Christians United for Israel and pastor of the Cornerstone megachurch in San Antonio, Texas, has decidedly claimed the mathematical ability to determine that exact date of Jesus' return based on this book's

---

[79] Ibid., p. 106.
[80] Ibid., p. 107.
[81] Ibid., p. 108.

previously explained eschatological assumptions (see **The Future According to the Futurist**). In an interview on Trinity Broadcasting Network (TBN) in which he described the dispensational prediction of the final Antichrist's "end times" plan to sign a seven-year peace treaty with Israel, Hagee confidently stated, "If you can tell me the day the Antichrist will sign that treaty, I can tell you, *to the day* [emphasis added] that Christ will come back."[82] As of today, Hagee Ministries has 2.6 million Facebook followers, nearly a million followers on Twitter, and his church boasts a 17,000-member congregation while his books are on the bestseller lists of *The New York Times* and *USA Today*.

Doomsday preachers have had their time in the spotlight because of their predictions about Jesus' return. One such pastor, Harold Camping, found popularity from his brazen, repeated predictions about the world's end. Though he had made such estimates early in his ministry, Camping gained notoriety for predicting that God's judgment day would arrive on 21 May 2011, which turned out to be just two years before his own death. His unwavering confidence in this revelation jumpstarted a public campaign into which he invested tens of millions of dollars and dispatched numerous followers around the country to spread the message, some of whom had "quit their jobs and sold all their possessions" to support the cause.[83] One man reportedly spent more than $140,000 of his personal savings on advertisements to bolster the efforts.[84]

When the projected date passed without incident, Atheist groups around the country held public celebrations mocking Camping's movement using as it as a clear example of how religious fundamentalism can leave no room for reason.[85] As would be expected of a religious

---

[82] Praise on TBN, "John Hagee: The Rapture and the Second Coming of Christ." *YouTube*. Uploaded on September 21, 2021. https://youtu.be/5fw4ge8Gyzc.

[83] CBS/AP, "Harold Camping, radio host who predicted world's end, dead at 92." December 17, 2013. https://www.cbsnews.com/news/harold-camping-radio-host-who-predicted-worlds-end-dead-at-92.

[84] US & Canada, "'Rapture:' Believers perplexed after prediction fails." May 22, 2011. https://www.bbc.com/news/world-us-canada-13489641.

[85] US & Canada, "'Rapture' apocalypse prediction sparks atheist reaction." May 21, 2011. https://www.bbc.com/news/world-us-canada-13468131. There was a two-day "Rapture After Party" held in Fayetteville, North Carolina, with groups in Washington state, Texas, Florida, and California.

leader discovered to have issued an incorrect calculation, Camping amended the prediction, moving it six months into the future. This, too, expired, forcing him to issue an apology and concede that his penchant for end of the world forecasting should cease.

Consider the money wasted on billboard and radio ads that the church might have used for those in need or the families that availed themselves of all financial and material belongings to preach a message with no scriptural support. Camping fostered a dangerous culture within his ministry that favored personal revelation over God's Word. The Bible explicitly states that such precise knowledge of Jesus' return was available to no one but God the Father. Is it a wonder that the world mocks Christianity for its own lack of self-control and judiciousness? Camping's ministry did not exercise wisdom or stewardship. Instead, it discharged reckless eschatology that left people scared, deceived, and penniless.

Apparently, many have disregarded Lewis' advice – and scripture.

The mystical nature of predictive prophecy has been taken to perilous extremes in today's American evangelical landscape. This practice has been belittled, mishandled, and abused by countless televangelists looking to make a dollar off the average American's weakness for feeding personal desire. What scripture describes as a sacred communication medium between God and a trusted intermediary has evolved into a loose cannon fired off by any leader feeling "led by the Spirit" to offer superficial inspiration to a desperate congregation.

How many evangelical pastors became so politically entranced by President Donald Trump after his surprise 2016 victory that they openly and authoritatively prophesied his follow-up, "God-ordained" triumph in the 2020 election – only to witness his ultimate defeat to Joe Biden? Unfortunately, many of those pastors had to address their miscalculation by apologizing and repenting before their congregations for getting it wrong. Christian, you need to realize something about those predictions. Those pastors were not simply incorrect; that error make them false prophets.

Regrettably, what many congregants experience as "prophecy" today is mostly a blurry combination of shallow and ambiguous words of encouragement typically offered as an attempt to demonstrate a leader's ability to commandingly exercise the gifts of the Spirit (I Cor. 12:7-11). This is done with a tactic similar to those used at physic readings by which the actor employs imprecise terminology through shotgun-style inquiries that cover as many subjects as possible and are based on the highest probability for producing an emotional response. As the church crowd's reaction grows, the leader's spiritual dexterity gains increased credibility, thereby reinforcing their reliability as an authoritative voice from God. Indeed, prophecy is often the most stimulating proclamation for modern audiences earnestly obsessed with signs and wonders.

Prophecy was a revered spiritual gift bestowed upon a trusted servant of God. It did not sit on a retail shelf awaiting selection after a consumer's personal deliberation to use in accordance with their individual determinations or will. This gift was given by the Spirit (I Cor. 12:4) and served a distinct purpose to edify the Body of Christ. Divine prophecies were targeted and specific revelations, directly from the Almighty, to someone whom He anointed to be a message carrier. They were, therefore, not lab animals with which the believer experimented. Prophecy was not a "stab in the dark" with which one would do better next time.

A prophet spoke on behalf of God, and because God is not a liar, there was no guessing game. Such was the gravity of prophecy in Judaism that Mosaic Law placed an exceptional warning on mishandling its sanctity: "But the prophet who speaks a word presumptuously in My name which I have not commanded him to speak, or which he speaks in the name of other gods, that prophet shall die" (Deut. 18:20). For pastors who flippantly engage the charismatic side of faith to manipulate the atmosphere of their Sunday morning service – proceed with extreme caution.

As one scholar noted, there were three primary features of prophecy that "recur across works of various authors of early Jewish literature: 1) its empowerment through God's Spirit, 2) its trustworthiness as true and evident knowledge, and 3) its infallible capacity to foretell future events."[86] Prophecies had parameters by which to be assessed, and when spoken, the people were commanded to test them "to see whether they

---

[86] Albert Hogeterp, "Prophecy and the prophetic as aspects of Paul's Theology." *Stellenbosch Theological Journal* Vol. 4, No. 2, 2018) pp. 169-196. p. 175.

are from God" (I John 4:1, Deut. 18:21-22). A person who speaks is not permitted to qualify their Sunday morning "feelings" as revelation from God simply by virtue of being a church leader. True prophets were identified by not only their propensity to prophesy unwelcome news to their peers, often making them outcasts in their own community, but more importantly, the accuracy of those predictions. I pray, therefore, that you understand that this spiritual gift's purpose and nature is not to be trivialized.

Here is the point: God's prophecies are flawless. We must examine them in detail because when observed in their truth, they accomplish numerous purposes in the believer's life. Appreciating the exactness of God's promises will increase knowledge for defending one's beliefs and understanding the nature of His Being as just and trustworthy. Seeing prophetic truth in its fulfillment will solidify the foundations of one's faith that no foothold of the enemy could begin to crack. Indeed, Jesus prophesied to His disciples for purposes of protection against future deceptions and preparation for events in Jewish history. He warned that without such grounding, "The evil one comes and snatches away what has been sown....He has no firm root in himself, but is only temporary, and when affliction or persecution arises because of the word, immediately he falls away" (Matt. 13:19-21). Without faith it is impossible to please God, and yet the evidences of His faithfulness surround us as world history demonstrates His character and sovereignty, so we can see His glory. He is, undeniably, the quintessential story-teller.

The Christ-follower is called to love God. One shows such love through obedience and therefore, should develop the ability to read scripture correctly to understand what such obedience looks like. This book will not attempt to convince you that the author is absolutely and indisputably correct about eschatology. In fact, the objective is to introduce the believer to a new world of biblical understanding, reading scripture in a straightforward and uncomplicated manner that does not weave a tangled web of unverifiable prophecy from arbitrary verses that only creates confusion. Indeed, an incorrect understanding of biblical prophecy can levy several devastating consequences upon the Body of Christ – and those around us. It cannot be denied that one's eschatological outlook can affect one's entire worldview and, by extension, how they live their life.

It was a warped interpretation of the book of Revelation that gave famed Waco, Texas cult leader David Koresh (Branch Davidians) his power. Research on his apocalyptic beliefs abounds, offering analysis on everything from his emphasis on the seven seals of Revelation to his interpretation of the United States government representing the book's two-horned beast (Rev. 13:11). But at the foundation of his teaching was the framework that God reveals progressive forms of salvation to mankind throughout world history. In other words, each generation gets a new piece of the puzzle. This concept of progressive revelation inevitably allows for radical interpretations and additions to sacred biblical theology. This is a staple form of teaching given by most cult leaders.

People become increasingly susceptible to manipulation when they are convinced that God is constantly revealing hidden information given exclusively to them. And they are particularly vulnerable when interpreting this information in the context of the immediate environment. Koresh's accusation, for example, that the United States government was one of the crucial, antagonistic figures of Revelation gave the book a remarkably personal feel to their circumstances. It sparked simultaneous concerns of fear, yet spiritual obligation among the cult's followers that triggered a dutiful separation from the world with a fierce physical defense of personal property. While Koresh may never have asserted an exclusive claim to be a reincarnation of Jesus Christ, he believed he was the Lamb who could open Revelation's seven seals of judgment.

However, the individual messianic claims made by Koresh are irrelevant. The issue is that if one has a fragile grasp of biblical eschatology, deception becomes a powerful tool for any charismatic cult leader. According to two biblical scholars who had been tasked by the FBI to negotiate with Koresh during the standoff with law enforcement at the compound, all that might have been needed to avoid catastrophe was to persuade the leader of a differing interpretation of Revelation.[87] However, time was of the essence for government negotiators and the Waco compound was raided before this teaching could be administered. Up to 80 men, women, and children were killed during the government assault with numerous survivors prosecuted and imprisoned for their roles in the armed rebellion. This author admits the extreme nature of this example; however, many cults are formed and nurtured within the premise of apocalyptic imminence. And when biblical truth is replaced with personal revelation and an incorrect interpretation of eschatology the results can literally, be fatal.

There are other instances of lethal consequences because of bad eschatology. In 2020, during the Covid-19 pandemic, one young man became so convinced that the vaccine and its PCR tests were the mark of the beast from Revelation that he left his family to separate from the world and ride out the inevitable apocalypse "off the grid."[88] Having been persuaded by a social media influencer of the necessity for finding a remote spot on earth that the virus had not yet reached, he journeyed into the South Pacific on a small boat with another man who shared his fear, thinking they could escape Satan's apocalyptic attack.

After searching through risky weather, the boat's captain expressed the need to dock at a local refuge. However, to do so required everyone on board to be tested for Covid-19. Such a mandate caused the young men to jump overboard into the waters of the world's largest ocean as, according to the boat's captain, they were convinced by the media guru to be "afraid of taking the Covid test."[89] If it was the "mark of the beast," it would not only keep them from riding out the end of all things, but jeopardize the status of their eternal souls. More than two years later, the men have not been found. Indeed, this "mark of the beast" has

---

[87] Malcolm Gladwell. "Sacred and Profane: How not to negotiate with believers." *The New Yorker*, March 24, 2014. (March 31, 2014 issue). These two theologians were Philip Arnold and James Tabor.

[88] Randi Kaye and Anne Clifford, "They planned to 'ride out the end of the world.' They would up lost at sea." *CNN*, Updated January 19, 2023. https://www.cnn.com/2023/01/17/us/isaac-danian-covid-missing-south-pacific/index.html.

[89] Ibid.

penetrated the deepest recesses of American culture instilling fear with every new development of digital technology.

Misplaced futuristic interpretations of biblical prophecy also present a unique stumbling block for the gospel itself. Allow me to elaborate. Jesus once warned Jewish leaders, "You are from below, I am from above; you are of this world, I am not of this world. Therefore, I said to you that you will die in your sins, for unless you believe that I am He, you will die in your sins" (John 8:23-24). His purpose was to establish that their rejection of His role as Israel's Messiah would result in their destruction and condemnation. Believing Paul's gospel as outlined in his first letter to the Corinthians is reliant on the belief that Jesus of Nazareth fulfilled that identity. This belief, thus, is at the foundation of the gospel message.

Unsurprisingly, skeptics have devised an underhanded, yet clever, argument to disprove Christ's messianic claims. Christopher Hitchens (1949-2011) – one of the world's most renowned atheists, who travelled the globe to discredit and dismantle organized religion – frequently attempted to paint Jesus as a liar who self-engineered the fulfillment of OT messianic prophecies for personal benefit. In one debate with theologian Doug Wilson, Christian pastor in Moscow, Idaho, Hitchens invoked the futuristic interpretation of Jesus' Olivet Discourse (Matthew 24) as one such flaw in the Savior's teaching.

Hitchens pointed out that, in Matthew 24:30, Jesus stated that "all the tribes of the earth will mourn, and they will see the Son of Man coming on the clouds of the sky with power and great glory." As mentioned in this book's narrative of the Olivet Discourse, this verse is widely interpreted by evangelicals to be Jesus' promise of His future Second Advent at the end of the world. But as Hitchens astutely pointed out, Jesus also declared four verses later, "Truly I say to you, this generation ('genea') will not pass away until all these things take place" (Matt. 24:34). According to Hitchens' argument, Jesus promised His Return would occur within that generation ("genea"). If Jesus did not come back within that generation as He predicted – an assertion attested to by the evangelical church as it awaits His Second Coming – then reasonable thinkers are enabled to portray Him as a false prophet, liar, and certainly not the promised Messiah. Such an argument is similarly levied by famous British philosopher and author Bertrand Russell who said of Jesus in his lecture, "Why I Am Not a Christian":

> He certainly thought that his second coming would occur in clouds of glory before the death of all the people who were living at that time. There are a great many texts that prove that. He says for instance, "Ye shall not have gone over the cities of Israel until the Son of Man be come." Then He says, "There are some standing here, which shall not taste death until the Son of man comes into His kingdom." And there are a lot of places where it is quite clear that he believed that His Second Coming would happen during the lifetime of many then living. That was the belief of His earlier followers. And it was the basis of a good deal of His moral teaching. When he said, "take no thought for the 'morrow" and things of that sort, it was very largely because He thought that the Second Coming was going to be very soon. And that all ordinary and mundane affairs did not count. I have, as a matter of fact, known some Christians who did believe that the Second Coming was imminent. I knew a person who frightened His congregation terribly by telling them that the Second Coming was very imminent indeed. But they were much consoled when they found that he was planting trees in his garden. The early Christian did really believe it. And they did abstain from such things as planting trees in their gardens because they did accept from Christ the belief that the Second Coming was imminent. In that respect, clearly, He was not so wise as some other people have been. And he was certainly not superlatively wise.[90]

These avowed, highly intellectual atheists are using Jesus'

---

[90] Religion, Atheism, Science, "Why I am Not a Christian by Bertrand Russel, (1927)." *YouTube*, Uploaded January 17, 2013, https://youtu.be/NnDYvvevLZk.

Olivet Discourse against Him in an attempt to disprove His claim of Messiahship. And with an exclusively futuristic interpretation; the dispute is entirely legitimate. For if the church is still waiting for Jesus' return, then He lied to those to whom He was speaking ("this generation"). This problem forces Christian scholars who purport a future reading to begin changing the meaning of words in the text to defend their interpretation.

For example, these scholars are quick to alter the definition of "genea," offering multiple connotations for the Greek term such as "race" (which has its own Greek word) or "ethnicity" in an attempt to expand the characterization to a group identity that can be stretched over millennia as it fits within their theological supposition. One popular futurist interpretation is that the word "generation" is linguistically tied with "all these things" by which they mean that the future generation that sees all the signs that Jesus mentioned in the prophecy will be the generation spoken of. Such an understanding solidifies the belief that Jesus was speaking of a distant, future group of people. Greek concordances will confirm that this manipulates the basic meaning of the term.

As one can see, Hitchens' challenge puts the Christian apologist on their heels, scrapping for a counter punch, but unable to find one except through altering the meaning of their own text. This is all because evangelicals refuse to consider another interpretation other than their malleable, futuristic approach. Famed author C.S. Lewis even acknowledged the validity of Russell's argument against Jesus' messiahship because His promise in the Olivet Discourse did not come true, noting that the church has no response to the point, and lamented that because of this conundrum, Matthew 24:34 "is certainly the most embarrassing verse in the Bible."[91]

Yet another problem with unchecked eschatology is the direction it provides for how the church sees its position in present world affairs, especially when influencing political stances toward Israel. While the church knows that most Jews continue to reject Jesus, it also knows that it cannot abandon them. The scriptural promise of blessing and

---

[91] C.S. Lewis, *The World's Last Night and Other Essays*, (New York: Harcourt, Brace and Company, 1952), 98.

curse based on a nation's treatment of Israel weighs on the American mindset: "And I will bless those who bless you, and the one who curses you I will curse" (Gen 12:3). The power of this verse drives the foreign policy of a country in which seven out of ten citizens declare allegiance to Christianity. It is worthy of note, according to one author, that "the American constituency most supportive of Israel is not Jews but fundamentalist and evangelical Christians. The support of the caucus stems from a distinctive reading of the Old Testament and a unique eschatology (a belief about death, judgment, and the end of the world), in which Israel plays a pivotal role."[92]

However, evangelicalism's steadfast commitment to Israel based on its desire for God's favor can result in blind support for modern Israeli initiatives, right or wrong. For example, one thing for which Israel presently strives is the rebuilding of the Jewish temple that was destroyed in AD 70. Judaism believes such a temple is necessary for the future messianic kingdom in which all people and nations will worship at its alter. And who is the church to oppose Israel's desires? Indeed, the Jews are God's chosen people.

But the primary justification for Christian support in restoring this temple is rooted in the evangelical church's own eschatology. Futurists believe that Paul prophesied the appearance of a future Antichrist figure during the "last days" in his second letter to the Thessalonians: "Let no one in any way deceive you, for [the day of the Lord] will not come unless the apostasy comes first, and the *man of lawlessness is revealed, the son of destruction*, who opposes and exalts himself above every so-called god or object of worship, so that he takes his seat in the temple of God, displaying himself as being God" (II Thes. 2:3-4, emphasis mine). Paul described a man who would desecrate the "the temple of God" by placing himself in authority within the Holy of Holies and claim to be God.

If this popular understanding conveys that this "man of lawlessness" is the future Antichrist, then the prophecy requires a temple to defile. The implication then is that before Jesus returns, there must be another temple standing in Jerusalem. By supporting Israel's efforts, Christians

---

[92] Paul D. Miller, "Evangelicals, Israel, and US Foreign Policy," *Survival*. Vol. 56, Issue 1. pp. 7-26, 2014.

believe they are helping facilitate Jesus' Second Coming and the end of the world. Erecting a third temple would certainly be an unmistakable confirmation of the "end-times" for both Judaism and futurist Christians.

The following thought might seem elementary, but this author must ask how evangelicals can support the restoration of the building that God, Himself, demolished in AD 70 as punishment against the Jews for their rejection of the salvation He brought them? How can a believer support the reinstitution of a religious system of recurrent sacrificial offering that they believe Jesus made obsolete through His work on the cross? Why does the church preach a gospel to the unbeliever about justification by faith alone through which no physical offering is acceptable before God, yet support Israel's efforts to implement a system of physical atonement for their justification? Because, church, your theological and philosophical corruption of biblical texts has created a total misunderstanding of eschatology.

Read Paul's passage again about the supposed Antichrist. Paul used an adverb and participle describing the "present time" (Strong's concordance), to comfort the Thessalonians that the "man of lawlessness" was, then, being contained: "You know what restrains him *now*," (2:6) "The mystery of lawlessness is *already* at work," and "He who *now* restrains." (2:7, emphasis mine). He warned them to "stand firm and hold to the traditions which you were taught" (II Thes. 2:15) because an apostasy would soon occur that would be led by some man of perdition. Why would Paul use events that would not occur for another 2,000 years to urge first-century Thessalonians to remain in the faith? He would not. Futurists have simply decided that this description fits the mold of their end-times Antichrist.

Such an apostasy described by Paul was also predicted by Jesus in His Olivet prophecy when He warned the disciples that their Great Commission would be treacherous: "Then they will deliver you to tribulation, and will kill you, and you will be hated by all nations because of My name. At that time many will *fall away* and will betray one another and hate one another" (Matt. 24:9-10, emphasis mine). Paul's character must have been alive at the time of the letter's composition but was presently being kept from asserting his purpose before an appointed time. This is further verified in that this person would be destroyed at the Lord's Coming (II Thes. 2:8). If Jesus promised his arrival within that generation, it is further evidence that this man lived at that time.

This is not the place for an extensive study of Second Thessalonians, rather an abridged lesson in reading scripture properly to avoid the consequences of misplaced eschatological assumptions.

How about the general draw of doomsday philosophies? Christian evangelicals the world over await God's wrath upon what they see as a condemned planet filled with wicked inhabitants. Consider the message coming from the pulpit at Grace Community Church, pastored by eminent evangelical minister John MacArthur. In his fierce opposition to the perceived hysteria of climate change activism, he has unashamedly taught that God has "cursed" this "disposable planet" and that if what humans presently see before them worries them, they should know that "this is nothing like what's going to happen next time" when "He will destroy [it] in an instant."[93] Indeed, in futurist eschatology, the "end of the world" is merely common sense theology if the Bible prophesies an eventual "new heaven and a new earth" (Is. 65:17, Rev. 21:1).

This author shares Dr. MacArthur's sentiment that Christians should not fret about apocalyptic consequences from ever-changing climates. God promised that "all flesh shall never again be cut off by the water of the flood, neither shall there be again a flood to destroy the earth" (Gen. 9:11) indicating that any claim of current rising sea levels should not create mass panic among believers. However, his claim that God has deemed this planet as a throwaway item is an extremely careless teaching and does not match with the words of the same scripture for which he desperately pleads his own congregation's faithfulness.

In persuading his listeners of Earth's hopeless status, MacArthur ignores multiple verses that establish God's creation as everlasting in its goodness: "He established the earth upon its foundations, so that it will not totter [be moved] forever and ever" (Psalm 104:5), "A generation goes and a generation comes, but the earth remains forever" (Ecc. 1:4), and to Noah, He promised, "I will never again curse the ground on account of man, for the intent of man's heart is evil from his youth; and

---

[93] Christian Discernment. "John MacArthur on Global Warming and Environmentalism." *YouTube*, Uploaded October, 28, 2018, https://youtu.be/mSZ1f9eSfxQ.

I will never again destroy every living thing, as I have done" (Gen. 8:21). These verses should reinforce the Christian efforts toward responsible stewardship over what God has granted mankind rather than looking to carelessly plunder its resources before He returns for its obliteration.

Also consider the potential consequences of an obsession with waiting for the rapture of the church. It, too, has led some to concede life's ambitions as utterly senseless because they were convinced of its imminency. Likewise, the notion of a pending Christian escape can produce a short-term thinking process when addressing important issues. Many Christians are ill-prepared for trials (which Jesus promised) because they believe they will be whisked away before they must endure them. And rapture fever can be so intense for some believers that its proponents will forsake fellowship with other Christians who merely ask questions about its theological grounds. Would God have His people divide over such an issue?

The future rapture of the church has even been entered into the statement of faith for some denominations, establishing the concept as official doctrine and emphasizing its importance as a matter of fact rather than debate. Therefore, for church membership, one must adhere to such theology. Yet the very concept of a pre-tribulation "rapture" – a secret Christian extraction prior to a worldwide tribulation – cannot be derived from even one passage in the entire Bible. This might seem a shocking concept for most Americans, but how would they know? Only one out of ten read their Bible on a daily basis. Looking at scripture through the preterist lens, there will not be a pre, mid, or post-tribulation rapture because there is no future Great Tribulation period (see **Narrative of Matthew 24,** Dan. 9:27).

The Savior, Himself, rebuked the idea of a pre-tribulation rapture. John 17:15 states that Jesus once offered a prayer to God the Father, thanking Him for the disciples and asking for His providence over their lives: "I do not ask you to take them out of the world but that you keep them from the evil one." This represents a specific request, by Jesus, for the disciple's protection through trial, not a direct removal from their earthly circumstance. Jesus asked that His followers remain; rapture advocates demand to leave. Why? Because they are rewards members looking to cash out. And in their haste, if someone is only looking to catch the next train out of town, you will find them sitting on the bench at the station – waiting to depart.

Allow me to demonstrate how rapture proponents remove verses from other scriptural contexts to promote their fictitious concept. One popular gospel tract, made available from the largest retailer in the world, proposes that the pre-tribulation rapture will, indeed, be the "greatest day of the believer's existence" as it represents the moment when they arrive in Jesus' presence.[94] For support, it cites Revelation 22:4 which states, "They will see His face, and His name will be on their foreheads." In making this connection, the gospel tract has, thus, specified that Revelation 22:4 is confirmation of the rapture because it identifies the moment when the believer meets Jesus. Simple enough.

There are three problems with this. The first is context. Revelation 22 is a passage discussing life within the New Jerusalem (Rev. 21), an establishment that, according to futurists, does not arrive until after the millennial kingdom (Rev. 20) which comes after the seven-year tribulation period, which, itself, is preceded by – the rapture. This leads to the second issue – timing. This verse states that it is in the New Jerusalem that His followers will finally see Him face to face, yet the city comes down from heaven 1,007 years *after* the rapture. The third problem is language. As one can see, not only is the word "rapture" absent in the verse, it is found nowhere in the entire book of Revelation. This verse has, thus, intentionally been pulled from Revelation 22 – where it is being utilized to describe one particular time, setting, and circumstance – and directly used to support an entirely different event. This is how futurist eschatology operates. Its proponents concoct an "end of the world" scenario and proceed to locate scattered verses that can sustain their thesis, however vaguely. What an incredibly damaging hermeneutic!

This author would argue, however, that the most devastating component of rapture theology is that it contradicts Jesus' message about the promised reality of God's kingdom. Because rapture proponents teach a Christian removal from earth, they must emphasize the

---

[94] Tim Johnson. "The Rapture." *Moments With The Book,* Gospel Series #204, p. 2. https://mwtb.org/products/the-rapture. This tract is available through Wal-mart.com.

perpetually evil nature of the present world to highlight the necessity of such a separation. In other words, Christians do not belong here. The inevitable conclusion is that Satan is still the "god of this world" (II Cor. 4:4) who wields enormous power and influence as he "prowls around like a roaring lion, seeking someone to devour" (I Peter 5:8).

Such a devastating notion can be found in the writings of the man who pioneered rapture theology in the mid-nineteenth century, John Nelson Darby. In his teaching on the future Second Coming, he taught: "It is Satan, and not Christ, who is now the prince and god of this world. It is strange how many people fancy that the cross put an end to that. It was exactly the contrary. The cross was the one grand demonstration – and there never was such a demonstration before – that Satan is the prince and god of this world."[95] Not only does this contradict scripture's clear teaching that Jesus received all "authority...in heaven and on earth" (Matt. 28:18) upon His ascension, but it also denies that Jesus accomplished two of the objectives that were set before Him: to destroy the works of the devil (I John 3:8) and usher in God's kingdom (Matt. 12:28, 16:28, 25:34, Mark 1:15, Luke 17:21, John 18:36).

If Satan still has dominion, then Jesus failed. Such is not a gospel of "good news," but of fear that has created a backwards perspective for the Christian walk. When the world shows seeming signs of deterioration, rapture advocates must celebrate because they believe their time to flee such wickedness fast approaches. Did you catch that? The worse things become, the more excited they become. Many who claim to be God's followers earnestly seek to leave the kingdom that He promised *is* already setup (Dan. 2 & 7) and will never suffer defeat. After all, why stay to help a fractured world, when it's that very broken nature that requires the Christian's extradition? These sad ironies of rapture theology are deeply regrettable.

The examples listed in this section are the tip of the iceberg regarding the consequences of an eschatology that promotes fear. Please understand that misunderstanding biblical prophecies can have serious consequences for the Body of Christ. Eschatology contributes greatly to the formulation of an individual's worldview and affects how one treats

---

[95] John Nelson Darby, *Lectures on the Second Coming.* (London: W.H. Broom Paternoster Row, 1868), p. 31.

others as we walk through life together. It is one thing to seek "hope" in possible future events; it is another to manipulate scripture to manifest that perceived "hope." Reading the majority of biblical prophecies as having been fulfilled answers the difficult questions that a futurist perspective only exacerbates.

Interpreting biblical prophecies as though some are past is not heretical, but entirely biblical. History provides the parameters by which to make such measurements, while an entirely futuristic approach makes prophecy flexible to present circumstances. Christopher Hitchens' doubtlessly considered his Olivet Discourse assertion to be an effective argument against Jesus' Messiahship. However, Doug Wilson responded without hesitation, calmly replying that Jesus did not promise that *His* generation would see the consummation of all things but that, "He promised He was going to come back and destroy Jerusalem – which he did."[96]

Church, what does the phrase "iron sharpens iron" (Prov. 27:17) mean to you? Based on the reaction that this author has received from the evangelical community when confronting them with such a divergent interpretation of past fulfillment of certain scriptures – it is difficult to say. I once penned a series of articles that posed biblical and theological challenges to the concept of the rapture. One of the first reader responses included an immediate personal attack claiming that I was a "condemned by Jesus, false teacher." No curiosity, no civility, no desire for elaboration or exchange; just hostile condemnation. Friends, such thoughtless accusations signal a heart of stone that boasts in the fleshly pride of personal wisdom and self-righteousness.

Differing interpretations among the Body will produce questions that generate friction. And it is friction that will sharpen. Such inquiries will encourage all involved to dive more deeply into God's Word and should excite the church into a pursuit of further understanding. Instead, much of the church merely surrounds itself with like thinkers, thereby exponentially affirming its own understanding, and proceeds to eliminate opposing perspectives, even from within its own family. And

---

[96] American Vision, "Answering Hitchens on the End of the World." *YouTube.* Uploaded June 22, 2022. https://youtu.be/1EacWyM7FDw, Doug Wilson holds a partial preterist, post-millennialist eschatology.

once the church thinks it has all the answers, there is nothing further to learn.

Such complacency, thus, produces an inevitable, intellectual dullness among the adherents, and soon they are unable to answer questions defending their own faith to a pagan world that possesses truly hostile intent. When a Christian dismisses a fellow "brother in Christ" in response to asking tough questions to become more intimate with God through His Word, it demonstrates the characteristics of the very hard-heartedness that it attributes to an unsaved world.

This author does not rely upon denominational authority; my only authority is God's Word in the pages of scripture. The good news is that Jesus of Nazareth's death paid a sin debt that God required for redemption and reconciliation, while His resurrection proved Who He was and completed the process of justification for those who will receive it. The life truly saved emanates the fruits of repentance that serves the God of Israel through obedience.

My faith should, therefore, be observed not through my perfect theological knowledge about the Trinity or water baptism, but by the spirit of repentance brought forth by the Holy Spirit in a transformed life. This book does not disregard these cherished doctrinal beliefs, but merely points out that if the gospel is stipulated, in Paul's letters to the Corinthians and Romans, as a genuine belief that Jesus died for sin and was raised from the dead, then one's salvation is not contingent upon an infallible understanding of the timing of Jesus' Second Advent.

It is, however, apparently required for membership in some churches.

How can one combat the perils of reckless eschatology? Study God's Word. And let us begin with the book many Christians freely quote, but very likely misunderstand – Daniel. Because Daniel is saturated with prophecy, it is flooded with symbolism and figurative language, leaving some of the terminology indefinite. The book's mysterious nature, however, requires us to enter scholar mode. Composition, literary style, context, and language are paramount for an accurate interpretation, but the willingness of the reader to engage in dialogue that challenges established beliefs is equally important. One can recite scripture without the actual desire to learn what it means. Be prepared that the following information might seem overwhelming, but such is the effort that scholars exert over a lifetime of biblical exegesis for topics of this nature.

Unfortunately, most congregants hear little from these experts who are behind the scenes compiling the material that pastors attempt to disseminate from the pulpit on Sunday mornings. Be patient, pray for wisdom, and engage the text because when grasped in its fullness, one will never read it the same. Salvation in Jesus Christ is rooted in one's belief in who He said that He was (John 8:24). Daniel confirmed that identity. The proof of the pudding – is in the eating. Christ was the incarnate One who lived the sinless life, was killed on the cross, buried, and raised again, and in doing so, purchased the world – a bounty that he will collect when your time comes.

Please read with an open mind because the intent of this commentary is to encourage a more profound understanding of God's Word – nothing more. Daniel laid out events that prophesied the future of Israel up to the destruction of Jerusalem and the Jewish temple in AD 70; prophecy that included the coming – and death – of the Messiah.

Please engage the Bible and enjoy the opportunity to study God's Word.

DANIEL CHAPTER 1

Verse 1

"In the third year of the reign of King Jehoiakim of Judah, Nebuchadnezzar king of Babylon came to Jerusalem and besieged it."

The historical narrative of King Jehoiakim of Judah, Israel's southern kingdom, begins with his identification as the second of son King Josiah (1 Chr. 3:15), whose Hebrew name was Eliakim.

- In 609 BC, Jehoiakim was installed as king of Judah by Pharoah Neco, who killed Josiah in his endeavor to stabilize Egyptian power in the region (II Kings 23:34). Jehoiakim is, thus, made entirely subservient to Egypt, a fact signified by Eliakim's name change to Jehoiakim as instituted by Neco (II Chr. 36:4).

- In 605 BC, Nebuchadnezzar II, who shared Babylonian military leadership duties with his father, King Nabopolassar, defeated Pharoah Neco's armies in Syria and Palestine (II Kings 24:7, Jer. 46:2) and solidified Babylon's power in the region. This removed Egyptian forces which he pushed back south. Nebuchadnezzar then marched on Judah in his pursuit of destroying the Egyptian armies, laying siege to Jerusalem.

- In 604 BC, Nebuchadnezzar, in an effort to dismantle Pharoah Neco's influence further, subjugated Jehoiakim, making him dissolve his Egyptian alliance and become a "vassal" to Babylon, a fact recorded in II Kings 24:1: "In his days, Nebuchadnezzar king of Babylon came up, and Jehoiakim became his servant for three years...." In a further demonstration of surrender, he removed some Jewish elites to Babylon.

- In 601 BC, Nebuchadnezzar attacked Egypt. This incursion was a massive failure for the Babylonian king and caused great rebellions within his kingdom. Among the discontented was the kingdom of Judah. Jehoiakim condemned the attempted invasion and ceased paying tribute to Babylon, thereby placing Judah in a state of revolt: "Then [Jehoiakim] turned and rebelled against [Nebuchadnezzar]" (II King 24:1).
- In 599/598 BC, as confirmed by the Babylonian Chronicles, in this sixth year of Nebuchadnezzar's reign, the king of Babylon responded by sending troops to Judah and Palestine to suppress the rebellion and make an example of Judah.
- In 598 BC, Jehoiakim's eleventh year as king (II Kings 23:36, II Chr. 36:5), his reign ended and "he slept with his fathers" (II Kings 24:6) when he was killed while in custody of Babylonian forces (December).
- In 598/597 BC, Jehoiakim's son, Jehoiachin, replaced him as king at the height of the Jewish revolt. The successor contributed little to the resistance effort.
- In 597 BC, Jerusalem was directly sieged and captured, which the Babylonian Chronicles confirm as having occurred in the seventh year of Nebuchadnezzar's reign. Jehoiachin was removed into custody (II Kings 24:12), and Nebuchadnezzar installed a new king, Zedekiah (II Kings 24:17). Upon Jerusalem's seizure, Nebuchadnezzar removed some of the treasury by pillaging the temple (II Kings 24:12-15, II Chronicles 36:9-10) and took nearly 10,000 Jews into captivity.

Historians find difficulty in the chronology of Daniel's first verse. They believe it contradicts a separate biblical account of Jehoiakim's reign as told by Jeremiah: "The word that came to Jeremiah concerning all the people of Judah, in the fourth year of Jehoiakim the son of Josiah king of Judah, that [was] the first year of Nebuchadnezzar king of Babylon" (Jer. 25:1). The surrounding events are further verified later in the prophet's writing in that "concerning the army of Pharoah

Neco of Egypt, which was by the Euphrates River at Carchemish, which Nebuchadnezzar king of Babylon defeated in the fourth year of Jehoiakim the son of Josiah, king of Judah" (Jer. 46:2).

The two authors seem to offer contrasting information regarding Nebuchadnezzar's actions against Judah, which Jeremiah claims began during Jehoiakim's fourth year, while Daniel attests the third. Another problem facing apologetic scholars is that the most likely independent sources for historical corroboration do not mention a siege against Jerusalem around 605 BC. The Babylonian Chronicles, an extensive series of ancient tablets that record major events in Babylonian history, indicate that Nebuchadnezzar's first siege occurred in 597 BC at the end of the reign of Jehoiakim's son, Jehoiachin, when he captured the city.

Jewish commentators are aware of both problems and reconcile the passage through their traditional interpretation of Jewish history. According to Rabbi Shlomo Yitzchaki (Rashi), a renowned Jewish commentator who lived during the eleventh century, the Jewish Seder Olam – a work that provides a biblical chronology of the Jews from their very beginning – confirms that it was during Nebuchadnezzar's eighth year (597 BC) that Jehoiakim was overcome: "In his first year [Nebuchadnezzar] conquered Nineveh, and in his second year he advanced and vanquished Jehoiakim, who served him for three years and rebelled against him for three years. That was the eleventh year of the reign of Jehoiakim: five years before he vanquished him, three years that he served him, and three years that he rebelled against him. And then Jehoiakim died under his hand, and in his stead, Nebuchadnezzar enthroned Jehoiachin, his son" (Rashi Commentary on Daniel).

According to Rashi's calculations, Jehoiakim was a servile ruler installed by Neco in 609 BC, whose reign lasted for five years. He was preserved as such for an additional three years under Nebuchadnezzar, thus, making his first eight years representative of a puppet king installed by foreign rulers. From his installation in 609 BC until his rebellion against Nebuchadnezzar in 601 BC, any power Jehoiakim retained was under a foreign thumb and answerable to superior pagan authority. However, when Jehoiakim refused to continue paying tribute to Nebuchadnezzar after the king of Babylon's attempted invasion of Egypt in 601 BC, the king of Judah initiated a break from this encumberment of pagan rule under which he served as an instrument and proxy. His rebellion lasted for three years when Nebuchadnezzar besieged Jerusalem, killing Judah's king (598 BC), and a few months later captured the city (597 BC).

However, Rashi believed that the historical timeline made it impossible for Nebuchadnezzar's "siege" to have occurred during Jehoiakim's "third year" as stated by Daniel. Instead, he supposed that what Daniel meant by "third year" was not following Jehoiakim's installment by Neco in 609 BC, but when he rebelled against Nebuchadnezzar in 601 BC, when he refused to continue tributes to Babylon. In this rebellion, Jehoiakim asserted himself as no longer beholden to foreign powers, but a truly autonomous king initiating his legitimate reign. The siege spoken of by Daniel, according to Rashi, was Nebuchadnezzar's attack on Jerusalem in 597 BC that initiated the exile, an event supported by the Babylonian Chronicles. Thus, the recorded histories can be harmonized.

Such an interpretation is not entirely unreasonable. However, it stretches the meaning of traditional Hebrew language by applying a figurative explanation to literal terminology.

The lack of corroborating evidence of a 605 BC siege in the Babylonian Chronicles does not mean that one did not occur. After Nebuchadnezzar defeated the Egyptian armies at Carchemish (Syria and Palestine) in the first half of 605 BC, he followed them south. However, he stalled upon learning of his father's death in August 605 BC, and he was obligated to return to Babylon for his inauguration as king in September. By that time, Nebuchadnezzar's pursuit of the Egyptian forces would have driven him south into the regions of Israel and Judah that summer, putting him into direct confrontation with Neco's underling, Jehoiakim. OT passages verify this inevitability and indicate Nebuchadnezzar's forceful actions against Jehoiakim prior to Jerusalem's capture in 597 BC. For example, this could be understood in the narrative from the second book of Kings which states, "In [Jehoiakim's] days, Nebuchadnezzar king of Babylon came up, and Jehoiakim became his servant for three years" (24:1, II Chr. 36:6). Indeed, according to one scholar, the Hebrew language for "came up" that described the circumstances of Nebuchadnezzar's arrival do not exclude the notion that a siege occurred.[97]

Additionally, the Babylonian historian Berossus noted that when "Nebuchadnezzar learned of his father's death [605 BC]...he ordered some of his friends to bring the Jewish, Phoenician, Syrian, and Egyptian prisoners together with the bulk of the army and the rest of the booty to Babylon."[98] The presence of Jewish captives in the spoils of Nebuchadnezzar's military campaign of 605 BC, thus, implies that Judah was among the places pillaged by Nebuchadnezzar.

There is little reason to doubt that a siege of Jerusalem occurred in the summer of 605 BC, except for its omission in the Babylonian Chronicles. This is especially true if it was short lived. The remaining issue is the difference between Jeremiah and Daniel in their description of the timing. This can be reconciled with an assessment of the calendar systems employed by each prophet which, in their contexts, were different. Daniel used the Hebrew calendar system of *Tishri*, which is marked by the holiest day of the year for Jews, Yom Kippur (Day of Atonement). It occurs sometime in September-October which initiated the start of a Jewish new year. According to *Tishri*, if Jehoiakim was not installed until after October of 609 BC, the start of a Jewish new year, then he would have had to wait an entire year for his first official year to begin. This would have brought his third year to the summer of 605 BC, when Nebuchadnezzar arrived at Jerusalem.

Jeremiah, on the other hand, is held to have adhered to the Babylonian/Assyrian dating system which marked *Nisan* as the first month of the new year and occurred in March-April. Jehoiakim's reign would have, thus, started six months earlier than Daniel's date in March/April 608 BC. Jeremiah then would have considered Nebuchadnezzar's first year (summer 605 BC) to be Jehoiakim's fourth year. The accounts do not contradict themselves but are synchronized within the context of each author's method of calculating dates and is not as devastating to the account's credibility as scholars have long held.

---

[97] Mark K. Mercer, "Daniel 1.1 and Jehoiakim's Three Years of Servitude," *Andrews University Seminary Studies*, Vol. 27, No. 3, 1989, pp. 187-188. p. 184.

[98] Stanley Mayer Burstein, ed. *The Babyloniaca of Berossus*, Vol. 1, fascicle 5, Malibu: Undena Publication, 1978), p. 27.

For the sake of history, Nebuchadnezzar waged yet another attack upon Jerusalem (II Kings 25:1-3, Jeremiah 39, II Chronicles 36) in the fifth Jewish month *Av* (August) in 586 BC. This resulted in the complete destruction of the city and Solomon's temple while the remaining Jews were taken into captivity. This desolation had been prophesied by the prophet Ezekiel around 592 BC, six years before, but five years after Nebuchadnezzar's initial assault against Jehoiachin. The final siege of Jerusalem is progressively described in Ezk 4:1-3 with God's departure from His temple in Ezk. 10:1-22 and the horrors of the curse upon Israel foretold in Ezk. 20-23.

Verse 2

"The Lord gave Jehoiakim king of Judah into his hand, along with some of the vessels of the house of God; and he brought them to the land of Shinar, to the house of his god, and he brought the vessels into the treasury of his god."

Some things Nebuchadnezzar took in his 605 BC confrontation with Judah, others he left, as this was not a matter of destruction, but subjugation (Jer. 27:19). This verse also acknowledges that God ordained Jehoiakim's defeat, which is unsurprising when considering the verses that deplore His rulership: "And he reigned eleven years in Jerusalem: and he did evil in the sight of the Lord his God… and his abominations which he did" (II Chr. 36:5, 8), and "Therefore thus says the Lord in regard to Jehoiakim, the son of Josiah, king of Judah, 'they will not lament for him…'" (Jer. 22:18). However, II Chronicles also seems to verify the result of Nebuchadnezzar's move against Jerusalem as told by Daniel. It is said that "Nebuchadnezzar king of Babylon came up against [Jehoiakim] and bound him with bronze chains to take him to Babylon" (II Chr. 36:6).

Nebuchadnezzar also brought some of the articles of the house of the Lord to Babylon and put them in his temple at Babylon (II Chr. 36:6-7). Jehoiakim was not a man surrendered to God, and the sins of the nation haunted the people, thus God sanctioned a Babylonian victory (Jer. 22:25). The plunder from this assault was removed for personal boasting and offered to the Babylonian gods, while the subjugation of Jehoiakim was possibly made public by a brief captivity in Babylon, as mentioned in the above verse. Jehoiakim would have returned to Jerusalem, however, to begin his role as a Babylonian "vassal" for the following three years.

Verses 3-7

"Then the king ordered Ashpenaz, the chief pf his officials, to bring in some of the sons of Israel, including some of the royal family and of the nobles, youths in whom was no defect, who were good looking, showing intelligence in every branch of wisdom, endowed with understanding and discerning knowledge, and who had ability for serving in the king's court; and he ordered him to teach them the literature and language of the Chaldeans. The king appointed for them a daily ration from the king's choice food and from the wine which he drank, and appointed that they should be educated three years, at the end of which they were to enter the king's personal service. Now among them from the sons of Judah were Daniel, Hananiah, Mishael and Azariah. Then the commander of the officials assigned new names to them; and to Daniel he assigned the name Belteshazzar, to Hananiah Shadrach, to Mishael Meshach and to Aazariah Abed-nego."

Upon this suppression of Jerusalem, many members of Jewish status were sent to Babylon and assessed for integration depending on their abilities. The exiles, most likely, included members of noble status like Daniel, who exhibited privilege, wisdom, and education. The Babylonians considered themselves masters of arts and sciences, but especially witchcraft and sorcery that required intelligent minds to dabble in matters of fortune telling. The best and brightest could be assimilated to contribute to the nation's welfare.

These Jewish men were enrolled into a training program in which they would be groomed to serve the king and Babylonian court. They would become accustomed to the elements of royalty and were, thus, fed well. Three years into captivity (602 BC), Daniel would be prepared for service. In his role, Daniel's Babylonian name became Belteshazzar, and here is an introduction to characters that inform the most noteworthy tales of biblical history. According to Jewish commentator Rashi, Daniel was renamed after the Babylonian god, "Bel" in combination with the term "Teshazzar" meaning wisdom.

Verses 8-13

"But Daniel made up his mind that he would not defile himself with the king's choice food or with the wine which he drank; so he sought permission from the commander of the officials that he might not defile himself. Now God granted Daniel favor and compassion in the sight of the commander of the officials, and the commander of the officials said to Daniel, 'I am afraid of my lord the king, who has appointed your food and your drink; for why should he see your faces looking more haggard than the youths who are your own age? Then you would make me forfeit my head to the king.' But Daniel said to the overseer whom the commander of the officials had appointed over Daniel, Hananiah, Mishael, and Azariah, 'Please test your servants for ten days, and let us be given some vegetables to eat and water to drink. Then let our appearance be observed in your presence and the appearance of the youths who are eating the king's choice food; and deal with your servants according to what you see.'"

This passage begins the narrative of Daniel receiving favorable status before Nebuchadnezzar. His elevation to influential positions within Babylonian leadership must have stemmed from his unquestionable fidelity to the God of Israel, despite the oppression that was expected in captivity. Rashi identifies the "pulse" as beans. Daniel's adamant refusal to accept the non-kosher baking habits of the pagans, in accordance with Mosaic law, was instrumental in maintaining his close relationship with God. Such obedience thereby gained God's favor. The officer over the king's stewards feared for his own life when asked to give Jews special treatment as the king's orders were to prepare these men for service in accordance with the Nebuchadnezzar's established expectations.

Verses 14-16

"So he listened to them in this matter and tested them for ten days. At the end of ten days their appearance seemed better and they were fatter than all the

youths who had been eating the king's choice food. So the overseer continued to withhold their choice food and the wine they were to drink, and kept giving them vegetables."

Though beans and water would be their only sustenance, the physical appearance of Daniel's group improved progressively more than the others despite the seeming lack of the required nutritional standards set by the king. Such begins the definitive overtone, throughout the book, that God has unchallengeable and personal sovereignty over not only Israel, but Babylon and the nations of the world as His will is brought forth.

Verses 17-20

"As for these four youths, God gave them knowledge and intelligence in every branch of literature and wisdom; Daniel even understood all kinds of visions and dreams. Then at the end of the days which the king had specified for presenting them, the commander of the officials presented them before Nebuchadnezzar. The king talked with them, and out of them all not one was found like Daniel, Hananiah, Mishael and Azariah; so they entered the king's personal service. As for every matter of wisdom and understanding about which the king consulted them, he found them ten times better than all the magicians and conjurers who were in all his realm."

Their continued obedience to God was rewarded with an honored place in the courts of Babylon, as Daniel became one of the most revered and trusted servants at Nebuchadnezzar's disposal. In this position, Daniel would be God's mouthpiece to prophesy the future of nations, especially the fate of the present kingdom.

Verse 21

"And Daniel continued until the first year of Cyrus the king."

Babylon was conquered in 539 BC by the Medo-Persians so this reference denotes his years of service under Babylonian dominion. The year 538 BC was the "first year" of the Medo-Persian reign; however, not yet under Cyrus. As will be indicated later, the Medes were given initial authority over the conquered Babylonian Empire, led by Darius, who exercised power for only a year before the Persians assumed complete control.

Daniel's position of influence in the Babylonian government is not only an indication of God's favor upon his life, but follows in God's instruction to the Jewish people who were exiled. During captivity, they were not to be hostile or combative toward their captors, and despite Daniel's clear aversion to certain pagan practices, he readily walked through the doors that God opened. Indeed, Jeremiah had relayed counsel through his prophecy about the exile that while the Israelites were in Babylon they were to "build houses and live in them; and plant gardens and eat their produce. Take wives and become the fathers of sons and daughters, and take wives for your sons and give your daughters to husbands, that they may bear sons and daughters; and multiply there, and do not decrease. Seek the welfare of the city where I have sent you into exile, and pray to the Lord on its behalf, for in its welfare you will have welfare" (Jer. 29:4-7).

The personal challenge for Daniel would be assimilation without forfeiting fidelity. The book of Daniel demonstrates a lesson on such an achievement.

DANIEL CHAPTER 2

Verse 1

"Now in the second year of the reign of King Nebuchadnezzar, Nebuchadnezzar had dreams; and his spirit was troubled and his sleep left him."

Under the assumption that a siege of Jerusalem occurred in 605 BC and knowing that positive evidence exists indicating that Jewish prisoners were removed to Babylon during Nebuchadnezzar's return to be named king (Berossus), one must conclude that Daniel was among Judah's intelligentsia and elite that had been captured that year. According to the first chapter, the Jewish men, including Daniel, who had been brought back engaged in a training program that lasted for three years (Dan 1:5). This is stated to have been completed by Chapter 1's end as Daniel was presented to Nebuchadnezzar near the end of the chapter (1:19). Therefore, if Daniel tells a fluid narrative, the established timeframe for the commencement of events that open this chapter would be around 602 BC. Yet it opens, "in the second year of the reign of Nebuchadnezzar," which would have been 604 BC.

This chronology has puzzled commentators for centuries, and many radical explanations have been proposed. Rashi has posited, for example, that Daniel's "second year" was the time following the destruction of the temple in 586 BC, an event that would have precipitated Nebuchadnezzar's total dominion over Israel. This is differentiated from the tribute-centric overlording of the previous 15 years. Most Christian commentators, on the other hand, either ignore the difficulty or generate further confusion by speculating about the several numerological methods employed by ancient authors when writing about historical events.

However, why is it impossible for the narrative surrounding Nebuchadnezzar's dream to have occurred during Daniel's training period? Indeed, Daniel 1:17 stated that before those men were presented to Nebuchadnezzar for personal service, "God gave them knowledge and intelligence in every branch of literature and wisdom; Daniel even understood all kinds of visions and dreams." It seems that God had granted Daniel such special inspiration that his interpretive ability was present prior to completing his training. Having a strong interpreter of future events was important to all nations, but none more so than the Babylonians; therefore, such a trait even in one of the foreign exiles would have garnered immediate attention from leadership.

As one scholar asserts "Dan. 2 does not necessarily follow Dan 1 chronologically. In addition, the text of Dan. 2 suggests that he was not finished with his training. After all, Daniel was evidently not among those who were unable to interpret the dream (v. 2-11; cf v. 27), nor had he even been informed of the matter (v. 15). Thus. it is entirely possible that Dan. 2 records an incident that took place after the story in Dan. 1:8-17, but before the end of the three-year period."[99] The first chapter of Daniel may simply have offered an abridged summation of his history under the entire dominion of Babylonian rule, while the second chapter provides an important anecdote during his stay.

For this commentary, Daniel is presumed to relate that around 604/603 BC, the king suffered a concerning dream.

Verses 2-6

"Then the king gave orders to call in the magicians, the conjurers, the sorcerers and the Chaldeans to tell the king his dreams. So they came in and stood before the king. The king said to them, 'I had a dream and my spirit is anxious to understand the dream.' Then the Chaldeans spoke to the king in Aramaic: 'O King, live forever! Tell the dream to your servants, and we will declare the interpretation.' The king replied to the Chaldeans, 'The

---

[99] Mercer, "Daniel 1.1 and Jehoiakim's Three Years of Servitude," pp. 187-188.

command from me is firm: if you do not make known to the dream and its interpretation, you will be torn limb from limb and your houses will be made a rubbish heap. But if you declare the dream and its interpretation, you will receive from me gifts and a reward and great honor; therefore declare to me the dream and its interpretation."

The Greek description of such practitioners was those who perform arts of magic through incantations and formulas from which their power was derived from idol worship. This supports the reality that, though we worship the one true God, there are spirits that offer human access to supernatural abilities. To these people, Nebuchadnezzar articulated his distress from his recent dream that had caused confusion through its symbolism. Despite the outward confidence, of those present, in providing an interpretation, Nebuchadnezzar warned them that should they fail to assist him he would inflict a generational punishment upon them. The penalty included a literal dismemberment which was common in eastern nations. However, success would garner boundless rewards from a grateful sovereign.

Verses 7-12

"They answered a second time and said, 'Let the king tell the dream to his servants, and we will declare the interpretation.' The king replied, 'I know for certain that you are bargaining for time, inasmuch as you have seen that the command from me is firm, that if you do not make the dream known to me, there is only one decree for you. For you have agreed together to speak lying and corrupt words before me until the situation is changed; therefore tell me the dream, that I may know that you can declare to me its interpretation.' The Chaldeans answered the king and said, 'There is not a man on earth who could declare the matter for the king, inasmuch as no great king or ruler has ever asked anything like this of any magician, conjurer, or Chaldean. Moreover, the thing which the king demands is difficult, and there is no one else who could declare it to the king except gods, whose dwelling place is not with mortal flesh.' Because of this the king became indignant and very furious and gave orders to destroy all the wise men of Babylon."

Nebuchadnezzar informed these conjurers that the matter escaped him, alluding to the fact that he would expect those boasting of divine revelation to not only tell him the meaning but also the content from which the interpretation is derived. Nebuchadnezzar immediately suspected their treachery as they continuously asked additional questions to buy themselves time. When confronted they beseeched him of the impossibility of the task. As such, Nebuchadnezzar's anger drove him to order the execution of these soothsayers.

Verses 13-16

"So the decree went forth that the wise men should be slain; and they looked for Daniel and his friends to kill them. Then Daniel replied with discretion and discernment to Arioch, the captain of the king's bodyguard, who had gone forth to slay the wise men of Babylon; he said to Arioch, the king's commander, 'For what reason is the decree from the king so urgent?' Then Arioch informed Daniel about the matter."

The language suggests that the decree was swiftly being executed by the time word had reached Daniel of impending punishment. He did not understand the chaos. Once Arioch had explained, however, that Nebuchadnezzar was plagued by his dream, Daniel believed that within God's mercy, the task of interpretation could be achieved. Thus, he sought not only to appease this wrath called upon those who could never accomplish the task, but also to spare those who were never charged with this interpretive responsibility in the first place.

The question can be asked, if Daniel was sought for death because his lot was among the wise men, was his training not yet complete? The answer should be in the negative; for why had Daniel not been summoned into Nebuchadnezzar's court when his desire for the dream's interpretation had first been brought to them? Daniel and his "colleagues" were, most likely, in a position of general acceptance among the court but had not completed the full training and been relegated to positions of subordinance. Nebuchadnezzar's fury at those soothsayers must have been so great that it extended to every branch of the tree of witchcraft and fortune-telling within the Babylonian ranks, which would have left none outside the coming rage.

Verses 17-19

"Then Daniel went to his house and informed his friends, Hananiah, Michael, and Azariah, about the matter, so that they might request compassion from the God of heaven concerning this mystery, so that Daniel and his friends would not be destroyed with the rest of the wise men of Babylon. Then the mystery was revealed to Daniel in a night vision. Then Daniel blessed the God of heaven,"

As true followers of God, Daniel and his friends submitted themselves in humility, requesting that God aid their effort to do good in the sight of the king. As would be expected, they desired to be spared, and God responded by showing Daniel the dream and its meaning.

Verses 20-23

"Daniel said, 'Let the name of God be blessed forever and ever, for wisdom and power belong to Him. It is He who changes the times and the epochs; He removes kings and establishes kings; He gives wisdom to wise men and knowledge to men of understanding. It is He who reveals the profound and hidden things; He knows what is in the darkness. And the light dwells in Him. To You, O God of my fathers, I give thanks and praise, for You have given me wisdom and power; even now You have made known to me what we requested of You, for You have made known to us the king's matter.'"

Thus begins a Davidic-like psalm of praise and worship. Daniel realized whatever wisdom he attained was not of his own accord but that of the One who gave it. This is a profound example of the prostrate nature with which we should approach the God of Israel in our own prayers. His sovereignty is such that the seasons are at his behest, but as will be seen, "remov[ing] kings" would also represent a significant portion of the dream itself. Daniel praised God, not only for giving the revelation but what the revelation represented about God's power.

Verses 24-26

"Therefore, Daniel went in to Arioch, whom the king had appointed to destroy the wise men of Babylon; he went and spoke to him as follows: 'Do not

destroy the wise men of Babylon! Take me into the king's presence, and I will declare the interpretation to the king.' Then Arioch hurriedly brought Daniel into the king's presence and spoke to him as follows: 'I have found a man among the exiles from Judah who can make the interpretation know to the king!' The king said to Daniel, whose name was Belteshazzar, 'Are you able to make known to me the dream which I have seen and its interpretation?'"

It appears that Arioch, having been given the responsibility of executing the king's decree, retained enough reason to understand that disobeying orders would have been trumped by the joy of having the larger problem solved – interpreting the dream. Thus, Arioch presented Daniel, knowing that any failure similar to that of the soothsayers would most likely result in everyone's death, including his own. However, should Daniel make good on his promise, the reward might be great for him, as well.

Verses 27-30

"Daniel answered before the king and said, 'As for the mystery about which the king has inquired, neither wise men, conjurers, magicians nor diviners are able to declare it to the king. However, there is a God in heaven who reveals mysteries, and He has made known to King Nebuchadnezzar what will take place in the latter days. This was your dream and the visions in your mind while on your bed. As for you, O king, while on your bed your thoughts turned to what would take place in the future; and He who reveals mysteries has made known to you what will take place. But as for me, this mystery has not been revealed to me for any wisdom residing in me more than in any other living man, but for the purpose of making the interpretation known to the king, and that you may understand the thoughts of your mind.'"

Daniel again demonstrated his humble virtue by giving all credit to the God of Israel. The young prophet was able to recite the contents of the dream itself and its meaning, proving to Nebuchadnezzar the divine truth behind the explanation. Daniel's call for the king to remember from whom the interpretation came drew a sharp distinction with the pagan sorcerers and established that there is only one true God before whom all should demonstrate reverence.

The ancient Hebrew phrase "latter days" is translated into English as "in the last days." Popular evangelical understandings about "end-times" events often lead to the presumption that most biblical references to "the last days" point to the end of the world. But, according to the Cambridge Bible for Schools and Colleges, this phrase described the "closing period of the future so far as it falls within the range of view of the writer using it."[100] Such an understanding makes context the deciding interpretive factor, which is especially significant since the phrase is used fourteen times in the OT.

Verse 28 stipulates that God has made information known to Nebuchadnezzar – the king of a sixth-century empire – through a dream that predicts four successive world empires after his own. These empires are all verified in history as having occurred. Within this passage's context, the "latter days" most likely refer to the final days laid out in the dream in which the fifth kingdom (divine) would be established. And since this kingdom is setup *during* the fourth, so must its closing years be included in the timeframe.

Additionally, there were two ages in Jewish Rabbinic tradition: their age (Judiac, Mosaic Law, Old Covenant, etc.) and the age to come (Messianic, New Covenant, etc). And a significant point that will be seen in Daniel is that the latter – the fifth kingdom – has no prescribed end. One this fifth kingdom would be established; the last days must have already occurred because a kingdom that has no end has no "latter days." Here, the sense is simply related as forthcoming times, not those at the consummation of all things sometime in the indefinite future even extending into the twenty-first century.

Daniel's interpretation will give Nebuchadnezzar a peek at the end of his own empire but also what would follow and to the future of Daniel's own people.

---

[100] Cambridge Bible for Schools and Colleges, "Chapter 2. Nebuchadnezzar's Dream," https://biblehub.com/commentaries/cambridge/daniel/2.htm.

Verses 31-34

"You, O king, were looking and behold, there was a single great statue; the statue, which was large and of extraordinary splendor, was standing in front of you, and its appearance was awesome. The head of that statue was made of fine gold, its breast and its arms of silver, its belly and its thighs of bronze, its legs of iron, its feet partly of iron and partly of clay. You continued looking until a stone was cut out without hands, and it struck the statue on its feet of iron and clay and crushed them."

The king's dream presented the image of a colossal statue with incomparable greatness and progressively changing metal compositions with differing values. In popular culture, gold is the standard by which all other valuables are measured. Further down the statue follows silver, bronze (primarily copper), and iron. Iron had far less monetary value, but was considered exceptionally strong. At the base, which should ordinarily form the strongest part of the structure, clay was mixed with the iron, leading to instability.

Though the statue was made of the strongest and most valuable earthly elements assembled by humans, it would be cast down by a small stone. The phrase "without hands" is a contrast with the worldly kingdoms that had been built before it. Each of these metallic elements represented one of the four successive pagan kingdoms that were forged by physical construction through brick and mortar. The stone, which represents God's divine kingdom, will not be.

Verses 35-36

"Then the iron, the clay, the bronze, the silver and the gold were crushed all at the same time and became like chaff from the summer threshing floors; and the wind carried them away so that not a trace of them was found. But the stone that struck the statue became a great mountain and filled the whole earth. This was the dream; now we will tell its interpretation before the king."

Such would be the destruction of this statue that it would be cast away without memory, while the stone that crushed it would cover the entire earth. "Like the chaff" is representative of divine judgments in the OT (Is. 41, Jer. 51). Isaiah 2:2 offers imagery for a mountain such as one in Israel that would garner the attention and worship of the world: "Now it will come about that in the last days the mountain of the house of the Lord will be established as the chief of the mountains and will be raised above the hills, and all the nations will stream to it."

This also carries an astounding correlation to how Jesus described the kingdom that had been brought upon first-century Israel when He began His public ministry (Matt. 3:2, Mark 1:15) in that it was "like a mustard seed, which a man took and sowed in his field; and this is smaller than all other seeds, but when it is full grown, it is larger than the garden plants and becomes a tree, so that the birds of the air come and nest in its branches" (Matt. 13:31-32). The point seems to be that God will destroy these elements with something unexpected and it will grow into a dominion that overtakes and extends past the power exerted by these formidable entities.

Verses 37-38

"You O king, are the king of kings, to whom the God of heaven has given the kingdom, the power, the strength and the glory; and wherever the sons of men dwell, or the beasts of the field, or the birds of the sky, He has given them into your hand and has caused you to rule over them all. You are the head of gold."

History did not fail to demonstrate the accuracy of this interpretation. Nebuchadnezzar's Babylonian Empire = head of gold. Such a title as "king of kings" is bestowed upon Nebuchadnezzar (Ezk. 26:7) to denote his position as the first and the standard. He has been placed into his position by the God of the universe who made the creation over which the king now rules.

Verse 39

"After you there will arise another kingdom inferior to you, then another third kingdom of bronze, which will rule over all the earth."

Cyrus the Great's Medo-Persian Empire = the chest (Media)

and arms (Persia) of silver. This empire's reign immediately followed Babylon's fall in 539/538 BC.

Alexander's Greek Empire = belly (Macedonia) and thighs (Greece) of bronze (copper). This immediately followed Persia's fall to Alexander the Great.

Verse 40

"'Then there will be a fourth kingdom as strong as iron; inasmuch as iron crushes and shatter all things, so, like iron that breaks in pieces, it will crush and break all these in pieces.'"

The Roman Empire = legs of iron. Its power would be unprecedented, and it would crush everything in its path. The Roman Empire immediately followed the fall of Greece. These four sequential empires would hold dominion over Israel and the known world beginning in the early seventh century until the last came to a close, after which no empire has accomplished that which these four did.

Verses 41-43

"'In that you saw the feet and toes, partly of potter's clay and partly of iron, it will be a divided kingdom; but it will have in it the toughness of iron, inasmuch as you saw the iron mixed with common clay. As the toes of the feet were partly of iron and partly of pottery, so some of the kingdom will be strong and part of it will be brittle. And in that you saw the iron mixed with common clay, they will combine with one another in the seed of men; but they will not adhere to one another even as iron does not combine with pottery.'"

The fourth kingdom would be divided; though maintaining a level of strength from the iron, it would contain weakness from the clay. On one hand, the superficial explanation is that Rome was indeed divided into two kingdoms by the time of its demise, Western and Eastern (AD 286). Other more profound explanations lend toward the clay's identity as Israel. It was described as God's clay throughout the OT: Jeremiah 18:2-6, Isaiah 29:13-16, 45:9, 64:8, and Lamentations 4:2. Additionally, the relationship between the Roman government and the apostate leadership of Israel was necessary for the Jewish elite to maintain their status and power. However, another interpretation rests upon the "combin[ing]" mentioned in the final portion of the verse.

By the end of the Roman Empire, the Germanic peoples from the north had begun to infiltrate provincial territory, and rather than go to war, the empire preferred assimilation. Therefore, the ethnicity and linguistic characteristics of surrounding nations were allowed to influence the unity of the empire, and eventually it succumbed. As Rashi contributes, "They will intermarry with the other nations but they will not be at peace and truly cleave to them wholeheartedly, and their laws will differ from the laws of the other nations." Roman historian Tacitus agreed that Rome's lust for ruling exceeded that of any other craving. Roman leadership professed to have sovereign authority even when it came at the expense of integrating foreign cultures; they simply wanted control as far as they could reach.

Verses 44-45

"In the days of those kings the God of heaven will set up a kingdom which will never be destroyed, and that kingdom will not be left for another people; it will crush and put an end to all these kingdoms, but it will itself endure forever. Inasmuch as you saw that a stone was cut out of the mountain without hands and that it crushed the iron, the bronze, the clay, the silver and the gold, the great God has made known to the king what will take place in the future, so the dream is true and its interpretation is trustworthy."

Sometime during the reign of the fourth kingdom (Roman Empire), God's promised kingdom would arrive ("stone"). It would not be a kingdom that passed one to the next like the previous, sequential empires; it would be everlasting, and it would reign over all nations. It will have no end, and no kingdom will stand against it. Jewish commentators emphasize this kingdom as that of the Messiah. Indeed, if this passage describes their messianic kingdom, which they also postulate must be initiated by the Messiah, then it must have started during the Roman Empire. And yet, they are still looking.

Most significantly, the new kingdom would be made "without hands" meaning it was not physical, but spiritual.

If one is to understand the world today through God's eyes, then this point is paramount: Daniel has articulated, through a divine revelation, that God's promised, messianic, otherworldly kingdom – the kingdom of heaven – would arrive during the Roman Empire. It would seem that if one still awaits its arrival, they call God a liar.

Verses 46-47

"Then King Nebuchadnezzar fell on his face and did homage to Daniel, and gave orders to present to him an offering and fragrant incense. The king answered Daniel and said, 'Surely your God is a god of gods and a Lord of kings and a revealer of mysteries, since you have been able to reveal this mystery.'"

Nebuchadnezzar was so humbled by Daniel's revelation, the king paid deference to him in such a way to resemble that given to the gods of Babylon. Such revelation could only come from the prophet's access to the divine. The king of Babylon must, then, have recognized, to some, degree, the true source from which Daniel's ability was derived – the God of Israel.

Verses 48-49

"Then the king promoted Daniel and gave him many great gifts, and he made him ruler over the whole province of Babylon and chief prefect over all the wise men of Babylon. And Daniel made request of the king, and he appointed Shadrach, Meshach, and Abed-nego over the administration of the province of Babylon, while Daniel was at the king's court."

The Babylonian monarchy was divided into provinces ruled by deputy governors. Daniel's wisdom was considered utmost in the kingdom and most valuable to the Babylonian king. Finally, if this anecdote occurred before the completion of Daniel's formal training, was it possible for Daniel to be elevated to such positions of rulership? In all likelihood, this is a summation of the rewards Daniel received from Nebuchadnezzar; in other words, he did not receive these numerous promotions all at once. This was a process that could have occurred over many years but was described in summation in the present verse.

DANIEL CHAPTER 3

Verses 1-2

"Nebuchadnezzar the king made an image of gold, the height of which was sixty cubits and its width six cubits; he set it up on the plain of Dura in the province of Babylon. Then Nebuchadnezzar the king sent word to assemble the satraps, the prefects and the governors, the counselors, the treasurers, the judges, the magistrates and all the rulers of the provinces to come to the dedication of the image that Nebuchadnezzar the king had set up."

To construct a golden image of such size would have required an enormous quantity of the precious resource. According to some commentators, such as Charles Ellicott or John Gill, the statue would have been made as described by Isaiah, constructed of wood, but covered in plates of gold. The cubit proportions would have made the statue around 90 feet tall. Dura was a valley to the southeast of Babylon. According to Jewish teaching (Talmud), this was the valley of "dry bones" into which Ezekiel was dropped in the vision of Ezekiel 37.

Verses 3-6

"Then the satraps, the prefects and the governors, the counselors, the treasurers, the judges, the counselors, the treasurers, the judges, the magistrates and all the rulers of the provinces were assembled for the dedication of the image that Nebuchadnezzar the king had set up; and they stood before the image that Nebuchadnezzar had set up. Then the herald loudly proclaimed: 'to you the command is given, O peoples, nations and men of every language, that at the

moment you hear the sound of the horn, flute, lyre, trigon, psaltery, bagpipe and all kinds of music, you are to fall down and worship the golden image that Nebuchadnezzar the king has set up. But whoever does not fall down and worship shall immediately be cast into the midst of a furnace of blazing fire."

The local leaders were to inform the people that the statue was to be worshipped at the herald's sound. This implementation of idol worship by Nebuchadnezzar demonstrated his unparalleled arrogance, seemingly blind to his glaring inadequacies. The dream which Daniel interpreted must have reinforced Nebuchadnezzar's understanding of his glorified role as king of the world's greatest empire. To defy the edict would result in being thrown into a blazing furnace.

Verses 7-12

"Therefore at that time, when all the peoples heard the sound of the horn, flute, lyre, trigon, psaltery, bagpipe and all kinds of music, all the peoples, nations and men of every language fell down and worshiped the golden image that Nebuchadnezzar the king had set up. For this reason at that time certain Chaldeans came forward and brought charges against the Jews. They responded and said to Nebuchadnezzar the king: 'O king, live forever! You O king, have made a decree that every man who hears the sound of the horn, flute, lye, trigon, psaltery, and bagpipe and all kinds of music, is to fall down and worship the golden image. But whoever does not fall down and worship shall be cast into the midst of a furnace of blazing fire. There are certain Jews whom you have appointed over the administration of the province of Babylon, namely Shadrach, Meshach, and Abed-nego. These men, O king, have disregarded you; they do not serve your gods or worship the golden image which you have set up.'"

The Babylonian subjects, predictably, abdicated. But there were those who sought to punish the Jews and desired Nebuchadnezzar's punishment for dedicating worship to their own God. The king's blind conceit presented an opportunity to inflict revenge against Daniel for the esteem that Nebuchadnezzar had granted upon him despite his foreign status. So Daniel's three companions, whom he had appointed to leadership positions, were informed upon for defying the order.

Verses 13-14

"The Nebuchadnezzar in rage and anger gave orders to bring Shadrach, Meshach, and Abed-nego; then these men were brought before the king. Nebuchadnezzar, responded and said to them: 'Is it true, Shadrach, Meshach, and Adeb-nego, that you do not serve my gods or worship the golden image that I have set up?'"

Declaring himself to be king of kings, Nebuchadnezzar was offended that anyone would not prostrate. As Bible commentator Alexander MacLaren points out, "The crime of the three was not that they worshipped wrongly, but that they disobeyed…at all events, the worship required was an act of obedience to him, and to refuse it was rebellion. Idolatry is tolerant of any private opinions about gods, and intolerant of any refusal to obey authority in worship."[101] It is interesting to note that scripture previously describes Nebuchadnezzar's extreme passions igniting immediate emotional responses (Dan. 2:12); however, here he questioned them first rather than demanding their swift execution. Most likely, this was another instance of divine providence resulting from the Jews' unquestionable loyalty to the God of Israel.

Verses 15-18

"'Now if you are ready, at the moment you hear the sound of the horn, flute, lyre, trigon, psaltery and bagpipe and all kinds of music, to fall down and worship the image that I have made, very well. But if you do not worship, you will immediately be cast into the midst of a furnace of blazing fire; and what god is there who can deliver you out of my hands?' Shadrach, Meshach, and Abed-nego replied to the king: 'O Nebuchadnezzar, we do not need to give you an answer concerning this matter. If it be so, our God whom we serve is able to deliver us from the furnace of blazing fire; and He will deliver us out of your hand, O king. But even if He does not, let it be known to you, O king, that we are not going to serve your gods or worship the golden image that you have set up.'"

---

[101] Alexander MacLaren, "MacLaren Expositions of Holy Scripture" https://biblehub.com/commentaries/maclaren/daniel/3.htm.

There is little for them to explain; they will not worship another god. Such fidelity is at the peak of the religious obligation that defined their covenant with the God of Israel. If every action had a reaction, then Israel's national blessing or curse was contingent upon their faithfulness. Here is a shining example of true faith. These men were certain that their God had the capacity to save them at His impulse, yet humbly embraced that the outcome was based upon His sovereign will and they were but His subjects. Israel has always understood its role to be a light in the world and was instructed to demonstrate God's character and blessing. The world was intended to look upon the Jews for what this relationship looks like. Whether God chose to spare their lives, they would serve Him for having such power as the Creator of all things.

Verses 19-23

"Then Nebuchadnezzar was filled with wrath, and his facial expression was altered toward Shadrach, Meshach and Abed-nego. He answered by giving orders to heat the furnace seven times more than it was usually heated. He commanded certain valiant warriors who were in his army to tie up Shadrach, Meshach and Abed-nego in order to cast them into the furnace of blazing fire. Then these men were tied up in their trousers, their coats, their caps and their other clothes, and were cast into the midst of the furnace of blazing fire. For this reason, because the king's command was urgent and the furnace had been made extremely hot, the flame of the fire slew those men who carried up Shadrach, Meshach and Abed-nego. But these three men, Shadrach, Meshach and Abed-nego, fell into the midst of the furnace of blazing fire still tied up."

The rage described is intended to help us visualize the merciless characteristics of a tyrannical king's wrath. Nebuchadnezzar's cruelty was evident in his threat to eradicate even the families of the magicians and soothsayers of Babylon should they fall short of his demand for acceptable interpretations. Here it was displayed by his ordering the furnace to temperatures seven times greater than normal. The king could see their resolve and ordered them bound and cast into the fire. Because of his fury, the orders were directed with immediacy, and without having time for suitable preparation, the soldiers who executed the commands were killed because of heat's extreme nature, as it so fiercely engulfed the surrounding area.

Verses 24-25

"Then Nebuchadnezzar the king was astounded and stood up in haste; he said to his high officials, 'Was it not three men we cast bound into the midst of the fire?' They replied to the king, 'Certainly, O king.' He said, 'Look! I see four men loosed and walking about in the midst of the fire without harm, and the appearance of the fourth is like a son of the gods.'"

It becomes readily apparent, however, that the punishment inflicted upon these men was harmless to their persons as they walked around the furnace with ease – accompanied by a visible guardian. What is one's reaction to such a phenomenon? How many more signs could Nebuchadnezzar be given to verify the power of Israel's God that would persuade him? Jewish commentators interpret the fourth man to be an angel. Many English translations read "son of God" in a theological attempt to reinforce Jesus Christ's eternal presence throughout the OT. However, Christian expositors maintain the true rendering to be "like the son of gods," because the Aramaic is plural. This more likely denotes a figure under the control of God's divine counsel in the heavenly realms (Psalm 82:1-7). It is not an affront to the Christian faith or denial of the Savior's person to admit that the language used here expresses that this figure is an angel walking with them.

Verses 26-29

"Then Nebuchadnezzar came near to the door of the furnace of blazing fire; he responded and said, 'Shadrach, Meshach and Abed-nego come out, you servants of the Most High God, and come here!' Then Shadrach, Meshach and Abed-nego came out of the midst of the fire. The satraps, the prefects, the governors and the king's high officials gathered around and saw in regard to these men that the fire had no effect on the bodies of these men nor was the hair of their head singed, nor were their trousers damaged, nor had the smell

of fire even come upon them. Nebuchadnezzar responded and said, 'Blessed be the God of Shadrach, Meshach, and Abed-nego, who has sent His angel and delivered His servants who put their trust in Him, violating the king's command, and yielded up their bodies so as not to serve or worship any god except their own God. Therefore I make a decree that any people, nation or tongue that speaks anything offensive against the God of Shadrach, Meshach and Abed-nego shall be torn limb from limb and their houses reduced to a rubbish heap, inasmuch as there is no other god who is able to deliver in this way.'"

What else is the king to do but welcome them out in a state of awe amid perplexity? No one could go into the fire to finish the job, and what harm would come to them at the hands of men outside of the fire? People gathered to witness the incomprehensible event, while the king was led to praise the name of the one true God. Throughout scripture, signs accompanied the work of the Almighty, yet people were so easily dissuaded. The disciples were filled with such skepticism of Jesus' revived body that he had to eat in their presence to demonstrate that he was, indeed, resurrected in the flesh (Luke 24:41-43). Thomas the disciple would not believe in the resurrected Jesus until he could place his finger inside the wounds (John 20:27).

How easy is it for the believer, today, to retain their faith without signs such as this? And yet Jesus said, "Blessed are they who did not see and yet believed" (John 20:29). One important note in understanding Nebuchadnezzar's mindset is that, despite the power of this event, it did not drive him to deny the existence or power of the gods he had always worshipped, but he did recognize the superiority of the God of Israel. Therefore, the worship of this God would be tolerated.

Verse 30

"Then the king caused Shadrach, Meshach and Abed-nego to prosper in the province of Babylon."

Nebuchadnezzar, thus, restored their positions and pronounced blessing over their time in Babylon.

DANIEL CHAPTER 4

Verses 1-7

"Nebuchadnezzar, the king to all peoples, nations, and men of every language that live in all the earth: 'May your peace abound! It has seemed good to me to declare the signs and wonders which the Most High God has done for me. How great are His signs and how mighty are His wonders! His kingdom is an everlasting kingdom and His dominion is from generation to generation. I Nebuchadnezzar, was at ease in my house and flourishing in my palace. I saw a dream and it made me fearful; and these fantasies as I lay on my bed and the visions in my mind kept alarming me. So I gave order to bring into my presence all the wise men of Babylon, that they might make known to me the interpretation of the dream. Then the magicians, the conjurers, the Chaldeans and the diviners came in and I related the dream to them, but they could not make its interpretation known to me.'"

It should be brought to the Bible student's attention that, in standard English versions, the first three verses of the present chapter are placed at the close of Chapter 3 in the Hebrew Bible. The purpose is probably insignificant except to create more emphasis on Nebuchadnezzar's seemingly kingdom-wide policy shift in religious affairs. However, the present chapter introduces a personal anecdote from the king, which provides an important moral lesson for the Bible reader about life lived with the knowledge of God's sovereignty.

Nebuchadnezzar used an Aramaic term describing his contemporary state as one of pure joy; a place of bliss in which the glory of his position had provided security and fulfillment. God had placed the king into the role of a universal monarch over the earth. So, to receive another dream that seemingly involved destruction without explanation would certainly be cause for a change in his disposition.

Humbled by God in the previous chapter, the king then guaranteed the freedom of religion for the Jewish exiles, while ironically prohibiting freedom of speech toward the rest of his kingdom. Though his citizens were permitted to worship their pagan gods, they were forbidden to blaspheme the God of Israel. Nebuchadnezzar informed his spiritual advisors of the dream's substance, clamoring for an interpretation that they were of course unable to provide.

Verses 8-9

"But finally Daniel came in before me, whose name is Belteshazzar according to the name of my god, and in whom is a spirit of the holy gods; and I related the dream to him, saying, 'O Belteshazzar, chief of the magicians, since I know that a spirit of the holy gods is in you and no mystery baffles you, tell me the visions of my dream which I have seen, along with its interpretation.'"

Daniel, having acquired the reputation for divine wisdom after his interpretation of the great statue (Dan. 2), was called to resolve the king's dilemma. Though the true sovereignty of the God of Israel had been confirmed to Nebuchadnezzar, his reluctance to abandon his partiality to the gods of Babylon is reiterated in his explanation about the Babylonian name he bestowed upon Daniel.

Verses 10-12

"Now these were the visions in my mind as I lay on my bed: I was looking, and behold, there was a tree in the midst of the earth and its height was great. The tree grew large and became strong and its height reached to the sky, and it was visible to the end of the whole earth. Its foliage was beautiful and its fruit abundant, and in it was food for all. The beasts of the field found shade under it, And the birds of the sky dwelt in its branches, and all the living creatures fed themselves from it."

The tree was described as one of incomparable beauty and stature that provided nourishment for all living things. It gave food, shelter, rest; in essence the world received all sustenance from it. This describes the zenith of Nebuchadnezzar's magnificence as king of the most powerful empire on earth.

Verses 13-17

"I was looking in the visions in my mind as I lay on my bed, and behold, an angelic watcher; a holy one, descended from heaven. He shouted out and spoke as follows: Chop down the tree and cut off its branches, strip off its foliage and scatter its fruit; let the beasts flee from under it and the birds from its branches. Yet leave the stump with its roots in the ground, but with a band of iron and bronze around it in the new grass of the field; and let him be drenched with the dew of heaven, and let him share with the beasts in the grass of the earth. Let his mind be changed from that of a man and let a beast's mind be given to him, and let seven periods of time pass over him. This sentence is by the decree of the angelic watchers and the decision is a command of the holy ones, in order that the living may know that the Most High is ruler over the realm of mankind, and bestows it on whom He wishes And sets over it the lowliest of men."

Who is the holy watcher? The language suggests an angelic being from heaven who was assigned to cut down this tree that sustains physical life for all beings. Thus begins an exposition on how everything that the tree offered would be taken from it, yet its structure would remain intact. Despite its power and glorious appearance, it would be cast down. The image of placing "a band of iron" would be like chaining someone for restraint. The very one who represents the tree would become like the beasts that it once sheltered and gave provision.

The holy ones are most likely a reference to the divine counsel holding angelic authority. Their purpose was to reveal to all nations and peoples that the universe belongs to only one God, not Babylon's harem of pagan deities.

Verse 18

"'This is the dream which I, King Nebuchadnezzar, have seen. Now you, Belteshazzar, tell me its interpretation, inasmuch as none of the wise men of my kingdom is able to make known to me the interpretation; but you are able, for a spirit of the holy gods is in you.'"

The following question might be asked: if Daniel had been the only one able to interpret the previous dream, why would Nebuchadnezzar not have called on him first? It is reasonable to assume that Nebuchadnezzar had suspected the dream's unfavorable outcome and desired to receive a more promising explanation from a group of men interested in pleasing him.

Verses 19-22

"Then Daniel, whose name is Belteshazzar, was appalled for a while as his thoughts alarmed him. The king responded and said, 'Belteshazzar, do not let the dream or its interpretation alarm you.' Belteshazzar replied, 'My lord, if only the dream applied to those who hate you and its interpretation to your adversaries! The tree that you saw, which became large and grew strong, whose height reached to the sky and was visible to all the earth and whose foliage was beautiful and its fruit abundant, and in which was food for all, under which the beasts of the field dwelt and in whose branches the birds of the sky lodged – it is you O king; for you have become great and grown strong, and your majesty has become great and reached to the sky and your dominion to the end of the earth.'"

In his contemplation Daniel became distressed at the uncomplimentary interpretation he would be required to give the king, even hesitating to relay the explanation. He thus employed a diplomatic and gentle approach by reassuring the king of his own wishes, that the misfortune Daniel was about to describe should happen to Nebuchadnezzar's enemies rather than him ("would that the dream were for your enemy...").

The tree represented Nebuchadnezzar. His glory and power had become such that the nations of the world were his to command and they found their sustenance from his unparalleled power and innovation.

Nebuchadnezzar had made Babylon the most magnificent city in the known world, expanded economic opportunities through amassing the wealth by his military victories, and increased agricultural output to unprecedented levels through advanced methods of production. The surrounding provincial leaders had become unquestionably dependent on the king's reliable provision.

To concede Nebuchadnezzar's glorified status was quite legitimate.

Verses 23-27

"In that the king saw an angelic watcher, a holy one, descending from heaven and saying, 'Chop down the tree and destroy it; yet leave the stump with its roots in the ground, but with a band of iron and bronze around it in the new grass of the field, and let him be drenched with the dew of heaven, and let him share with the beasts of the field until seven periods of time pass over him,' this is the interpretation, O king, and this is the decree of the Most High, which had come upon my lord the king: that you be driven away from mankind and your dwelling place be with the beasts of the field, and you be given grass to eat like cattle and be drenched with the dew of heaven; and seven periods of time will pass over you, until you recognize that the Most High is ruler over the realm of mankind and bestows it on whomever He wishes. And in that it was commanded to leave the stump with the roots of the tree, your kingdom will be assured to you after you recognize that it is Heaven that rules. Therefore, O king, may my advice be pleasing to you: break away now from your sins by doing righteousness and from your iniquities by showing mercy to the poor, in case there may be a prolonging of your prosperity."

Daniel conveyed that the sovereign Creator had decided that Nebuchadnezzar would fall despite his achievements. The angel's duty was to oversee this destruction. A message for the follower of God was made clear through Nebuchadnezzar's example: the God of Israel will cut someone down to build them back up, within His sovereignty. Many consider pride with little regard, but God desires a repentant heart: "For you do not delight in sacrifice, otherwise I would give it, You are not pleased with burnt offering. The sacrifices of God are a broken spirit; a broken and contrite heart, O God, You will not despise" (Psalm 51:16-17).

Quite an unimaginable sequence of events for royalty, Nebuchadnezzar would be cast out from among humanity to live as a beast of the field. He would live like them even so far as to rely upon the morning dew for bathing. Rashi called the time periods "seven seasons," and described them as "recompense for the temple, which he destroyed, which was built in seven years." The purpose of such misery was to bring about the king's recognition that everything he had was from the one true God, Yahweh. The stump and root must remain as proof that the king would return to his position.

Daniel gave Nebuchadnezzar the path to redemption: do good to others. The Jewish exiles had suffered in their captivity, and Nebuchadnezzar's generosity toward God's people would count as a positive start toward his reconciliation with Creator.

Verses 28-30

"All this happened to Nebuchadnezzar the king. Twelve months later he was walking on the roof of the royal palace of Babylon. The king reflected and said, 'Is this not Babylon the great, which I myself have built as a royal residence by the might of my power and for the glory of my majesty?'"

Thus begins a succinct description of the fulfillment of the interpretation. After one year, during which the king may have administered the mercy advised by Daniel through generosity, he viewed his charity as further proof of his glorified status. He continued to look upon his achievements with unmitigated pride and acknowledged nothing outside of himself for the kingdom's authority and success.

Verses 31-33

"While the word was in the king's mouth, a voice came from heaven, saying, 'King Nebuchadnezzar, to you it is declared: sovereignty has been removed from you, and you will be driven away from mankind, and your dwelling place will be with the beasts of the field. You will be given grass to

eat like cattle, and seven periods of time will pass over you until you recognize that the Most High is ruler over the realm of mankind and bestows it on whomever He wishes' Immediately the word concerning Nebuchadnezzar was fulfilled; and he was driven away from mankind and began eating grass like cattle, and his body was drenched with the dew of heaven until his hair had grown like eagles' feathers and his nails like birds' claws."

As we will see in the verses that follow, Nebuchadnezzar was struck with madness and driven out into the wild. There is call for an honest historical analysis over this incident. Critical scholars acknowledge the lack of corroborating, external sources that verify a seven-year period during Nebuchadnezzar's reign in which he was noticeably absent.

One expert on Old Testament studies, Professor Paul Ferguson, notes that ancient Babylonian records are quite prevalent up to the eleventh year of Nebuchadnezzar's reign (594/593 BC), "after which the chronicles are practically silent."[102] He described that "not only does the number of inscriptions suddenly drop, but also their content radically changes. Earlier preoccupation with religion wanes, and attention is turned to places and politics. Prayers show evidence of being copied from earlier sources."[103] This observation establishes that a break in previously meticulous records might indicate an unusual circumstance, especially when one considers that ancient histories often abstained from recording unfavorable events in the life of kingly figures who were considered to be god-like. Such an absence during Nebuchadnezzar's reign might have been intentionally neglected by Babylonian historians to avoid embarrassment.

There is, however, one ancient document that might offer an additional form of substantiation regarding Nebuchadnezzar's state at that time. A Babylonian cuneiform tablet in a British Museum may have provided contextual evidence that Nebuchadnezzar might have suffered from instability in his mental faculties. Published in 1975 by A. K. Grayson, a small fragment of Babylonian antiquity appears to portray the famous king of Babylon as the fragment's subject:

---

[102] Paul Ferguson, "Nebuchadnezzar, Gilgamesh, and the 'Babylonian Job.'" *Journal of the Evangelical Theological Society*, Vol. 37, no. 3, (September 1994), pp. 321-331. p. 322.

[103] Ibid.

> Nebuchadnezzar considered
> His life appeared of no value to [him,....]]
> and (the) Babylon(ian) speaks bad counsel to Evil-
> merodach [...]
> Then he gives an entirely different order but [...]
> He does not heed the word for his lips, but cour[tier(s)- - -]
> He does not show love to son and daughter [...]
> ...family and clan do not exist [...]
> His attention was not directed towards promoting the
> welfare of Esagil [and Babylon]
> He prays to the lord of lords, he raised [his hands (in
> supplication) (...)]
> He weeps bitterly to Marduck, the g[reat] gods... [...]
> His prayers go forth to [...] (Brackets indicate breaks in
> text on the original tablet)[104]

It seems that the subject described had given little value to his own life, gave conflicting orders with corrupted direction to his subordinates, and seemingly forfeited love for his children and recognition of family. In addition, the ruler had seemingly abandoned the administrative duties focused on the well-being of his kingdom. All these indicate an unbalanced mentality for the leader described in the passage.

Evil-merodach was Nebuchadnezzar's oldest son who is said to have released Jehoiachin – Judah's king at the time of Nebuchadnezzar's capture of Jerusalem – from captivity upon his ascension to Babylon's throne (2 Kings 25:27-30). Esagil was the place of worship for Babylonian's chief deity, Marduck. While Nebuchadnezzar is the subject of the first few lines, it is plausible that Evil-merodach became the focus of the rest of the passage as Grayson admits that its latter theme might be a description of inappropriate behaviors in Marduck's temple.

---

[104] "New Light on Nebuchadnezzar's Madness." *Ministry*. April 1978. httsp:// www.ministrymagazine.org/archive/1978/04/new-light-on-nebuchadnezzars-madness. Cited as A.K. Grayson, Babylonian Historical-Literary Texts. "Toronto Semitic Texts and Studies," No. 3. (Toronto: University of Toronto Press, 1975), pp. 87-92. Tablet no. BM 34113 (sp 213).

This extra-biblical evidence is not conclusive of a seven-year hiatus because of the king's madness. But this fragment remains an extraordinary discovery that lends further insight into the time of Nebuchadnezzar's reign and Babylon's history that could validate portions of the biblical narrative.

Verses 34-37

"But at the end of that period, I, Nebuchadnezzar, raised my eyes toward heaven and my reason returned to me, and I blessed the Most High and praised and honored Him who lives forever; For His dominion is an everlasting dominion, and his kingdom endures from generation to generation. All the inhabitants of the earth are accounted as nothing, but He does according to His will in the host of heaven and among the inhabitants of earth; and no one can ward off His hand or say to Him, 'What have You done?' At that time my reason returned to me. And my majesty and splendor were restored to me for the glory of my kingdom, and my counselors and my nobles began seeking me out; so I was reestablished in my sovereignty, and surpassing greatness was added to me. Now, I, Nebuchadnezzar, praise, exalt and honor the King of heaven, for all His works are true and His ways just, and He is able to humble those who walk in pride."

Only upon his recognition of Jehovah as the one true God were Nebuchadnezzar's senses restored, and he was allowed to return to his throne. Not only did he retain his position, but he received more glory than he previously experienced. Such is often the case with the appreciation of one's complete dependence upon God's mercy and gratitude for His blessing.

DANIEL CHAPTER 5

Verse 1

"Belshazzar the king held a great feast for a thousand of his nobles, and he was drinking wine in the presence of the thousand."

According to numerous Jewish traditions, Belshazzar was Nebuchadnezzar's second-born child. King Nebuchadnezzar's first-born son, Evil-merodach (II Kings 25:27, Jer. 52:31), assumed his father's stead during his seven-year "madness" hiatus from the previous chapter and became king following Nebuchadnezzar's death around 562 BC. Evil-merodach enjoyed a substantial reign, after which Belshazzar assumed the kingship for a short time.

The historical reliability of this feast has support. Rashi believes that Isaiah, who wrote numerous generations before Belshazzar's reign, prophesied this gathering (Is. 21:5). Jewish historian Josephus confirmed that Belshazzar hosted a great feast after having spent a day fighting against Darius and Cyrus around 539 BC, at the approximate time of Babylon's fall. Renowned Greek historians Herodotus and Xenophon likewise support this feast. The problem for modern scholars is less the verification of whether the event occurred but who was king at the time.

While Jewish tradition is firm in its interpretation of ancient history, Babylonian records and numerous documented accounts from secular historians show Nabonidus to be the final Babylonian king when Cyrus captured Babylon in 539 BC. How can one reconcile these two contrasting narratives since even most Christian scholars concede the weight of the evidence found in the Babylonian Chronicles? If one uses these records to corroborate favorable biblical information, then one cannot discard them when they provide data of a conflicting nature.

The Babylonian royal succession began with the death of Nebuchadnezzar II in 562 BC. His son Evil-merodach ascended to the throne for two years. He was assassinated by Neriglissar (Jer. 39:3), who was not in the bloodline, but Evil-merodach's brother-in-law. Neriglissar's son, Labashi-marduck, followed in sequence for an extraordinarily brief stint that historian Berossus records ended at the hands of his own friends who had plotted against him. Following this, Nabonidus, one of the plotters with great respect among the military members, was named the new king of the Babylonian dynasty. According to extra-biblical sources, Nabonidus was, thus, the last king of Babylon, while his son, Belshazzar, served as the crown prince. But according to Daniel, Belshazzar was the final king.

Because records do not explicitly verify that the title of "king" was ever conferred to Belshazzar, critics have unsurprisingly highlighted this contrast with the prophet's claim, appealing that Daniel cannot be the paragon of historical credibility that Christian scholars avow. The prophet indeed stands by himself against external sources. However, Jeremiah prophesied the future of the world under the thumb of the Babylonian Empire as God had established nearly a century before: "Now I have given all these lands into the hand of Nebuchadnezzar king of Babylon, My servant, and I have given him also the wild animals of the field to serve him. All the nations shall serve him and his son and his grandson until the time of his own land comes; then many nations and great kings will make him their servant" (Jer. 27:6-7). The implication could be that only two kings followed in the next thirty-two years of Babylonian dominion. However, the greater point is that it would be the second and third *generations* from Nebuchadnezzar's line that would reign before Babylon's appointed time arrived; not necessarily two men.

History has given indicators as to Belshazzar's eventual role in the kingdom. Documents verify that around 553 BC, Nabonidus departed Babylon for a military campaign. Among those he left to oversee Babylon's welfare during his absence was his son, Belshazzar, who he named a co-regent. This is verified by the "Verse Account of Nabonidus," which indicates that Belshazzar had been "entrusted" with the kingship. Nabonidus did not return to Babylon until a little over a decade later. Admittedly, however, as noted scholar William H. Shea points out, this "is not the same as making him king."[105] Though records do not list a date at which Belshazzar was ever conferred with the title of "king," if Nabonidus delivered to Belshazzar the "keys to the kingdom" through a possible co-regency, then addressing him by the royal term as Daniel did would not have been surprising. This was especially true because of Daniel's familiarity with co-regencies, a common leadership arrangement within Israel's own political structure.

Christian apologist scholar Dr. Shea has conceded the difficulty in establishing the truth of Belshazzar's kingship without any independent corroborating evidence and offers two possible solutions to the problem. Both suggest that Belshazzar was named king just prior to Babylon's fall in 539 BC, though they fall under differing circumstances. Just before the city's capture, there was much political and military activity in the surrounding regions that required Nabonidus' attention. If Nabonidus departed for a military engagement, he may have conferred kingship upon his son knowing that he might not return from battle. This was a practice with existing precedent among ancient royal families. This may also have been the purpose of the feast. And if a thousand nobles were intoxicated at the party – including the new king – is it a wonder that Babylon fell so easily?

A second notion is that Belshazzar might have named himself "king" just prior to Babylon's collapse. As these military engagements inched closer to the capital, Nabonidus' armies had been severely defeated. In fact, the capitulation of a large Babylonian stronghold, Sippar, had occurred two days before Persia's attack on Babylon in 539 BC. The rumor was that Nabonidus had fled after such devastating defeats amid what he could only assume would be further impending disasters for the empire. Shea believed that warning of this Persian advance would easily have reached Belshazzar's ears prior to their arrival to the Babylonian capital.

Consequently, Belshazzar may have conferred the duties of defending the kingdom upon himself: "With his father's meeting defeat and fleeing before the enemy, the most direct course of action open

---

[105] Shea, "Nabonidus, Belshazzar, And the Book of Daniel," p. 135.

to him to [e]nsure his acquisition of such power and authority was to occupy the throne of Babylon himself. In view of the turn of political and military events, it would have been logical for Belshazzar to have proclaimed himself king at this moment."[106] Such an action, in which a crown prince installed himself as king with the knowledge that his father's permanent absence or death was imminent, was also not without precedent in ancient kingdoms.

In either instance, such a hasty installment would never have made the Babylonian record books. However, Belshazzar is consistently granted the title of "king" throughout this chapter, meaning Daniel suffered no qualms in conferring the distinction for historical purposes. Also, if Shea's hypothesis is correct, such a short timeframe does not preclude Daniel's designation of Belshazzar as king in the rest of the book. This will be seen in Chapters 7 and 8.

One fact's exclusion from extra-biblical sources does not delegitimize its veracity, rather other considerations can and should be evaluated. Once again, the Bible will assume precedence but with considerable exploration.

Verses 2-4

"When Belshazzar tasted the wine, he gave orders to bring the gold and silver vessels which Nebuchadnezzar his father had taken out of the temple which was in Jerusalem, so that the king and his nobles, his wives and his concubines might drink from them. Then they brought the gold vessels that had been taken out of the temple, the house of God which was in Jerusalem; and the king and his nobles, his wives and his concubines drank from them. They drank the wine and praised the gods of gold and silver, of bronze, iron, wood and stone."

Having the valuables from His temple disparaged and abused in such a manner by a pagan kingdom would have been quite an affront to God. Likewise, this sacrilege would offend the Jewish people. Belshazzar's intent was to demonstrate Babylon's superiority in conquering nations and the gods who were enlisted to protect them. Indeed, the king's

---

[106] Ibid., p. 142.

insolence against Israel's sacred possessions may have been the final straw against God as it coincided with the timing of Babylon's fall as a nation. Daniel's reference to Nebuchadnezzar as Belshazzar's father is simply representative of lineage, similar to how Jewish tradition mentions the "fathers" of its faith, Abraham, Jacob, and Isaac. None of these men were literally Daniel's father, but were honored as such through Jewish legacy and tradition.

Verses 5-6

"Suddenly the fingers of a man's hand emerged and began writing opposite the lampstand on the plaster of the wall of the king's palace, and the king saw the back of the hand that did the writing. Then the king's face grew pale and his thoughts alarmed him, and his hip joints went slack and his knees began knocking together."

Have you ever wondered where the popular English axiom "writing on the wall" comes from? Look no further. The essence of the Hebrew language describing the king's witness to this phenomenon conveyed shock and horror to the point of physical contractions. It is also worthy of consideration that Belshazzar was the only person listed who witnessed the hand.

Verses 7-8

"The king called aloud to bring in the conjurers, the Chaldeans and the diviners. The king spoke and said to the wise men of Babylon, 'Any man who can read this inscription and explain its interpretation to me shall be clothed with purple and have a necklace of gold around his neck, and have authority as third ruler in the kingdom.' Then all the king's wise men came in, but they could not read the inscription or make known its interpretation to the king."

Having the same misfortune as Nebuchadnezzar in matters of initial interpretation, Belshazzar was desperate for an interpretation that his most trusted sorcerers and advisors could not deliver. Additionally, it is entirely reasonable to assume that, in the king's drunken state, his entire disposition had probably changed to sheer panic.

Verses 9-12

"Then King Belshazzar was greatly alarmed, his face grew even paler, and his nobles were perplexed. The queen entered the banquet hall because of the words of the king and his nobles; the queen spoke and said, 'O king live forever! Do not let your thoughts alarm you or your face be pale. There is a man in your kingdom in whom is a spirit of the holy gods, and in the days of your father, illumination, insight and wisdom like the wisdom of the gods were found in him. And King Nebuchadnezzar, your father, your father the king, appointed him chief of the magicians, conjurers, Chaldeans, and diviners. This was because an extraordinary spirit, knowledge and insight, interpretation of dreams, explanation of enigmas and solving of difficult problems were found in this Daniel, whom the king named Belteshazzar. Let Daniel now be summoned and he will declare the interpretation.'"

Since Belshazzar's female companions would have been with him at the feast, the entrance of the queen must refer to the queen-mother; however, Christian accounts differ on that identity. A woman clearly familiar with Daniel's exploits in service to the Babylonian royal line regarding matters of interpretation, she attempted to calm Belshazzar by comforting him that indeed Daniel would provide an answer.

Verses 13-16

"Then Daniel was brought in before the king. The king spoke and said to Daniel, 'Are you that Daniel who is one of the exiles from Judah, whom my father the king brought from Judah? Now I have heard about you that a spirit of the gods is in you, and that illumination, insight and extraordinary wisdom have been found in you. Just now the wise men and the conjurers were brought in before me that they might read this inscription and make its interpretation known to me, but they could not declare the interpretation of the message. But I personally have heard about you, that you are able to give interpretations and solve difficult problems. Now if you are able to read the inscription and make its interpretation known to me, you will be clothed with purple and wear a necklace of gold around your neck, and you will have the authority as the third ruler in the kingdom.'"

Here Belshazzar offered an explicit reference to his "father" who brought Daniel into exile. This was none other than Nebuchadnezzar. The Babylonian Chronicles do not affirm this relationship, while Jewish tradition does. Many Christian commentators will reconcile the language by asserting its definition as a generational reference to a particular predecessor rather than an immediately direct descendant, a common understanding in ancient eastern cultures (see commentary on Verse 2).

Verses 17-19

"Then Daniel answered and said before the king, 'Keep your gifts for yourself or give your rewards to someone else; however, I will read the inscription to the king and make the interpretation known to him. O king, the Most High God granted sovereignty, grandeur, glory, and majesty to Nebuchadnezzar your father. Because of the grandeur which He bestowed on him, all the peoples, nations and men of every language feared and trembled before him; whomever he wished he killed and whomever he wished he spared alive; and whomever he wished he elevated and whomever he wished he humbled.'"

Daniel had already experienced the rewards from Nebuchadnezzar and desired none of Belshazzar's offering. This was likely compounded by Daniel's probable awareness of Babylon's impending fall within the day as there would be little reason to be concerned for status in an empire that was about to be conquered. Also, by this time Daniel was much older, probably around 80 years of age. The glory of Nebuchadnezzar is reiterated for sake of the family lineage and to call upon his example.

Verses 20-21

"'But when his heart was lifted up and his spirit became so proud that he behaved arrogantly, he was deposed from his royal throne and his glory was taken away from him. He was also driven away from mankind, and his heart was made like that of the beasts, and his dwelling place was with the wild donkeys. He was given grass to eat like cattle, and his body was drenched

with the dew of heaven until he recognized that the Most High God is ruler over the realm of mankind and that He sets over it whomever He wishes.'"

Nebuchadnezzar's great lesson of Chapter 4 was that God had humiliated and removed him from his place of power because of his denial of the One who had first bestowed it. What had been prophesied of Nebuchadnezzar had befallen him. Out of such arrogance came destruction, a moral lesson that finds application in all generations.

Verses 22-23

"'Yet you, his son, Belshazzar, have not humbled your heart, even though you knew all this, but you have exalted yourself against the Lord of heaven; and they have brought the vessels of His house before you, and you and your nobles, your wives and your concubines have been drinking wine from them; and you have praised the gods of silver and gold, of bronze, iron, wood and stone, which do not see, hear or understand. But the God in whose hand are your life-breath and all your ways, you have not glorified.'"

Despite Nebuchadnezzar's example, Belshazzar followed in his footsteps. The "God who controls your life-breath" was a humbling realization that everything in the universe is at the Almighty's disposal.

Verses 24-28

"Then the hand was sent from Him and this inscription was written out. Now this is the inscription that was written out: MENE, MENE, TEKEL, UPHARSIN. This is the interpretation of the message: 'MENE' – God has numbered your kingdom and put an end to it. 'TEKEL' – you have been weighed on the scales and found deficient. 'PERES' – your kingdom has been divided and given over to the Medes and Persians."

The words listed here in Aramaic are equivalent to the Hebrew words for "counting," "weighed," and "slice" (divide). God had calculated the time for Babylon's determined end, and it was upon them. Because of the transgressions of the kings, He had seen that its line was without righteousness, which would result in its destruction and allotment to a forthcoming kingdom: the two-power kingdom of the Medes and the

Persians that was prophesied in Nebuchadnezzar's dream of the statue (see Chapter 2).

Verses 29-30

"Then Belshazzar gave orders, and they clothed Daniel with purple and put a necklace of gold around his neck, and issued a proclamation concerning him that he now had authority as the third ruler in the kingdom. That same night Belshazzar the Chaldean king was slain."

Fulfilling his promise of reward, Belshazzar blessed Daniel and further established his role in overseeing the kingdom. That night the armies of Medo-Persia entered the city, and the empire was conquered. The Chaldean line of kings was brought to an end. There is no doubt that the Judean exiles must have believed that their time in captivity had been fulfilled, as the Old Testament prophet Jeremiah had foretold the length of the Babylonian Empire to be seventy years. Thus, in their minds, the conquering of this kingdom must have initiated their return to Israel.

Verse 31

"So Darius the Mede received the kingdom at about the age of sixty-two."

The chronology of Daniel continues to confound scholars into the next chapter, primarily because of conflict between biblical and extra-biblical sources regarding historical records. Daniel's record of the overthrow of Babylon documents that Darius the Mede was given initial authority over the empire upon the invasion of the capital city by the allied Persian forces.

Rashi follows a very particular chronology as he examined the distinct time frame which Daniel is identifying based on the text's specific notation regarding Darius' age. Daniel's purpose, Rashi believed, was to demonstrate a supernatural confirmation by which these prophetic world events could be confirmed. The day Nebuchadnezzar first entered the temple was the same day that Darius the Mede was born. This day was not when Nebuchadnezzar destroyed the temple

(586 BC), but when He first conquered Jerusalem in 597 BC. At that time, Jehoiachin, son of Jehoiakim, was king of Judah (Israel's southern kingdom) and had ascended the throne during the kingdom's rebellion against Nebuchadnezzar after his failed attempt to invade Egypt (II Kings 24:8).

When Nebuchadnezzar finalized Jerusalem's capture, thereby suppressing Judah's revolt, he exiled this young king to Babylon with thousands of other Jews, a narrative confirmed by the Babylonian Chronicle and the prophet Jeremiah. The *Talmud* indeed teaches that the exile occurred in the eighth year of Nebuchadnezzar's reign (605-597 BC). Rashi thus noted that the time from Jehoiachin's exile at this destruction (597 BC) until Darius took authority over the Babylonian kingdom was sixty-two years. Rashi calculated that if Nebuchadnezzar ruled for forty-five years (605-560 BC) from which eight years is subtracted (597 BC) from Jerusalem's fall, thirty-seven years are left. This was followed by the twenty-three-year reign of his son Evil-Merodach and two years of Belshazzar.

However, the Nabonidus Chronicles provide a chronological sequence of leadership at the time of the fall of Babylon in which not only are numerous Babylonian kings from Jewish history omitted, but there are no independent records that verify the existence of Darius the Mede. How can the Bible reader reconcile this? Critics assert then that there is no evidence that anyone other than Cyrus would have assumed authority over Babylon, especially since it was Cyrus' forces who led the assault of the capital city. Darius the Mede is often considered to be fictional; a creation of the author of Daniel.

But, according to Lester Grabbe's research, published in "Another Look at the Gestalt of Darius the Mede," Babylonian documents do seem to verify that there was a year-long period toward the beginning of Cyrus the Great's reign over the Babylonian territories (538 BC) during which he was named "king of lands," rather than "king of Babylon."[107] Though such evidence is not overwhelming, the obvious implication is that some other man may have assumed the official title, making room in the historical line for an additional figure....

---

[107] Lester L. Grabbe, "Another Look at the Gestalt of Darius the Mede," *The Catholic Bible Quarterly*, Vol. 50, no.2, 1988. pp. 198-213. p. 199.

DANIEL CHAPTER 6

<hr>

Verse 1

"It seemed good to Darius to appoint 120 satraps over the kingdom, that they would be in charge of the whole kingdom,"

In 2014, Dr. Steve Anderson composed a dissertation aggressively addressing the historical problem of Darius the Mede. His extensive examination discovered that the Greek historian Xenophon (430-355 BC) suggested that there was a Median king who served as co-regent with Cyrus the Great immediately after the fall of Babylon. Xenophon called this king Cyaxares II. Anderson noted that Xenophon's history "agrees remarkably well with the book of Daniel and is supported by a surprising variety of other ancient sources" as well as acknowledging that the "view that Cyaxares II is Darius the Mede was the standard Jewish and Christian interpretation from Josephus and Jerome until Keil in the 1870's."[108]

According to Anderson, "Darius" was Cyaxares throne name, and contrary to critical scholarship, he was recognized as the lead authority in the realm as the Medes and Persians had formed a confederated government, rather than one immediately dominating and subjugating the other. Thus, he shared power with Cyrus as co-regent over Babylon. Anderson also notes that there do indeed exist a number of historical

<hr>

[108] Steven Anderson, "Darius the Mede: A Solution to his identity." *TruthOnlyBible – About the Bible, Christianity, and current events.* January 8, 2016, https://truthonlybible.com/2016/01/08/darius-the-mede-a-solution-to-his-identity/.

sources that mention a "King Darius" immediately after the fall of Babylon, but are not attributed the same level of popularity as the Babylonian Chronicles. Among them are the Babylonian historian Berossus (3rd century BC), Greek grammarian Valerius Harpocration, and Greek dramatist Aeschylus. Anderson's work might be the modern, definitive Christian work on the subject.

In the end, the inevitable conclusion for the Christian scholar, once again, should be that the biblical account will take precedence. Recall that if Jesus of Nazareth established Daniel as incontestably legitimate (Matthew 24:15), then any seeming contrasts can be reconciled.

Verse 2

"and over them were three commissioners (of whom Daniel was one), that these satraps might be accountable to them, and that the king might not suffer loss."

There were numerous provinces over which Darius administered authority. Immediately under him were three directors, one of which was Daniel. This seems to demonstrate the partiality exhibited by Darius for the Jewish prophet, a relationship that displeased those with status in the pagan circles of leadership. It should not surprise the reader to know that Babylonian records do not indicate Daniel's position of leadership. But Egyptian records do not list Joseph among the nation's rulers, either (Gen. 41:41).

Verses 3-4

"Then this Daniel began distinguishing himself among the commissioners and satraps because he possessed an extraordinary spirit, and the king planned to appoint him over the entire kingdom. Then the commissioners and satraps began trying to find a ground of accusation against Daniel in regard to government affairs; but they could find no ground of accusation or evidence of corruption, inasmuch as he was faithful, and no negligence or corruption was to be found in him."

Daniel's favor with God had ensured his security within the pagan ranks while the Jewish exiles awaited their return to the land of Israel. Similar to Joseph, God had bestowed Daniel with unique abilities that offered divine assistance to pagan leaders in a such a way that guaranteed both his survival and his role as an intermediary for God's plans. Daniel's upright nature and clear commitment to obeying God's laws kept him in such a moral standing that there was none who could bring an accusation against him.

Historical documents may have intentionally overlooked the reign of a man named Darius the Mede specifically because of Daniel's favorability with the king's court. The enormous political powers conferred to Daniel during this time may have angered even those responsible for record-keeping in the Babylonian priesthoods who may have chosen to manipulate the circumstances to avoid embarrassment. If true, it might contribute to the reason for scant records during the latter portion of Nebuchadnezzar's reign. Indeed, Daniel's star rose exponentially within a pagan royal hierarchy. This is the author's speculation; however, not an improbable proposition.

Verses 5-8

"Then these men said, 'We will not find any ground of accusation against this Daniel unless we find it against him with regard to the law of his God.' Then these commissioners and satraps came by agreement to the king and spoke to him as follows: 'King Darius, live forever! All the commissioners of the kingdom, the prefects and the satraps, the high officials and the governors have consulted together that the king should establish a statute and enforce an injunction that anyone who makes a petition to any god or man besides you, O king, for thirty days, shall be cast into the lion's den. Now, O king establish the injunction and sign the document so that it may not be changed, according to the law of the Medes and Persians, which may not be revoked.'"

Realizing their inability to bring an accusation of ill-repute against Daniel, the leaders manufactured a circumstance that required him either to transgress God's law or the laws of the nation he served. In other words, he would have to either offend his God or his king. Knowing that Daniel would choose the latter, which would pave an inevitable path to his removal from leadership, the pagan leaders encouraged Darius to pass a law that prohibited the worship of entities other than the king, the penalty for which would be death.

Verses 9-10

"Therefore King Darius signed the document, that is, the injunction. Now when Daniel knew that the document was signed, he entered his house (now in his roof chamber he had windows open toward Jerusalem); and he continued kneeling on his knees three times a day, praying and giving thanks before his God, as he had been doing previously."

Suspecting that to secure his new position in the Babylonian kingdom he must garner the loyalty of the nobles, Darius implemented the law while having no knowledge of the underhanded scheme. When Daniel learned of the decree, he immediately entered a state of supplication before God, facing the direction of the temple in Jerusalem, which was, then, destroyed. God required such an action of the Israelites when they had no way to access their temple (I Kings 8:48). Just because they resided in a foreign nation, they were not relieved of their covenantal duties to offer homage to Him.

Verses 11-14

"Then these men came by agreement and found Daniel making petition and supplication before his God. Then they approached and spoke before the king about the king's injunction, 'Did you not sign an injunction that any man who makes a petition to any god or man besides you, O king, for thirty days, is to be cast into the lions' den?' The king replied, 'The statement is true, according to the law of the Medes and Persians, which may not be revoked.' Then they answered and spoke before the king, 'Daniel, who is one of the exiles from Judah, pays no attention to you, O king, or to the injunction which you signed, but keeps making his petition three times a day.' Then as soon as the king heard this statement, he was deeply distressed and set his mind on delivering Daniel; and even until sunset he kept exerting himself to rescue him."

Daniel's prayer sessions were discovered and summarily reported as a violation of the recent law. These leaders painted such a picture of Daniel that the king might think that the Jewish sage had no regard for his authority, yet Darius' faith in this young man as decent and respectful produced fear on Daniel's behalf rather than anger against him. The relationship that seemed to have developed between the two led Darius set his mind to create a loophole for Daniel's forgiveness of the infraction. It may have occurred that Darius offered Daniel grace if he refused to temporarily engage in his prayer schedule. But Daniel's faith and obedience to God would not relent.

Verses 15-16

"Then these men came by agreement to the king and said to the king, 'Recognize, O king, that it is a law of the Medes and Persians that no injunction or statute which the king established may be changed.' Then the king gave orders, and Daniel was brought in and cast into the lions' den. The king spoke and said to Daniel, 'Your God whom you constantly serve will Himself deliver you.'"

In the end, Darius had no choice but to execute the law since any appearance of flexibility in the Medo-Persian judicial system could jeopardize its credibility. However, Darius knew Daniel's faith and seemed to share the prophet's confidence in his safety, most likely speaking such words in a state of desperate hope and encouragement.

Verses 17-18

"A stone was brought and laid over the mouth of the den; and the king sealed it with his own signet ring and with the signet rings of his nobles, so that nothing would be changed in regard to Daniel. Then the king went off to his palace and spent the night fasting, and no entertainment was brought before him; and his sleep fled from him."

Following his own edict, Darius ordered Daniel into the lion's den. For lack of more scholarly vocabulary – Darius was an emotional wreck. One of his most trusted advisors was surely going to be killed instantly.

And yet the faith that he knew Daniel possessed gave him a glimmer of hope that, somehow, the prophet would survive. He could not eat or sleep, and no political affair could keep his attention.

Verses 19-22

"*Then the king arose at dawn, at the break of day, and went in haste to the lions' den. When he had come near the den to Daniel, he cried out with a troubled voice. The king spoke and said to Daniel, 'Daniel, servant of the living God, has your God, whom you constantly serve, been able to deliver you from the lions?' Then Daniel spoke to the king, 'O king live forever! My God sent his angel an shut the lions' mouths and they have not harmed me, inasmuch as I was found innocent before Him; and also toward you, O king, I have committed no crime.'*"

At first opportunity, following a restless night, Darius rushed to affirm his hope of Daniel's deliverance – which God ensured. Because Daniel was certainly innocent before God, and had not instigated an unprovoked offense against the king, his protection was secured.

Verses 23-24

"*Then the king was very pleased and gave orders for Daniel to be taken up out of the den. So Daniel was taken up out of the den and no injury whatever was found on him, because he had trusted in his God. The king then gave orders, and they brought those men who had maliciously accused Daniel, and they cast them, their children and their wives into the lions' den; and they had not reached the bottom of the den before the lions overpowered them and crushed all their bones.*"

Darius, having fulfilled his lawful responsibility to execute Medo-Persian law and exact punishment upon any offender, swiftly removed Daniel from any further danger. But he also recognized that he had been swindled and responded to the slanderers without mercy. They and their families were exacted retribution through the same means by which Daniel had been condemned. Darius would be rid of those who intended to subvert his authority of placing those in his trust into leadership. Such was the swiftness of the punishment that the people could not even proceed through the cave before they were devoured by the lions.

Verses 25-28

"*Then Darius the king wrote to all the peoples, nations and men of every language who were living in all the land: 'May your peace abound! I make a decree that in all the dominion of my kingdom men are to fear and tremble before the God of Daniel; for He is the living God and enduring forever, and His kingdom is one which will not be destroyed, and His dominion will be forever. He delivers and rescues and performs signs and wonders in heaven and on earth, Who has also delivered Daniel from the power of lions.' So this Daniel enjoyed success in the reign of Darius and in the reign of Cyrus the Persian.*"

Darius was so overwhelmed by the evidence of God's goodness, grace, and power, that he issued a kingdom-wide decree that the God of Israel would suffer no insult from the people. Daniel's prosperity would find increase under Darius and continue into the rule of the Persian king, Cyrus the Great.

DANIEL CHAPTER 7

———————

Verse 1

"In the first year of Belshazzar king of Babylon Daniel saw a dream and visions in his mind as he lay on his bed; then he wrote the dream down and related the following summary of it."

Our conclusion in the commentary from Chapter 5 favored the likelihood that Belshazzar was officially named king just prior to the fall of Babylon in 539 BC, a proposition set forth by Dr. William Shea. If true, then such a fleeting title would certainly not be described in "years" of Belshazzar's reign, as Daniel has done in the present verse. In his work, "Nabonidus, Belshazzar, and the Book of Daniel," Dr. Shea proposed that Daniel was not alluding to a prolonged individual reign as Babylon's king at the end of the empire's dominion. Rather it is a reference to the time that Belshazzar had been named co-regent by Nabonidus during his recorded absence from Babylon (553-442 BC). He notes "Historically, these designations and the dates of 'first year' and 'third year' (as seen in Dan. 8:1) can only apply to the time when Belshazzar managed matters in Babylonia while his father was in Tema, and they clearly imply an awareness of this arrangement in the Neo-Babylonian kingdom."[109]

Daniel's kingly identification for Belshazzar in this timeline was rooted in the prophet's understanding of the national tradition of administering co-regencies. As Dr. Shea elaborated, Daniel "came from the kingdom of Judah where this custom was practiced. It is suggested,

---

[109] Shea, "Nabonidus, Belshazzar, And the Book of Daniel," p. 134.

therefore, that Daniel did what Jeremiah, Ezekiel, Nehemiah, and the writer of II Kings did: He evaluated this specific situation in Babylonia in terms of his own political heritage."[110] Additionally, if Daniel ever considered Belshazzar to be "king," then any historical reference would include the title, regardless of the timing of a given event. This is similar to the commonplace etiquette in addressing a high-ranking political official by their designation even after which they held their position ("Mr. President," "Senator," "Madam Secretary," etc.) If Daniel labelled Belshazzar as "king" at any point, such a designation would be required for posterity.

Daniel recalled a vision he received in what can only be assumed as around 552 BC during the first year of Nabonidus' absence from Babylon (553 – 543 BC). During this time, Belshazzar would have enjoyed a joint rule over Babylon as he would have been commissioned to rule in his father's stead.

Verses 2-3

"Daniel said, 'I was looking in my vision by night, and behold, the four winds of heaven were stirring up the great sea. And four great beasts were coming up from the sea, different from one another.'"

The beasts in Daniel's vision were representations. Such descriptions designated the arrival of powerful historical figures that would cause political and social agitation among the nations ("great sea"). Such tension would be accomplished by the uprising of four "beasts" coming out of the nations of the earth ("sea") which will be verified as kingdoms that would exert rule over their inhabited landscapes and hold dominion over Israel. The language telling of the "four winds" can be compared to other places in scripture. One example is Jeremiah 49:36: "I will bring upon Elam [Persian descent] the four winds from the four ends of heaven, and will scatter them to all these winds." Another instance is found in the book of Zechariah, "'...Flee from the land of the north,' declares the Lord, 'for I have dispersed you as the four winds of heaven...'" (Zech. 2:6). These verses used such language to describe destruction and

---

[110] Ibid., p. 145.

dispersion. For interpretive purposes, however, this vision expands upon the vision of Nebuchadnezzar's statue from Daniel 2.

Verse 4

"The first was like a lion and had the wings of an eagle. I kept looking until its wings were plucked, and it was lifted up from the ground and made to stand on two feet like a man; a human mind also was given to it."

A lion exudes strength, power, and fierceness. However, there can also be painted the picture of merciless victory. This vision directly parallels the gold head portion of Nebuchadnezzar's statue. Thus, this lion must be confirmed as representing the Babylonian Empire (See Jeremiah 4:7). Though the kingdom would be great, its "wings were plucked," describing its eventual downfall, and while this empire's power was without earthly compare, its weakness would be demonstrated when it was given "the heart of a mortal." Indeed, if you put a man's heart in a lion's body, the lion will not have the capacity to do what it is truly able.

First beast (Dan. 7) = Gold Head (Dan. 2) = Babylonian Empire (605 – 539 BC).

Verse 5

"And behold, another beast, a second one, resembling a bear. And it was raised up on one side, and three ribs were in its mouth between its teeth; and thus they said to it, 'Arise, devour much meat!'"

The "bear" is mentioned alongside the "lion" in I Samuel (17:34-37) as beasts from which deliverance is administered. The ferocity of a mother bear's defense of her cubs is also described II Sam. (17:8). But the lion and the bear are primarily contrasted with sheep or oxen to note the stark difference in their earthly natures; one is ferocious, the other meek. Because the beasts listed here parallel the statue in Daniel 2, the reader will know that this bear must be the Medo-Persian Empire. Since the statue has two parts (arms), we can surmise that the verse's "stood to one side" reference is a description of one of these entities standing by while the other reigns. When Babylon fell, the Medes reigned for one year before the Persians assumed dominance over the entire empire. It was during this brief stint that Darius the Mede was given authority, perhaps why his character is mostly buried in history. The three ribs most likely denote three entities that were conquered by the empire upon its widespread takeover, which could be Babylon, Lydia and Egypt.

Second beast (Dan. 7) = Silver chest (Dan. 2) = Medo-Persian Empire (539 – 330 BC).

Verse 6

"After this I kept looking, and behold, another one, like a leopard, which had on its back four wings of a bird; the beast also had four heads, and dominion was given to it."

It seems the OT aligns leopards with watchfulness and stealth (Hosea 13:7), yet they strike greatly at the opportune moment. Nebuchadnezzar's statue equivalent was the bronze belly. The "four heads" are the four kingdoms into which the empire was divided upon the death of the one who conquered Persia and ushered in this time of Greek dominion – Alexander the Great (323 BC). His generals each took control of their respective areas of the empire: Cassander over Greece, Lysimachus (Antigonus) over Thrace, Ptolemy over Egypt, and Seleucus over Syria.

Third beast (Dan. 7) = Bronze belly (Dan. 2) = Greek Empire (330 – 146 BC).

Verse 7

"After this I kept looking in the night visions, and behold, a fourth beast, dreadful and terrifying and extremely strong; and it had large iron teeth. It devoured and crushed and trampled down the remainder with its feet; and it was different from all the beasts that were before it, and it had ten horns."

The fourth beast corresponds with the iron legs of Nebuchadnezzar's statue. There is little to argue with regarding the strength that identifies this empire since Rome flattened everything in its path to dominion.

Two legs could represent the two kingdoms into which Rome was eventually divided (Western and Eastern); however, the clay foot of Daniel 2 has also been posited as Israel, which is compared to such material elsewhere in the OT (Isaiah 64:8, Jeremiah 18:6). Indeed, apostate Jewish leadership was dependent on Roman influence for their wealth and status in the first century, and Israel's stability was essential for Roman control over the region, which further suggests a tenuous relationship. It is highly reasonable to interpret these images as Israel and Rome having a political and social alignment and ultimately intertwined in future world history.

For example, in Revelation, it has been suggested that the "beast of the sea" is Rome while the "beast of the earth" is Israel, the two working off one another. What was "different" about the Roman Empire from its predecessors could be the monolithic nature of the previous three, whereas Rome was quite tolerant of numerous religious and cultural practices throughout the empire, ultimately choosing to make room for assimilation rather than imposition. Rome became a melting pot of diversity, mostly resulting from the vast area they conquered and their desire to maintain good standing by exhibiting open-mindedness. This was true of their relationship with Israel in that Rome allowed the Jews to practice their faith freely.

The ten horns are identified as "kings" of this fourth kingdom later in the chapter (Dan. 7:24).

Fourth beast (Dan. 7) = Iron legs and feet (Dan. 2) = Roman Empire (146 BC – AD 476).

Verse 8

"While I was contemplating the horns, behold, another horn, a little one, came up among them, and three of the first horns were pulled out by the roots before it; and behold, this horn possessed eyes like the eyes of a man and a mouth uttering great boasts."

A horn represents power. This "little horn" would come up from the first ten horns, not as a foreign entity, but an addition from the existing ten. If the ten horns from which a "little" one came were ten emperors of Rome, this horn must symbolize a powerful leader that comes from among them. The meaning for "pulled out before it," will be interpreted later in the chapter, but in Hebrew, the understanding is to "make low" or "make humble" indicating the notion that the "little horn" will either subdue three kings or get them under control in some form.

One must not forget that the interpretation of Daniel 2 created the expectation that the messianic kingdom – one that would never be destroyed – would arrive sometime during the fourth empire (Roman). This points to a first-century fulfillment for the existence of the players introduced in this passage. There must have been an event to facilitate the installation of this new kingdom, predictably one of magnanimity, that would eliminate its competition during that time period. The only occasion to have represented this, involving both Israel and Rome, was the total destruction of Jerusalem and the temple. By this, everything old was removed, making way for everything new. The changeover in world epochs was expected even in the minds of the disciples as Jesus relayed His Olivet Discourse about the temple. Thus, in order to ascertain the identity of the "little horn," the reader must assess the circumstances surrounding that event.

From the first emperor of Rome to the destruction of Jerusalem, there were ten "kings:" Julius Caesar, Octavian (Augustus), Tiberius, Caligula, Claudius, Nero, Galba, Otho, Vitellus, and Vespasian. These should be the same kings referred to in Revelation 17:12 and must be the ten horns, out of which would come an additional, eleventh "horn." The final emperor listed, Vespasian, was the father of the Roman general who destroyed Jerusalem – Titus. The latter would also become emperor in AD 79. The requirement of this figure coming out from the ten is fulfilled in the father/son relationship between Vespasian and Titus.

Jewish commentator Rashi, who lived over a thousand years ago in France, also believed the evidence for identifying the "little horn" points strongly to the Roman General Titus. Nero was the final emperor in the "Caesar" dynasty. Upon his suicide (AD 68), Galba, Otto, and Vitellus attempted to establish themselves as emperor in the imperial chaos, each having acquired their terms through vicious and, most likely, illegitimate means. They endured very brief reigns, each just months in length, immediately before the first Flavian emperor, Vespasian (Titus' father), who would serve for the subsequent decade. These were, most likely, the three kings who were subdued in their attempt to claim the Roman throne after Nero died (AD 68), but prior to Vespasian being given the title.

Jewish sources, including the *Babylonian Talmud*, also record that Titus was blasphemous ("arrogantly") and entered the sacred Jewish spaces with the intent of sacrilege. It is also well-established that the Roman emperors were historically notorious for requiring their subjects to worship them as gods during their reign.

Modern evangelical eschatology claims the "little horn" is a contemporary, future king that arises out of some ten-nation one-world confederacy under whose tyrannical authority the world will be placed in the "end-times." Daniel's character, however, clearly existed within the historical context of the four subsequent nations of the prophecy, coming out of a successive line of first-century kings. Thus, he was a figure in Jewish-Roman history, not some antichrist in the malleable future.

Verses 9-10

"I kept looking until the thrones were set up, and the Ancient of Days took His seat; His vesture was like white snow and the hair of His head like pure wool. His throne was ablaze with flames, its wheels were a burning fire. A river of fire was flowing and coming out before Him; thousands upon thousands were attending Him, and myriads upon myriads were standing before Him; the court sat, and the books were opened."

If one reads this chapter chronologically, then during this time of the Roman Empire, the Ancient of Days – the God of Israel – set up the thrones of judgment, and "books" containing the transgressions were opened and evils exposed. Such a process for how God passes judgment can be understood in Psalm 82: "God takes His stand in His own congregation; He judges in the midst of the rulers....I said you are gods, and all of you are sons of the Most High. Nevertheless, you will die like men and fall like any one of the princes. Arise, O God and judge the earth! For it is you Who possesses all the nations" (1, 6-8).

OT expert Dr. Michael Heiser has pointed out that the Hebrew word "Elohim" ("God") appears twice in the first verse of this psalm; the first singular, the second plural. The first "Elohim" was the God of Israel who stands among the second "Elohim;" the numerous "gods" in the heavenly realms.[111] This is "the court." Who are they?

Genesis offers insight. In the sixth chapter, the author wrote, "Now it came about, when men began to multiply on the face of the land, and daughters were born to them, that the sons of God saw that the daughters of men were beautiful; and they took wives for themselves, whomever they chose" (Gen. 6:1-2). A clear distinction between these "sons" and mortals was established two verses later: "The Nephilim were on the earth in those days, and also afterward, when the sons of God came into the daughters of men" (4).

The language describing these figures is the same used to identify those introduced in the book of Job when the "sons of God came to present themselves before the Lord, and Satan also came among them" (Job 1:6). It is clear from OT language that these beings were divine, residing with the God of Israel in the heavens, and that they comprised a formal, subservient group within which He executed sovereign authority over His creation. They marveled at His glory and power. These that present themselves (Job 1) are His heavenly hosts, or divine counsel.

According to Dr. Heiser, the throne with fire and wheels in the present verse seems to be an equivalent portrayal of the throne of God described in Ezekiel 1 further corroborating the appearance of Yahweh, and he noted that the attendance of numerous "thrones [in this verse] mark the presence of [God's] divine counsel."[112] Because of these factors, one must conclude that some culminating judgment event was scheduled to take place shortly during first-century events. With the "books" containing transgressions opened, God's divine counsel gathered as He prepared to pass judgment.

---

[111] Heiser, *The Unseen Realm.*
[112] Ibid.

Verses 11-12

"Then I kept looking because of the sound of the boastful words which the horn was speaking; I kept looking until the beast was slain, and its body was destroyed and given to the burning fire. As for the rest of the beasts, their dominion was taken away, but an extension of life was granted to them for an appointed period of time."

This judgment becomes quite significant if the narrative can be verified historically – which it can be. The arrogance of the "little horn" must have aroused God's anger as the "beast" would also be appointed to destruction. There are connections between John's Revelation and Daniel's prophecies that lend to the narrative of the immediate first-century circumstances. Revelation describes the "beast" in both the corporate and individual sense; Rome and the emperor Nero. Revelation 19:20 is a description of the "beast" being thrown into the fire, correlating with the portrayal given in these verses.

This particular "beast" might be representative of the Roman Caesaric dynasty, of which Nero was the final emperor and the most tyrannical toward Christians. From a corporate sense, the leadership of the Caesars which had been under the influence of Satan's entities was represented by Nero. When he committed suicide in AD 68, the Caesar dynasty ended after years of cruel, Christian persecution in the Roman capital, including his order to encamp around Jerusalem in AD 66 to quell insurrection. This must be the "beast" who "was slain, and its body was destroyed and given to a flame of fire.

The fourth beast is an amalgamation of the previous empires ("the rest of the beasts") that had ruled the world and held dominion over Israel. Romans incorporated the best aspects of each culture before it, a customary practice for victorious kingdoms in world history. These kingdoms do not erase all elements of the conquered cultures from the history books, rather they absorb and implement the finest practices of each into their own. Therefore, the "beasts" had all lived on through each subsequent kingdom, culminating in the Roman Empire, but obviously without any power and authority. The kingdom of God, then, replaced the dominion of the previous beasts, removing the pagan stranglehold of influence over the peoples under these empires.

This interpretation is supported by the fact that Christianity was eventually made Rome's official state religion. When Constantine interpreted certain events, during his early leadership years, as Christ-ordained (AD 312), he commenced a state-sponsored promotion of the Christian church, becoming its primary benefactor in hopes that its pious simplicity (one God; one religion) could unify the empire. Of course, the Roman Empire itself fell in AD 476, an ordained termination, but God's kingdom had initiated its march throughout the earth. What is the primary indicator of this kingdom's presence? It was the arrival of the Jewish Messiah in the first century.

Verses 13-14

"I kept looking in the night visions, and behold, with the clouds of heaven One like a Son of Man was coming, and He came up to the Ancient of Days and was presented before Him. And to Him was given dominion, glory and a kingdom, that all peoples, nations and men of every language might serve Him. His dominion is an everlasting dominion which will not pass away; and His kingdom is one which will not be destroyed."

As stipulated, the "Ancient of Days" is God the Father, Almighty, the Most Holy One. Next, Daniel witnessed "one like a man," which Jewish tradition teaches is a human being (someone like a human being), approaching God the Father to receive dominion over the promised kingdom. This could be none other than the Messiah, a fact attested to in both ancient and modern Jewish teachings.

Rashi's commentary interprets this "Son of Man," or "one like a man" as the "King Messiah." One popular modern Rabbi, Tovia Singer, who ardently denies Jesus' messiahship and frequently debates Christian evangelists on the subject, defends Daniel 7:13 as wholly messianic. Hear the words of Rabbi Michael Scobak from the group Jews for Judaism in one lecture: "He is the king of Israel. He is the king of the Jewish people. He is the leader of a nation. He is part of the nation." Despite the theological rifts, it is important for the Christian to grasp the Jewish concept of the messiah. He will be at the helm of Israel, having become one with them. According to Rabbinic traditions, however, the kingdom's three primary characteristics include a peace that covers the earth, that all inhabitants come to serve Him, and nothing will overcome it (everlasting). Until they see one who seamlessly administers these components – ushering in a physical kingdom of peace and dominion over which Israel will reside – they will continue waiting.

For the Christian apologist, this might be the most profound passage for Jesus of Nazareth followers regarding the doctrine of His Lordship. The narrative's fluidity, which has just described four successive empires, proceeds chronologically into the one that would come to destroy them all – God's kingdom. And it was to be setup during the Roman Empire (fourth kingdom). In the present passage, God's kingdom would be granted to its recipient through a spiritual exaltation that signifies the power and authority that comes with it. For the Christian, Jesus' life and ministry completely fulfills this prophecy in His proclamation that, as the Son of Man, he would return in His kingdom (Matt. 16:28). The reader should repetitiously note that this kingdom is prophesied in Daniel as having *no end*.

These verses provide surprising accord between Judaism and Christianity in the interpretation of its subject, but not its application. In general, both branches believe it represents the root of their faith. The difference is how one understands the nature of this kingdom. To the Jews, the messianic kingdom will be earthly and political over which the elect rule a physical world under God's perfect law. To the Christian, it is spiritual, slowly covering the earth and bringing more people to knowledge of, and obedience to, the God of Israel, which results in deliverance unto eternal life. This began with the advent of Jesus of Nazareth in the early first century. However, the official arrival of the consummated kingdom must be discerned.

The church traditionally interprets this verse as referring to the ascension of Jesus Christ (Acts 1:9), which, linguistically, is very reasonable. However, there are three reasons to question that direct link. First is the timing. Within the larger context of Daniel's narrative, this "coming of the Son of Man" occurs when the thrones of judgment have already been setup (9-10) during the Roman Empire. This is also after the "little horn" had spoken against the saints and the "beast" had been thrown into the fire (11-12). Jesus' ascension occurred shortly after His resurrection in AD 30, placing it outside Daniel's narrative of events. What grand judgment event took place in the first century exclusively involving Israel and the Roman Empire? It was the destruction of Jerusalem in AD 70 – forty years *after* Jesus' ascension to the right hand of God.

The second issue is that the kingdom era that Jesus was destined to usher in, and would receive dominion over, is one that has no end (Dan. 2:44). If Jesus went to God the Father to receive this kingdom at his ascension, it would have still been during the Judaic age (AD 30), which had not yet reached its own end. Jesus received power in heaven and on earth at His ascension to sit at the right hand of the Ancient of Days, but had not yet marshalled the future kingdom. Indeed, He had said during His public ministry that "there are some who are standing here who will not taste death until they see the Son of Man coming in His kingdom" (Matt. 16:28) confirming that this promised kingdom would not arrive until later in the time of that generation.

The third matter relates to the language in the present verse. Since this was directly quoted by the Savior in the Olivet Discourse, its meaning must correspond to how Jesus used it in Matthew as he narrated the fall of Jerusalem to His disciples using this exact imagery. The "coming of the Son of Man" must combine the two primary elements presented in these verses of Daniel's prophecy: the judgment presently taking place and the reception of the kingdom. Jesus did not use this phrase to describe His physical ascension; He did so to confirm that He would receive authority to judge Israel. Even some scholars who insist on Jesus' yet future Second Coming happily interpret this "coming" as His divine judgment on Jerusalem in AD 70. This verse cannot be referring to Jesus' ascension immediately after His death.

The language and context around the phrase "coming on the clouds" cannot be disregarded, and the indisputably divine nature of Jerusalem's destruction professed by even secular historians with no allegiance to the Christian disposition is profound. Historians Josephus and Tacitus record such accounts in their portrayals of what happened at the city. Josephus begins:

On the twentieth day of the month Artemisius, a certain prodigious and incredible phenomenon appeared; I suppose the account of it would seem to be a fable, were it not related by those that saw it, and were not the events that followed it of so considerable a nature as to deserve such signals; for, before sunsetting, chariots and troops of soldiers in their armor were seen running about among the clouds, and surrounding of cities.[113]

Likewise, states the Roman historian, Tacitus:

There had been seen hosts joining battle in the skies, the fiery gleam of arms, the temple illuminated by a sudden radiance from the clouds. The doors of the inner shrine were suddenly thrown open, and a voice of more than mortal tone was heard to cry that the Gods were departing. At the same instant there was a mighty stir as of departure. Some few put a fearful meaning on these events, but in most there was a firm persuasion that in the ancient records of their priests was contained a prediction of how at this very time the East was to grow powerful, and rulers, coming from Judea, were to acquire universal empire. These mysterious prophecies had pointed to Vespasian and Titus, but the common people, with the usual blindness of ambition, had interpreted these mighty destinies of themselves and could not be brought even by the disasters to believe the truth.[114]

Tacitus also provided verification that Daniel's prophecy was fresh in the minds of those familiar with the ancient scriptures, though in the priest's self-absorbed method of interpretation, Jews considered only themselves in regard to the prophetic. The devastation upon Jerusalem

---

[113] Josephus, *Wars*, 6.5.3.
[114] Tacitus, *Histories*, 5.13.

was the fulfillment of Jesus' proclamation in Luke's version of the Olivet Discourse as the "days of vengeance, so that all things which are written will be fulfilled" (Luke 21:22).

The narrative through the present verse has, thus, proceeded as a continuous prophecy. The Babylonian, Medo-Persian, Greek, and Roman Empires would hold dominion over Israel through subsequent centuries. The fourth empire would have ten notable kings up to the appointed event at Jerusalem, out of which would come an additional ruler, noted for his arrogance and persecution of God's people. The most likely candidate for the "little horn" is the Roman General Titus. After Nero committed suicide, there was a famous struggle over the empire known as the time of the "four emperors." Within one year three men, Galba, Otto, and Vitellius, each served as emperor through a brutal fight for the empire's control. It concluded with power being wrested away through their deaths into the hands of Vespasian, the father of Titus, who would eventually become emperor, himself.

The removal of these three men within the year eliminated the imperial infighting, and the subsequent installation of Vespasian instituted the beginning of the Flavian dynasty, of which Titus was an integral part. During this time, God's judgment thrones had been set up predictably to punish all the relevant players in the prophecy. And within the time of judgment, the Son of Man would come "with the clouds of heaven" and demonstrate authority to usher in the promised kingdom. The remaining implication is that the kingdom of God – one which would have no end – was established in the first century after the judgment levied upon the actors in the prophecy. In John's Revelation, its timing is identified when the seventh trumpet is blown: "Then the seventh angel sounded; and there were loud voices in heaven, saying, "The kingdom of the world has become the kingdom of our Lord and of His Christ; and He will reign forever and ever" (Rev. 11:15).

Verses 15-16

"As for me, Daniel, my spirit was distressed within me, and the visions in my mind kept alarming me. I approached one of those who were standing by

and began asking him the exact meaning of all this. So he told me and made known to me the interpretation of these things:"

The character present ("one of those standing") is seen by Jewish Rabbis as an angel who ministered to Daniel as he sought wisdom regarding his dreams. In the Hebrew language, its description of a human being is one who has the ability to progress because of free will. An angel on the other hand cannot become greater than they already are. The visual then is that the human is "moving forward" while the angel "stands still."

Daniel, unlike the major Prophets, does not seem to be speaking directly with God, but an angelic being. Prophets like Isaiah and Ezekiel were instructed to speak to Israel directly on behalf of God as their job was to inform the Jewish people of things that needed immediate correction regarding their covenantal relationship. Daniel, however, is being given an interpretation about distant, future events, meaning that he is receiving information that evaded even those men. Likewise, the book of Daniel offers prophecy that draws out direct interpretation of the visions given, which is not always the case in the OT. This interaction with the lesser beings of heaven seems to become more common as the time of prophecy draws to a close for the Judaic age. After Malachi, the final book of the OT, there is an intertestamental period of around 400 years where Israel received no prophecy at all.

Verse 17

"These great beasts, which are four in number, are four kings who will arise from the earth."

The angel gave a succinct summary of the vision because Daniel pled ignorance. In accordance with the parallel to the statue, Nebuchadnezzar was the "king" who was given the "kingdom" (2:37). Each kingdom experienced the reign of multiple kings, but all represented the same throne. These were the four kingdoms of Babylon, Medo-Persia, Greece, and Rome.

Verse 18

"But the saints of the Highest One will receive the kingdom and possess the kingdom forever, for all ages to come."

After these four earthly kingdoms, ruled by earthly kings, the new (fifth) kingdom established by God, that displaced them all, would be given to His true followers, the remnant of believers who followed Him and Him alone. These people would oversee it.

Jewish Rabbis teach that this verse confirms that it is the nation of Israel that will receive the kingdom alongside their Messiah. Therefore, the phrase "one like a man" from the thirteenth verse emphasizes a "people" rather than a pre-existent, supernatural god-man (Jesus) since their messiah is one of them. They admit, primarily because of Rashi's commentary, that this kingdom will only be given over to them when the Messiah is present and, thus, installed as King of Israel. If the nation receives the kingdom, it is only because the Messiah has received it first.

However, the Christian should possess the belief that the kingdom is active already. Jesus warned Israel at the start of His public ministry that this kingdom was on their doorstep: "From that time Jesus began to preach and say, 'Repent, for the kingdom of heaven is at hand' (Matt 4:17), "But if I cast out demons by the Spirit of God, then the kingdom of heaven has come upon you" (Matt. 12:28), "The time is fulfilled, and the kingdom is at hand; repent and believe in the gospel" (Mark 1:15), "...behold, the kingdom of God is in your midst" (Luke 17:21). Who, then, are the "high holy ones" if the kingdom is present? It could not be the nation of Israel in their Judaic context, for Jesus knew that they would reject the salvation that God had delivered and relayed the consequence: "Therefore I say to you, the kingdom of God will be taken away from you and given to a people, producing the fruit of it" (Matt. 21:43). But what is the nature of this kingdom?

- "My kingdom is not of this world. If My kingdom were of this world, then My servants would be fighting so that I would not be handed over to the Jews; but as it is, My kingdom is not of this realm." (John 18:36)

- "The kingdom of God is not coming with signs to be observed, nor will they say, 'Look, here it is!' or 'There!' for behold, the kingdom of God is in your midst." (Luke 17:20-21)
- "The kingdom of God is not eating or drinking but righteousness and peace..." (Rom. 14:17)
- "But the Jerusalem above is free; she is our mother." (Gal. 4:26)
- "But you have come to Mount Zion, and to the city of the Living God, the heavenly Jerusalem, and to myriads of angels." (Heb. 12:22)
- "Our citizenship is in heaven...." (Phi. 3:20)
- "Flesh and blood cannot inherit the kingdom of God." (I Cor. 15:50)

If Jesus sits at the right hand of God, then it is on a heavenly throne. And if He oversees a heavenly Jerusalem, then it must be inhabited by a present citizenry – those who have gone to be with the Lord. The implication is that God's saints – those who have submitted their lives to Him by accepting the accomplished work of Christ and saved by His perfect sacrifice – would rule this kingdom alongside him from this place of authority. In Jesus' Revelation to John, He encouraged readers, "He who overcomes, I will grant to him to sit with Me on My throne as I also overcame and sat down with My father on His throne" (Rev. 3:21).

The messianic kingdom is the kingdom of heaven; a spiritual realm of deliverance over which Jesus Christ holds all authority where the souls of His saints reign with Him in heaven while His church spreads its fruits on earth. It is not replacement theology to acknowledge that the Old Covenant has been exchanged for the New since Jesus "has made the first obsolete. But whatever is becoming obsolete and growing old is ready to disappear" (Heb. 8:13). This verse was written in the anonymous New Testament letter to the Hebrews around AD 60-62. The language suggests that the Old Covenant had not yet been fully removed but was prepared to be discarded. Less than a decade later, Jerusalem and Israel's glory and former method of sacrificial atonement – the temple – was dismantled to establish the new temple in the kingdom of God, Jesus Christ. Its inhabitants would, likewise, be temples of the Holy Spirit (I Cor. 6:19). The Law of Moses was no longer the centerpiece for faithful recompense, and the "good news" expressed by His church would spread like wildfire.

Verses 19-21

"Then I desired to know the exact meaning of the fourth beast, which was different from all the others, exceedingly dreadful, with its teeth of iron and its claws of bronze, and which devoured, crushed and trampled down the remainder with its feet, and the meaning of the ten horns that were on its head and the other horn which came up, and before which three of them fell, namely, that horn which had eyes and a mouth uttering great boasts and which was larger in appearance than its associates. I kept looking, and that horn was waging war with the saints and overpowering them."

Daniel was clearly distressed and pursued wisdom that was never given to the previous prophets of Israel. After the first compacted explanation from the angel, he hoped for additional clarity, especially regarding the elements of the final beast.

Titus ("little horn") waged direct war against God's people during his leadership in the Roman military. Jewish Rabbinic tradition interpreted the "holy ones" as all of Israel who were part of the over 1 million slaughtered in the siege of Jerusalem (Josephus). However, there were Christians and Jews in the city of Jerusalem during the siege that perished, even having remained from the remnant that previously removed themselves from the city to Pella (Eusebius). Only a select few were saved from the Great Tribulation of AD 70. But, Titus' intent is the key.

The Christian historian and writer Sulpicius Severus (AD 363-420) is considered an expert on Roman history. In his chronicle of the imperial events of the late first century, he noted that Titus was part of an inner-counsel debate as to whether the Jewish temple should be destroyed in the assault of Jerusalem. He thought such a feat of human accomplishment might be preserved for posterity; to revel in human architectural achievement. However – and this is crucial – Titus also believed that "the temple ought specially to be overthrown, in order that the religion of the Jews and of the Christians might more thoroughly be subverted: for that these religions, although contrary to each, had nevertheless proceeded from the same authors; that the Christians had sprung up from among the Jews; and that, if the root were extirpated, the offshoot would speedily perish."[115] This would seem to suggest that Titus fulfilled the prophetic vision of the additional horn "waging war" against Israel and anything that remained.

Verse 22

"Until the Ancient of Days came and judgment was passed in favor of the saints of the Highest One, and the time arrived when the saints took possession of the kingdom."

The persecution would continue until God avenged this remnant (Rev. 6:9-11) and bringing an end to the glory of the beast by replacing its dominion over them with a kingdom that He set up. The remnant would receive the keys to this kingdom under the rule of the Savior. Again, this is parallel to the kingdom in Daniel 2 that would crush the other kingdoms and would never be destroyed. Even though the narrative concludes by painting the picture of the Roman General Titus waging war against God's chosen and overwhelming them, God would ultimately avenge this destruction by ushering in the promised messianic kingdom by which the "beast" was destroyed and over which these martyrs reign.

The time spoken of in this verse must be the event that sparked the official changeover between the Judaic and Church ages because the promised kingdom had arrived. Jesus' appearance as the Jewish Messiah in AD 26 simultaneously kicked off God's rescue mission for His creation and His judgment of apostate Israel for their covenantal adultery, the result of which would be "the knowledge of God" being taken to the Gentiles (the rest of the world). Over the next generation (forty years), leading up to the destruction of Jerusalem, Jesus' followers

---

[115] Translated by Alexander Roberts, *Nicene and Post-Nicene Fathers, Second Series*, Vol. 11. Edited by Philip Schaff and Henry Wace. (Buffalo, NY: Christian Literature Publishing Co., 1894.) Revised and edited for New Advent by Kevin Knight. <http://www.newadvent.org/fathers/3505.htm>.

went out to persuade as many as possible of the truth of this gospel of the forgiveness of sins through Jesus, and the subsequent reconciliation with God through that sacrifice, in order that when the time of judgment upon Israel arrived (AD 70), the remnant was prepared and the transition from the Old Covenant age to the New Covenant age would be completed. This destruction of Jerusalem, then, initiated that exchange in world epochs from the Judaic age to the Messianic age, one in which this kingdom, given to Jesus and ruled by God's "holy ones" (martyrs of Rev. 6) began a new, global system in which the former order had passed away.

Verses 23-25

"Thus he said: 'the fourth beast will be a fourth kingdom on the earth, which will be different from all the other kingdoms and will devour the whole earth and tread it down and crush it. As for the ten horns, out of this kingdom ten kings will arise; and another will arise after them, and he will be different from the previous ones and will subdue three kings. He will speak out against the Most High and wear down the saints of the Highest One, and he will intend to make alterations in times and law; and they will be given into his hand for a time, times, and half a time."

Fourth beast = fourth kingdom = Rome.

Ten horns come out of it = ten kings (first ten emperors of the empire).

Last one after them = "little," or eleventh (not in text), horn = Roman General Titus.

The three kings "humbled" were, most likely, the three men fighting for Roman emperorship after Nero's death that were supplanted by Titus' family (Flavians) by AD 69.

Commentators are unified in the analysis of Hebrew terms for "time" (See Daniel 4:16). The consensus indicates that a "time" is one; "times" is two, and "dividing time" is half of one. The literal meaning would suggest this count is three and one-half of whatever timeframe is being suggested in the context (days, months, years). This would be the time that Israel is given into the hands of the "little horn," Titus. Did this occur?

This author believes it did. Titus began his assault of Jerusalem in late April AD 70. Within three weeks, on 11 May, he had breached the two outer walls of the city.[116] However, he could not hold his position. The Jews fought back with unexpected resolve and held the wall for three days, when on 14 May, the Romans finally took possession. Controlling this wall meant access to the heart of the city. When the last and inner most wall fell on 28 May, Roman forces gained unhindered access to every square inch of Jerusalem. No one was safe any longer.

This might be the starting point from which the people were given directly into Titus' hands for destruction. The calculation of 3½ months at 29½ days per month is 103¼ days. Counting forward this number would arrive at 11 September. Titus completed his objective of officially sacking the city on the fourth day of the month however, the following days he ordered that the soldiers reap the rewards of their incursion. A general plundering ensued as the soldiers viciously looted the city's many treasures, after which Titus held a three-day celebration for the Roman soldiers to revel in their victory.[117] After the festivities, he re-organized His forces sending some to other posts while deciding which legions would remain at the city. Thus, a week later, he left for Caesarea.

From the time that Titus breached the innermost wall, thereby gaining unfettered access to the entire city – including the temple – to the days he concluded his campaign and left for Caesarea could be the 3½ month timetable in which the city was given to the "little horn."

Verses 26-27

"But the court will sit for judgment, and his dominion will be taken away, annihilated and destroyed forever. Then the sovereignty, the dominion and the greatness of all the kingdoms under the whole heaven will be given to

---

[116] Josephus, *Wars*, 5.8.1.

[117] Thomas Lewin, *The Siege of Jerusalem*, Bradley Cobb, ed. (Cobb Publishing, [1863] 2016.), p. 85.

the people of the saints of the Highest One; His kingdom will be an everlasting kingdom, and all the dominions will serve and obey Him.'"

The judgment spoken of would come upon this persecuting power of the fourth beast while the theme of God's kingdom being established and given to His followers is abundant and clear.

Verse 28

"At this point the revelation ended. As for me, Daniel, my thoughts were greatly alarming me and my face grew pale, but I kept the matter to myself."

Though much of this vision was intended to give Jews a proper understanding of God's future plans regarding the Messiah and the arrival of His kingdom, Daniel was, literally, sick about these prophecies and kept it close to the vest.

DANIEL CHAPTER 8

Verses 1-2

"In the third year of the reign of Belshazzar the king a vision appeared to me, Daniel, subsequent to the one which appeared to me previously. I looked in the vision, and while I was looking I was in the citadel of Susa, which is in the province of Elam; and I looked in the vision and I myself was beside the Ulai Canal."

Daniel received a second vision around 551 BC in the third year of Nabonidus' absence from Babylon (553 – 542 BC). During this time, Belshazzar would have enjoyed his joint rule (coregency) over the kingdom as he would have been left to rule in his father's stead. Shusan (Susa) was the capital of Elam (Persia) in modern-day Iran.

Verses 3-4

"Then I lifted my eyes and looked, and behold, a ram which had two horns was standing in front of the canal. Now the two horns were long, but one was longer than the other, with the longer one coming up last. I saw the ram butting westward, northward, and southward, and no other beasts could stand before him nor was there anyone to rescue from his power, but he did as he pleased and magnified himself."

A different kind of animal was used to describe a conquering entity. It spread far and wide from its base and proceeding in such a manner that no one could stand against it. The ram had two horns indicating that this entity must have been comprised of two parts, one being better, or stronger, than the other though coming second ("coming up last"). This will be identified as the Medo-Persian kingdom (Dan. 8:20). Persia would become far greater than the Medes but would also come second in its rule over Babylonian territories as the Medes would assume leadership for the first year, under Darius.

Verse 5

"While I was observing, behold, a male goat was coming from the west over the surface of the whole earth without touching the ground; and the goat had a conspicuous horn between his eyes."

Daniel then saw another animal from the opposite direction that covered the inhabited earth, after the ram. This will be identified as the kingdom of Greece (Dan. 8:21). The "horn" can be identified as a king because of the ancient practice of anointing one with oil out of a horn. The "horn" that led this empire would be mighty and visible – Alexander the Great. Alexander was born in 356 BC to a life that would become rife with legend. Tutored by Aristotle and trained by the nation's leading military experts, the young man became king in 336 BC upon the assassination of his father. He became quite fierce, power hungry, and paranoid.

Rashi noted that the Hebrew language for not "touching the ground" means it looked like one skipping through the air. The surface understanding is that this described the swiftness with which this empire covered its ground in an almost effortless manner. However, there is another unique interpretation in that the "ground" could be a metaphorical reference to Israel. Throughout the Bible, the land of Israel is referred to as "the land" or "earth" ("ge"), especially regarding eschatological references in which Israel is the "earth" while the Gentile nations are the "sea." With that understanding, it might be inferred that the Greek armies speedily conquered the entire Persian territory while leaving Israel unscathed.

Verses 6-7

"He came up to the ram that had the two horns, which I had seen standing in front of the canal, and rushed at him in his mighty wrath. I saw him come beside the ram, and he was enraged at him; and he struck the ram and shattered his two horns, and the ram had no strength to withstand him. So he hurled him to the ground and trampled on him, and there was none to rescue the ram from his power."

Daniel begins a description of the encounter between these two powerful entities. In retrospect, the Greek Empire ("goat") led by Alexander the Great ("horn") attacked Persia ("ram") defeating it with great fury. Alexander conquered Persian lands as far away as India.

Verse 8

"Then the male goat magnified himself exceedingly. But as soon as he was mighty, the large horn was broken; and in its place there came up four conspicuous horns toward the four winds of heaven."

The vision proceeds with a divine elaboration on the goat (third empire of Daniel's previous vision). Once the empire ascended to global power, the "horn" would break; i.e., the great leader would die. This occurred with Alexander the Great's death in 323 BC. The "four heads" from the "beast" vision (Dan. 7:6) take control after the original horn breaks off. History shows that Alexander did not name a successor to his empire. These "four conspicuous horns" are the generals that assumed leadership over the empire which upon Alexander's death was divided into four parts.

Verses 9-11

"Out of one of them came forth a rather small horn which grew exceedingly great toward the south, toward the east, and toward the Beautiful Land. It grew up to the host of heaven and caused some of the host and some of the stars to fall to the earth and it trampled them down. It even magnified itself to be

equal with the Commander of the host; and it removed the regular sacrifice from Him, and the place of His sanctuary was thrown down."

Out of these four Greek Empires would arise a "small horn." This horn was different from the "little horn" in the previous chapter based on several observations, among them the characteristics that describe it, what it accomplished, and the kingdom out of which it came forth. The "little horn" came from the fourth, while this "small horn" came from the third. All external evidence points to Antiochus IV Epiphanes (Illustrious), who descended from the dynasty of Seleucus. Christian commentator Albert Barnes offers a line of succession for this family:

- Seleucus Nicator, 312-280 BC
- Antiochus Soter (I), 280-261 BC
- Antiochus Theos (II), (261-247 BC
- Seleucus Callinicus, 247-226 BC
- Seleucus Ceraunus, 226-223 BC
- Antiochus the Great (III), 223-187 BC
- Seleucus Philopater, 187-176 BC
- Antiochus Epiphanes (IV), 176-164 BC[118]

Antiochus conquered Egypt in 170 BC ("south") and, according to the Maccabean scrolls, invaded countries to the east (Armenia, Syria, etc.) which included plundering Palestine (1 Mac. 1-3:37). His conquests would culminate in sacking Jerusalem in 167 BC. The "beautiful land" (Israel) is described in a similar manner in Jeremiah 3:19 and Ezekiel 20:6 and 15. When Antiochus desecrated the temple, he removed the sacrificial system adhered to by Jewish law. His defilement included setting up the statue of a Greek god and ordering that a pig be slaughtered in the holy place.

It must be affirmed with certainty, at this point, that the "little horn" (Dan. 7) and the "small horn" (Dan. 8) are two different biblical characters with historical identities. They are also not future eschatological figures.

---

[118] Albert Barnes, *Barnes Notes*, "Daniel 8." https://biblehub.com/commentaries/barnes/daniel/8/htm.

Verse 12

"And on account of transgression the host will be given over to the horn along with the regular sacrifice; and it will fling truth to the ground and perform its will and prosper."

This circumstance was permitted by God as a punishment for the transgressions of the Jewish people against Him. From 168-167 BC, Antiochus had Jerusalem disciplined for what he perceived to be dishonor by Jewish citizens against his name. His directives resulted in oppression and sacrilege in Jewish holy spaces. The Jewish "truth" flung to the ground was the Mosaic law given to Israel which Antiochus was allowed to suppress during this time, even ordering ancient Jewish documents to be cut into pieces.

Verse 13

"Then I heard a holy one speaking, and another holy one said to that particular one who was speaking, 'How long will the vision about the regular sacrifice apply, while the transgression causes horror, so as to allow both the holy place and the host to be trampled?'"

Jewish interpretations suggest the "holy one" to be an angel speaking to another angel. The question posed hoped to address how long God would permit this punishment against His people. One of the "transgression[s]" was the engraved pagan idols placed in the temple to be worshipped.

Verse 14

"He said to me, 'For 2,300 evenings and mornings; then the holy place will be properly restored.'"

First and foremost, the Hebrew text does not say "days," though many English translations have inserted it. The textual problem becomes one of verbiage as the reader is left to surmise what the number "2,300" might represent. The reference to "evenings and mornings" suggests one twenty-four-hour day, which might be seen as 2,300 days (six years and six months). After this, then, Israel would be vindicated. However, it could also refer to the sacrifices themselves which were offered once in the morning and once in the evening (Exodus 29:38-42). The punishment involved the regular implementation of the daily sacrifices being placed on hold during this time period, leading the reader to assume that they would resume at the eventual restoration. The previous verse also specifically inquired how long the "daily sacrifice" would be disrupted. Two sacrifices a day would be the equivalent of 1,150 days in calendar time.

Though the exact date that the sacrifices ended is not known, the Maccabees do supply the date that Antiochus installed abominations in the temple to replace the sacrifices that the Jews could offer: 15 December (Hebrew month Kislev) 167 BC. However, this should probably not be the starting point. The second book of Maccabees describes that Antiochus' efforts to end the sacrifices began even before: "The king sent a certain old man of Antioch, to compel the Jews to depart from the laws of the fathers and God: and to defile the temple that in Jerusalem...."[119]

Prior to placing abominations in the temple, he had "issued a decree that all nations in his empire should abandon their own customs and become one people. All Gentiles and even many of the Israelites submitted to this decree. They adopted the official pagan religion, offered sacrifices to idols, and no longer observed the Sabbath."[120] Part of this decree had instructed that no further offerings be given in the temple. And to ensure its implementation, Antiochus sent his underlings to make it impossible by replacing the alters of the Jews with His own atrocities within its holy places.

The appropriate starting point might be when the decree was issued, a day lost in the annals of history. But if one counts backward from the time of the temple's rededication and thus the restoration of the sacrifices, then God's Word will certainly speak for itself. That day was 25 December, 164 BC.

If Daniel considered a typical Jewish year to have 354 days (lunar calendar), then one arrives at 1,072 days. Also important to the Hebrew

---

[119] 2 Maccabees 6:1-2.
[120] 1 Maccabees 1:41-43.

calendar was the "leap" year. To ensure that Passover fell in the spring season, they added one month to the necessary years to align the timing with their appropriate seasons. Over the three-year period when the temple was being desecrated, two were "leap" years. This means that there were sixty "leap" days for which to account. This calculation of the possible timeframe is: three years of 354 days each (3 x 354 =1,072) + two "leap" months of thirty days each (2 x 30=60) + 15 December to 25 December (10) = 1,134 days. This leaves eighteen days. In that span could Antiochus have issued the decree and sent his generals to Jerusalem to oversee its implementation directly? This would have been at the end of November 167 AD.

Verses 15-16

"When I, Daniel, had seen the vision, I sought to understand it; and behold, standing before me was one who looked like a man. And I heard the voice of a man between the banks of Ulai, and he called out and said, 'Gabriel, give this man an understanding of the vision.'"

The answer to this vision must come from heaven, alone. The voice must be of God, commanding the angel Gabriel to interpret the vision.

Verse 17

"So he came near to where I was standing, and when he came I was frightened and fell on my face; but he said to me, 'Son of man, understand that the vision pertains to the time of the end.'"

Good news: there is a precise time determined for the achievement of the vision.

Because the context is describing the reign of the Greek Empire and the appearance of Antiochus (IV) Epiphanes, to whom the passage is clearly referring, the "end" cannot possibly be describing the end of the world. Christians do have the proclivity to presume that anytime the word "end" or "last" appears in scripture, it must be a reference to the end of the world. This is not so and leads to enormous consequences when interpreting scripture. It could be the "end" of the time prophesied for what would befall the Jewish people, the "latter generations" of the Judaic age (which would have been 400 years from the time of this vision), or simply when the "2,300" expired. In the Jewish tradition, it is "the end of many days" (Rashi).

Verses 18-21

"*Now while he was talking with me, I sank into a deep sleep with my face to the ground; but he touched me and made me stand upright. He said, 'Behold, I am going to let you know what will occur at the final period of the indignation, for it pertains to the appointed time of the end. The ram which you saw with the two horns represents the kings of Media and Persia. The shaggy goat represents the kingdom of Greece, and the large horn that is between his eyes is the first king.*"

These verses confirm the prior analysis.

Ram = Medo-Persia

Goat = Greece

King = Alexander (the Great) of Macedon.

Verse 22

"*The broken horn and the four horns that arose in its place represent four kingdoms which will arise from his nation, although not with his power.*"

Four kingdoms divided the Greek Empire upon Alexander's ("broken horn") death. They were certainly not as strong as Alexander and began to fight with each other over the subsequent years: Cassander over Greece, Lysimachus (Antigonus) over Thrace, Ptolemy over Egypt, and Seleucus over Syria.

Verse 23

"*In the latter period of their rule, when the transgressors have run their course, a king will arise, insolent and skilled in intrigue.*"

Near the latter years of this kingdom, when Israel's sins and transgressions had filled God's cup of wrath, Antiochus Epiphanes would be cleared to plunder Jerusalem and desecrate the temple. This was the punishment against Israel for their covenantal disobedience: God departed the temple and allowed its devastation.

Verses 24-25

"His power will be mighty, but not by his own power, and he will destroy to an extraordinary degree and prosper and perform his will; he will destroy mighty men and the holy people. And through his shrewdness He will cause deceit to succeed by his influence; and he will magnify himself in his heart, and he will destroy many while they are at ease. He will even oppose the Prince of princes, but he will be broken without human agency."

The assumption is that Antiochus Epiphanes will accomplish these incredible feats, but not of his accord. He will be empowered by the enemy but permitted by God Almighty. This leader would destroy the Jewish people ("holy ones"). He will also speak with blasphemy toward heaven ("oppose the Prince of princes") since declaring war against Israel was akin to doing so against God, Himself. However, it would take surprisingly little to produce this leader's death. It was not military power or strength that triggered his demise. Antiochus died of a mental illness far away from home, a passing that the Maccabees attribute as divine punishment for his crimes against Israel. The untold history of Antiochus is that this illness from which he suffered could have been melancholy or depression caused by the weight of his sins against God, triggering prayerful repentance before his death.[121]

Verses 26-27

"The vision of the evenings and morning which has been told is true; But keep the vision secret, for it pertains to many days in the future. Then I, Daniel, was exhausted and sick for days. Then I got up again and carried

---

[121] 2 Mac. 9:7, 8, 10.

on the king's business; but I was astounded at the vision, and there was none to explain it."

The angel confirmed, with the reference to the "evenings and mornings" the truth of the matter. Daniel was instructed not to teach this or reveal it but to keep it hidden until the appropriate time. Can one imagine the weight of this with a mandate of total secrecy?

DANIEL CHAPTER 9

"In the first year of Darius the son of Ahasuerus, of Median descent, who was made king over the kingdom of the Chaldeans – in the first year of his reign, I, Daniel, observed in the books the number of the years which was revealed as the word of the Lord to Jeremiah the prophet for the completion of the desolation of Jerusalem, namely, seventy years."

By the mid-620's BC, the Assyrians, who held dominion over the Medes and Babylonians, were in a state of civil war and unable to defend themselves against any unified revolt from their subject peoples. In an attempt to end their subjugation, the Medes and Babylonians formed an alliance in the late seventh century to conquer the once powerful Assyrian Empire which was becoming visibly weakened by internal affairs. Around 612 BC, the Medes captured the Assyrian capital, and it collapsed within the following three years. The Median kingdom experienced subsequent expansion and developed a regional realm of authority. Around 550 BC, the Persians, who had become subject to the Medes, began a successful revolt against the Median King. However, the conquest did not result in a total Median dismantling or defeat as the two began a confederation in which both administered dominion, though the Persians would exercise prominence.

While most critical scholarship will attest to Cyrus' Persian invasion of Babylon in 539 BC, the OT prophesied that it would be the Medes that would take initial control of Babylon. Writing generations before Babylon's dominion, the prophet Isaiah predicted, "Behold, I am going to stir up the Medes against them, who will not value silver or take pleasure in gold" (Is. 13:17). Likewise, did Jeremiah: "Sharpen the arrows, fill the quivers! The Lord has roused the spirit of the kings of the Medes, because His purpose is against Babylon to destroy it; for is the vengeance of the Lord, vengeance for His temple," (Jer. 51:11) and "Consecrate the nations against her, the kings of the Medes, their governors and all their prefects, and every land of their dominion" (Jer. 51:28).

Daniel's observation centered on Jeremiah's prophecy of the Jewish exile to Babylon (Jer. 29:10). If Daniel wrote around 539/538 BC, immediately after the fall of Babylon, then the seventy years were nearing completion from the original Babylonian invasion around 605 BC, when the very first Jews were displaced. Sabbatical years are important in Israel's history, especially regarding the original reason for the departure from their land at the hands of the Babylonians. In II Chronicles, Jeremiah's prophecy of the 70-year exile is explained as the restoration of the physical land through "enjoy[ing] its sabbaths" (36:20-22, Lev. 26:34-35).

Every seventh year, the land required an agricultural respite to rejuvenate itself, which the Israelites had neglected. Thus, the years in exile were equivalent to the number of sabbatical requirements that the Jews had not followed. Daniel believed that at the exile's culmination, God promised their redemption and a return to their heritage and homeland. He seemed to be questioning the circumstances, however, as signs were indicating that a swift return to independence might not be immediately imminent. This concern led him to contemplate as to whether the seventy-year count was being measured correctly and, by extension, the implications for the promises made to the Jewish people by which they had found comfort during their exile.

Verses 3-4

"So I gave my attention to the Lord God to seek Him by prayer and supplications, with fasting, sackcloth and ashes. I prayed to the Lord my God and confessed and said, 'Alas O Lord, the great and awesome God who

keeps His covenant and lovingkindness for those who love Him and keep His commandments."

Daniel's confession on behalf of his people was modest, thorough, and intense, remembering that it would not be their own righteousness from which mercy was produced, but God's holiness. To his credit, his manner was not one in which he made demands from God, but rather admiration and praise for His character and glory, lauding His loyalty despite the transgressions committed against Him by His own people. This represents how we should come before the Lord, humble and reverential while never assuming a position of victimhood.

Verses 5-11

"We have sinned, committed iniquity, acted wickedly and rebelled, even turning aside from Your commandments and ordinances. Moreover, we have not listened to Your servants, the prophets, who spoke in Your name to our kings, our princes, our fathers and all the people of the land. Righteousness belongs to You, O Lord, but to us open shame, as it is this day – to the men of Judah, the inhabitants of Jerusalem and all Israel, those who are nearby and those who are far away in all the countries to which You have driven them, because of their unfaithful deeds which they have committed against You. Open shame belongs to us, O Lord, to our kings, our princes and our fathers, because we have sinned against You. To the Lord our God belong compassion and forgiveness, for we have rebelled against Him; nor have we obeyed the voice of the Lord our God, to walk in His teachings which he set before us through His servants the prophets. Indeed all Israel has transgressed Your law and turned aside, not obeying Your voice; so the curse has been poured out on us, along with the oath which is written in the law of Moses the servant of God, for we have sinned against Him."

Daniel acknowledged the transgressions of His people as the cause of the Babylonian destruction of the Jewish nation. Even the Jewish commentators acknowledge that they "were constantly turning away from [God's] commandments" (Rashi). Daniel knew there was no question about the justification of God's chastisement of the Jewish people, yet he anticipated the eventual restoration of Israel's status.

For centuries, the prophets had warned Israel of the consequences of their disobedience and covenantal adultery, and still, the elect nation had turned. Even during their initial salvation and exodus from Egypt, they complained that God had forsaken them. Israel was never satisfied. Consequently, the covenant promises of curses were upon them (Deut. 28).

Verses 12-14

"Thus He has confirmed His words which he had spoken against us and against our rulers who ruled us, to bring on us great calamity, for under the whole heaven there has not been done anything like what was done to Jerusalem. As it is written in the law of Moses, all this calamity has come on us; yet we have not sought the favor of the Lord our God by turning from our iniquity and giving attention to Your truth. Therefore the Lord has kept the calamity in store and brought it on us; for the Lord our God is righteous with respect to all His deeds which He has done, but we have not obeyed His voice."

While some people would declare anger at God for their individual misfortune, Daniel substantiated Israel's sentence and declared God as righteous and just for His response. (See Ezekiel 8-11 for a description of the departure of God's spirit from the temple, thereby paving the way for its devastation.) If Israel turned away from God, all blessings previously promised Israel would become misfortune and punishment. Pestilence would destroy the land, their crops would be unfruitful, disease would ravage the people, and a Gentile nation would be divinely permitted to invade, overcome, and persecute until "[they] are destroyed" (Deut. 28:45).

Indeed, God promised that an outside nation would "besiege you in all your towns until your high and fortified walls, in which you trusted come down throughout your land and it shall besiege you in all your towns throughout your land which the Lord your God has given you. Then you shall eat the offspring of your own body, the flesh of yours sons and of your daughters whom the Lord your God has given you, during the siege and the distress by which your enemy will oppress you....the refined and delicate woman among you, who would not venture to set the sole of her foot on the ground for delicateness and refinement, shall be hostile toward the husband she cherishes and toward her son and her daughter, and toward her afterbirth which issues from between her legs and toward her children whom she bears, for she will eat them secretly for lack of anything else during the siege and the distress by which your enemy will oppress you in your towns" (Deut. 28:52-54, 56-57).

How can the sincere Bible reader consume this narrative of absolute judgment and not be moved by its graphically horrific doom? Indeed, God promised that "the Lord will delight over you to make you perish and destroy you" (Duet 28:63). Instead of the weakness of the human mind that pleads unfairness in seeming disaster, proclaiming, "O God, how could you?" as though they held sway over the cosmic scales of justice, Daniel praised God for keeping His promises. Please consider the significance of such a notion: Daniel is worshipping God for cursing His own people. This is not because God maintains a devious nature, but because it proves that God keeps His promises.

Verses 15-16

"And now, O Lord our God, who have brought Your people out of the land of Egypt with a mighty hand and have made a name for Yourself, as it is this day – we have sinned, we have been wicked. O Lord, in accordance with all Your righteous acts, let now Your anger and Your wrath turn away from Your city Jerusalem, Your holy mountain; for because of our sins and the iniquities of our fathers, Jerusalem and Your people have become a reproach to all those around us."

The focus of this lament can also be found in I Kings as the prophetic call to the nation's ridicule: "Then I will cut off Israel from the land which I have given them, and the house which I have consecrated for My name, I will cast out of My sight. So Israel will become a proverb and a byword among all peoples" (I Kings 9:7).

Verses 17-19

"So now, our God, listen to the prayer of Your servant and to his supplications, and for Your sake, O Lord, let Your face shine on Your desolate sanctuary. O my God, incline Your ear and hear! Open Your eyes and see our desolations and the city which is called by Your name; for we are not presenting our supplications before You on account of any merits of our own, but on account of Your great compassion. O Lord, hear! O Lord, forgive! O Lord, listen and take action! For Your own sake, O my God, do not delay, because Your city and Your people are called by Your name."

As Daniel cried for mercy [for His name's sake], he pled for God to further demonstrate His glory by extending mercy despite Israel's transgressions and restoring His city and sanctuary – that the world would be unable to deny His benevolence and sovereignty.

Verses 20-23

"Now while I was speaking and praying, and confessing my sin and the sin of my people Israel, and presenting my supplication before the Lord my God on behalf of the holy mountain of my God, while I was still speaking in prayer, then the man Gabriel, whom I had seen in the vision previously, came to me in my extreme weariness about the time of the evening offering. He gave me instruction and talked with me and said, 'O Daniel, I have now come forth to give you insight with understanding. At the beginning of your supplications the command was issued, and I have come to tell you, for you are highly esteemed; so give heed to the message and gain understanding of the vision.'"

Daniel's emphasis in prayer looked toward the temple rebuild ("on behalf of the holy mountain of God"), which would restore God's glory and defend His name. Gabriel's informed Daniel that a word from God, Himself, had been brought forth. While the Christian acknowledges the sovereignty of God in all human affairs, including decisions of a predetermined nature, the wording suggests that because of Daniel's desirable qualities and, no doubt, the intensity of his prayer, God chose to reveal privileged information. Daniel was a faithful adherent to his Jewish roots, of a noble family, and known for his piety and loyal observance of the Law. His reverence before the God of their blessed covenant brought him divine favor. Thus began a veiled explanation of Israel's future that brought definition to both future Jewish and Christian heritage. The following four verses are among the most profound in the entire Bible because of their salvific qualities and prophetic truth for God's true followers.

Verse 24

"Seventy weeks have been decreed for your people and your holy city, to finish the transgression, to make an end of sin, to make atonement for iniquity, to bring in everlasting righteousness, to seal up vision and prophecy and to anoint the most holy place."

Here begins one of the most intensively studied passages in the book of Daniel. This verse and the three that follow are the hinge upon which nearly all evangelical eschatology rests, and yet, many Christians greatly struggle to comprehend its meaning. Consequently, there are rampant variances of interpretation.

The Jewish exile from Israel under Babylonian captivity was always a spiritual issue as it was direct punishment for their habitual disobedience toward their divine covenant. Ultimately, it required a spiritual resolution. Professor of Old Testament Interpretation, Peter J. Gentry, has provided an outstanding analysis of the central point of this prophecy in Daniel: "Although the focus of the message is on the city and the people (Jerusalem and Israel), there are broader implications for the nations. This passage must be seen in the light of the Abrahamic and Mosaic Covenants. The Abrahamic Covenant promised blessings for the nations through the family of Abraham (Gen. 12:1-3). The Mosaic Covenant directed and instructed the family of Abraham how to live in a right relationship with God, a right relationship with one another in covenant community, and a right relationship to the earth (as stewards of creation), so that they could be the blessing to the nations."[122] With the Mosaic Covenant broken by Israel, it required the forgiveness of

---

[122] Peter J. Gentry. "Daniel's Seventy Weeks and the New Exodus" *Southern Baptist Journal of Theology*, 14.1 (2010), p. 32.

sins for its restoration and to open the path for blessings to flow to the nations. Israel, thus, had to be spiritually renewed.

The major prophets, especially Isaiah, held little back in their own warnings toward their people: "Your iniquities have made a separation between you and your God…your hands are defiled with blood and your fingers with iniquity…they conceive mischief and bring forth iniquity… their feet run to evil…therefore justice is far from us, and righteousness does not overtake us…we hope for light, but behold, darkness, for brightness, but we walk in gloom…for our transgressions are multiplied before You and our sins testify against us; For our transgressions with us, and we know our iniquities: transgressing and denying the Lord, and turning away from our God…the Lord saw and it was displeasing in His sight that there was no justice. And He saw that there was no man, and was astonished that there was no one to intercede" (Is. 59:1-16).

After enduring a lineage of disobedience that Isaiah described with damning terminology, the Lord revealed there was no one to correct such a nature of profound depravity. This would require a redemption that only God could provide; "Then His own arm brought salvation to him, and His righteousness upheld him" (Is. 59:16) so that "they will fear the name of the Lord from the west And His glory from the rising of the sun" (Is. 59:19).

For God to make things right for the Jews and to save His covenant people, to expiate their sin, idolatry, and apostasy, He would bring their final salvation through Himself: "A Redeemer will come to Zion, and to those who turn from transgression in Jacob" (Isaiah 59:20). Gabriel is, thus, establishing this vision to Daniel as the realization of Israel's only hope – the Rescuer who will end all these things and usher in "everlasting righteousness." This expression, according to J. Paul Tanner, is exceptionally unique, making its only appearance in the entire OT in this verse. He stipulates that it is unavoidably messianic, convincingly arguing that the book of Isaiah copiously recognizes that Israel's future righteousness is ushered in only by their Messiah and the kingdom He brings. This source of redemption described must be the Messiah.[123]

---

[123] J. Paul Tanner, "Is Daniel's Seventy-Weeks Prophecy Messianic? Part 2." *Bibliotheca Sacra* 166 (July-September 2009) pp.319-35. p. 330.

The Hebrew word "shabua" is consistently translated as "sevens," which can refer to days, weeks, or years depending on the context. Simply put, it is an established period multiplied by seven. Throughout history, scholars from nearly every corner of biblical scholarship agree that this reference is equivalent to "weeks of sevens," a conclusion surmised through an exhaustive spectrum of research ranging from the mathematical analysis of Jewish sabbatical years to a simple process of eliminating unreasonable time periods. For example, it would have been impossible for Jerusalem to have been rebuilt in 490 days. However, the sabbatical element is the likely connection for calculating the prophecy. One "seven" is a seven-year period in which seven weeks times seven years equals forty-nine years. Thus, seventy weeks times seven years equals 490 years. After this time is completed, the process for Israel's redemption would see its culmination.

As for the six components to be achieved within the timetable, the Hebrew phrase for "finish transgression" renders the notion of "holding back" transgressions, or sins, which cause rebellion against the Creator. As such, an appropriate translation should, most accurately, be read as "restraining rebellion," a description that alludes to the image of an insurgence that is no longer advancing. Similarly, the following phrase "to make an end of sin" does not mean that sin, itself, would cease, but rather that the recurrent process of righting sin would be brought to completion; in other words, one final offering would be made to address sin's condemnation. In making "atonement for iniquity," the language extracts the thought that iniquity (immorality) will be ultimately atoned for in the end.

The phrase "seal up vision" reinforced the finality of this restoration in that it would fulfill all Old Testament prophecy and prediction. Much debate, however, has centered around the interpretation of the final objective, the Hebrew "qodesh qadashim," most precisely translated as "the most holy." This is, unfortunately, a phrase that Daniel left somewhat indefinite and, therefore, subject to various renderings in Christian Bible translations. It should be transliterated as "Holy of Holies," which is the frequent biblical description of the inner sanctuary of the Temple in Jerusalem (I Kings 6:16, Ezekiel 45:3, Hebrews 9:3-4). Indeed, the Temple was the center of Jewish life. The inner sanctuary contained the only earthly dwelling for God's physical presence and commanded Israel's worship and lawful support. It was in this place that the anointed priests offered incense and the blood sacrifices to open the spiritual intersection between heaven and earth, honoring the Jewish covenantal commitment in appreciation for their Provider's gracious blessings and the pacification of His preeminent standards.

Since the need for Israel's reconciliation with God could not be accomplished of their own accord – thus, the underlying advocacy of Messianic undertones – the nation's settlement would inevitably lead to new kind of temple. If Gabriel's suggestion is that the Jewish Messiah would come to complete this reconciliation, then it becomes difficult to accept "qodesh qadashim" as purely restoring the physical inner sanctuary, because the established Jewish process of repeated offering and sacrifice was intended to be replaced. Their penitence had always been their covenant routine for recompensing sinful behavior while they were inhabitants of the Promised Land. The subject of this verse, conversely, would invalidate the entire process by providing a final reparation, replacing what they had previously implemented of their own effort through physical offering and sacrifice. An understanding of "anoint[ing] the most Holy" must correlate with the culmination of this reckoning. There would be a new "Holy of Holies," a new house for God's spirit, one that brought the fulfillment of God's redemption plan. This was represented by the Messiah.

The figurative methods Jesus utilized for reading himself into this reality are nearly unmistakable in the Gospels. For example, in John 2, Jesus compared His body to the Jewish Temple when He warned Jewish leaders, "Destroy this temple and in three days, I will raise it up" (19), to which they replied that it had taken "forty-six years to build this temple and you will raise it up in three days?" (20). Likewise, Matthew told that Jesus rebuked the Pharisees for their hypocrisy in the Law as they criticized His disciples for picking grain to eat on the Sabbath and reminded them of how King David "entered the house of God and ate the consecrated bread, which was not lawful for him to eat nor for those who were with him, but for the priests alone? Or have you not read in the Law, that on the Sabbath the priests in the temple break the Sabbath and are innocent? But I say to you something greater than the temple is here. But if you had known what this means, 'I desire compassion and not a sacrifice,' you would not have condemned the innocent. For the Son of Man is Lord of the Sabbath" (Matt. 12:4-8). Furthermore, when Jesus would forgive sins, Jewish leaders became incensed because He was claiming to do what could only be accomplished in the Temple. Jesus was appropriating the priestly authority bestowed through Temple rituals onto Himself, claiming to be the new Temple.

In ancient times, the purpose of "anointing" was to confer an individual with divine approval for a task or purpose, usually with oil. Jesus of Nazareth was divinely purposed to die for sins, "anointed... with the Holy Spirit and with power" (Acts 10:38), becoming the new residence of sacrifice and the place and subject of worship, service, and offering while the redeemed of God would, through Him, become a dwelling place for His Spirit. As such, this "anointing" could equate to the execution of God's plan to redeem sinners, for it is by the blood of the Lamb that one may enter into the Holy of Holies. The Lamb would come from Jewish lineage, but his death signaled the end of Jewish exclusivity as anyone could now have access to this redemption (John 4:22). Regarding the phrase "qodesh qadashim," its emphasis might be less on the person of the Messiah, but the vessel through which the work was accomplished.

If this author may extend humility as a lowly teacher, I do not know the unquestionable reference for the phrase "the most holy." I believe, however, based on context and language that the physical, inner sanctuary of the Jewish Temple and Jesus' sacrifice become spiritually interchangeable for describing the ultimate atonement, prophesied to occur during the designated timeframe and accomplished through the objectives in this verse.

Verse 25

"So you are to know and discern that from the issuing of a decree to restore and rebuild Jerusalem until Messiah the Prince there will be seven weeks and sixty-two weeks; it will be built again, with plaza and moat, even in times of distress."

The forward calculation of "seven weeks and sixty-two weeks" begins from a decree given to restore Jerusalem – which had been completely destroyed in the Babylonian invasion in 586 BC – until the advent of a mashiach nagid (Hebrew) or "an anointed one, a leader." This expression is used nowhere else in OT scriptures.

The term mashiach is liberally employed throughout the OT as a description of an anointed individual, most frequently given to a priest, king, or prophet as one entering into a distinct service for the Lord. The word "nagid" is chosen to define a "ruler" with an emphasis on kingship, one who comes to rule a kingdom. In Hebrew grammar, an adjective follows its noun (opposite English), meaning if mashiach was just a descriptor, the words would have been reversed to read "nagid mashiach." This literary method denotes mashiach as a noun, emphasizing that this is not a ruler who is anointed, rather a messiah who will also rule.

Paul Tanner argues that though the term "anointed" (mashiach) was given to numerous kings, most of these titles were accompanied by a qualifying pronoun, providing a more formal description and identifier such as "the Lord's anointed," "My anointed," (I Samuel 2:35) or "Your anointed" (Psalm 132:10).[124] The fact that mashiach, here, has no accompanying qualifier, calls into question the notion that this person is simply a historical, earthly king. The lack of a grammatical qualifier, most assuredly, adds to the credibility that this person has unprecedented distinctiveness and significance, whose inherent position does not require a qualifier for identification. In other words, He is, simply – the One. The term "mashiach nagid," therefore, exceedingly indicates the arrival of the Messiah, a distinguished champion, anointed with isolated purpose, who would arrive 483 years (49 years + 434 years) after the "word" given to restore Jerusalem.

As for the decree, only one conclusion can be drawn that most accurately fits the timeline, despite healthy debate in modern Christian scholarship. This should be Artaxerxes' decree in 458/457 BC because it aligned with Ezra's return with freedom to re-establish all essential components of Jerusalem, even including administrative and judicial components of the city. According to Peter Gentry, Ezra would have

---

[124] Tanner, "Is Daniel's Seventy-Weeks Prophecy Messianic? Part 2," p. 323.

been familiar with the previous commands from Cyrus and Darius to initiate the Jewish re-habitation of Jerusalem by permitting the Temple's reconstruction.[125] Because Jews would have understood the sanctity of the Temple and Jerusalem to be synonymous, this would have, undoubtedly, levied the expectation that the city's renovation would have been inevitable after even one command to rebuild the sanctuary.

Ezra returned with plans both to reassemble essential administrative functions, such as laws, political structures, and the judiciary (Ezra 7:7, 13-14, 25), and administer physical construction of the surrounding elements. In the book of Ezra, he thanked God for extending mercy, through the Persian kings, to "give us reviving, to raise up the house of our God, to restore its ruins, and to give us a wall in Judah and Jerusalem" (Ezra 9:9), indicating that resources had been allocated to rebuild fortifications. This is reinforced by the first chapter of Nehemiah, which succeeds Ezra, in which the namesake expressed concern that the existing walls of Jerusalem would be insufficient to protect the newly rebuilt temple, demonstrating that an attempt had been made to restore the walls after the first decree, but were inadequate.

It would take forty-nine years to rebuild the temple ("seven weeks") and another 434 years ("sixty-two weeks") for the Messiah to arrive. The simple calculation of 483 years forward from this decree in 458/457 BC, brings the reader to AD 26/27. At first glance, this date might hold little significance based on the traditional Christian understanding of the timeline of Jesus' life because orthodoxy assumes that Jesus was born at the turn of history (around 1 AD). Luke's gospel informs the reader that Jesus began His public ministry at around thirty years of age (Luke 3:23), and according to the Gospel accounts, Jesus taught through three Jewish Passover celebrations, meaning that somewhere between thirty-three and thirty-four years of age, He was crucified.

According to the same gospel accounts, Jesus was born while King Herod was still alive. The historical, scholarly consensus postulates that Herod died around 4 BC, a conclusion that rests primarily on the records of renowned Jewish historian Flavius Josephus. In his *Antiquities of the Jews*, He described that Herod's death was preceded by a lunar eclipse, but closely followed by the Jewish Passover celebration.

---

[125] Gentry, "Daniel's Seventy Weeks and the New Exodus," p. 36.

Historical records indicate four lunar eclipses occurring between 5 BC and 1 AD, with only one total obscurity.

The most applicable instance, however, was a partial lunar eclipse that occurred 29 days before Passover in March, 4 BC, seemingly fitting Josephus' account. This would mean that Jesus was born between 6-5 BC. Counting forward about thirty years, the reader arrives at AD 26/27 when Jesus was baptized in the Jordan river at the hands of John the Baptist. This marked the commencement of His public ministry as Israel's Messiah, perfectly corresponding with Jesus' own announcement in Mark's gospel that "the time is fulfilled and the kingdom of God is at hand" (Mark 1:14-15).

Daniel's prophecy indicates that the advent of the Messiah will occur at the expiration of the first 483 years of the "seventy-weeks."

Verse 26

"Then after the sixty-two weeks the Messiah will be cut off and have nothing, and the people of the prince who is to come will destroy the city and the sanctuary. And its end will come with a flood; even to the end there will be war; desolations are determined."

After the sixty-two-week period, this mashiach would be "cut-off," a phrase stemming from the Hebrew word "karath," which is often translated as "cut down." It was used in the OT to describe various functions such as cutting a garment (I Sam. 24:5) or a tree branch (Numbers 13:23), but most frequently as the description of someone being "cut-off" from his people (Ex. 12:19, Num. 19:13) in a manner that symbolized death rather than exile. Why did Daniel utilize "karath" when other Hebrew words may have sufficed? The words "harag" (kill) or "ratsach" (murder, assassination) may have similarly paralleled a violent death and conveyed a simpler message. That answer might come from the more reflective purpose that "karath" signified in Old Testament history. In Genesis 15, God began His covenant with Israel by requiring that Abram slaughter a heifer, a goat, and a ram (v. 9) and cut the carcasses in two, arranging the pieces of flesh opposite each other for sacrifice. Later, as Abram slept, a "flaming torch passed between the pieces" (17). On the day, the Lord made a covenant with Abram saying, 'To your descendants I have given this land, from the river of Egypt as far as the great river Euphrates'" (18).

The Hebrew phrase used for "made a covenant" was "karath berith." The true root use of the word "karath" means "to cut" as flesh.[126] This was precisely God's process for establishing His agreements with Israel – cutting covenants. In simplest terms, blood was shed, and a covenant was born. Gabriel was not simply informing Daniel that an "anointed one" will be killed, but that this mashiach would be "cut" to signify a more profound, spiritual parallel – this ferocious death would shed blood for a superior purpose. The mashiach would also, in the words of modern translations, "have nothing." The purest transliteration should render "and he has not," a phrase which should not be overanalyzed. Despite his kingly and sanctified status as an "anointed one," He will have nothing left at His death; no belongings, no successor, nothing with which to leave a corporeal legacy. This "Anointed One" would give His life for His people to "cut" a new covenant.

The "city and the sanctuary" are undisputed references to Jerusalem and its temple, which according to this prophecy, would be restored by the time of Messiah's arrival. The original reconstruction happened twenty years after the book of Daniel was written; however, this verse predicts that it will again be demolished. It will also occur after the death of the Messiah.

The "people" and the "prince" must be identified within the appropriate guidelines of interpretation which are "according to the context and normal rules of literature," says Peter Gentry. Because the context of this entire passage is about Israel and the path to its redemption, the clear subject is Israel. The word for "prince," is the same used in the previous verse – nagid. Grammatically, Gentry points out that there are no indicators suggesting the introduction of a different individual to the narrative. In essence, he notes, the mashiach who is "cut-off" and the nagid of the people who destroy Jerusalem, here, might be the same individual.[127] And if the "prince" (nagid) of this verse is the Messiah figure, who then are the "people" of the leader?" Gentry

---

[126] Gentry, "Daniel's Seventy Weeks and the New Exodus," p. 38.
[127] Ibid., p. 40.

concludes the unorthodox, but inevitable, answer – the Jewish people. Even Daniel has attested, to this point, that Israel was responsible for what befell them. God's role in either permitting or executing the temple's desecration and destruction based on Israel's actions and behavior was unquestionably a historical precedent.

In Ezekiel 9:4-7, God, Himself, issued a defilement of the temple when he commanded that blood be spilled in the temple courtyard. Why? Because of sins committed by the people, God's presence had left the temple; it had already been defiled. Its sanctity had, thus, already been removed. Likewise, Ezekiel 23:38-39 describes God's provoked anger that children were slaughtered in the temple, a defilement that Ezekiel mourns as one of His justifications for its destruction in 586 BC. This devastation, at the hands of the Babylonians, and the subsequent Jewish exile from Israel was, therefore, caused by their sin and idolatrous practices (Jer. 25:1-7, II Chron 36:14-21). The temple was not immune to annihilation and desecration if God's presence had departed. And He would handle the punishment in accordance with His will.

To defile something is to remove its holiness. In accordance with scripture, the spilling of blood, especially murder, would have accomplished such a desecration. In AD 66, relations between Jews and Romans were quickly deteriorating as the former experienced great physical abuse and maltreatment under the latter's rule. After enough scandalous events, such as one Roman governor looting the temple treasury to acquire funds for the empire, combined with enduring persecution of Jews within Jerusalem, a group of Jewish zealots took irreconcilable action. They viciously attacked the present Roman forces and anyone collaborating with them, which included priests in Jewish leadership. These leaders were unceremoniously slaughtered in the temple in this revolt, an event described by Jewish historian, Josephus.

Upon hearing of the incidents, the Roman Emperor Nero sent his forces to squash any advancing unrest. Within months the Roman army had surrounded Jerusalem and would remain for 3½ years, at which point his army of mercenaries would carry out its final destruction in AD 70. The city and the Temple would be destroyed, as described in in this verse, "with a flood," the common term used to describe an incalculable army, and "desolations" would continue until the end of the "war" (Jewish-Roman). Such destruction was the basis for Jesus' urgent warning to His followers in the Olivet Discourse to evacuate the city.

Verse 27

"And he will make a firm covenant with the many for one week, but in the middle of the week he will put a stop to sacrifice and grain offering; and on the wing of abominations will come one who makes desolate, even until a complete destruction, one that is decreed, is poured out on the one who makes desolate."

The nearest subject of a particular clause is usually identified as the antecedent (something that precedes something else) for a following pronoun. Therefore, the "he" who will "uphold a covenant" should be connected to the nearest syntactic subject. Since the "people" of the leader could not apply, the nearest option would be the mashiach (Messiah) of the preceding verse. The phrase "uphold a covenant" is unique but represents strengthening an agreement that can apply to various entities, primarily between a lord and his servants, as mutual beneficiaries. As the Israelites, and their relationship with God, are the primary object of the prophecy's introduction three verses before, the language must have involved some form of covenantal rehabilitation, firming up the former arrangement through a new method of atonement – the sacrifice of the Messiah. Indeed, Jesus' first ministry was to the Jews (Matt. 15:24), meaning that this New Covenant would be offered to them first ("the many").

If one connects Jesus' first advent with His priority to save the Jews, then Luke's description of Israel's primacy identifies "the many" in this passage. As he explains of Jesus' purpose, "And He will turn *many* of the sons of Israel back to the Lord their God" (Luke 1:16) and "Behold, this Child is appointed for the fall and rise of *many* in Israel..." (Luke 2:34, emphasis added). Thus, Jesus' baptism initiated His introduction as Israel's Messiah who had brought the New Covenant which began the final seven-week period ("one week"). Within this time frame, the Jews had the opportunity to accept God's redemption as it had finally been revealed.

Halfway through this final time period, "he" would cause "sacrifice and offering" – the premise of the previous covenant – to cease and be replaced with one final atonement. The Messiah would endure a violent, sacrificial death to bring the purpose of this covenant to fulfillment. Because there is no textual evidence of a time gap between the sixty-ninth and seventieth "sevens" of Daniel's prophecy, there is no reason to assume the years are not consecutive. Futurism inserts this time gap into Gabriel's 490 years in order to justify their eschatological assumptions about "end-times" events. In doing so, futurism adds to scripture something that is not there.

Following the timeline, the final seven-year period would begin at the anointing of the leader (Jesus' baptism) establishing his identity as the Redeemer, triggering Israel's opportunity to restore their true relationship with God, a consummation made available by the Messiah's atonement. However, seven years later, they would demonstrate their total rejection of God's plan by spilling the blood of one of their own who had tried to convince them of its truth – Stephen (Acts 22:20). By this act of desecration, Jesus' commitment to the Jews as His priority was removed, and the gospel went to the Gentiles (Matt. 21:43, Acts 13:46, Romans 1:16).

Speaking of the "one," Gabriel is referring to the source of the "desolation" brought about by the "abominations." Historically, this must refer to Titus Vespanian, who led the physical destruction of the city, but did so on the "wing of abominations," which was the temple's desecration by the Jewish zealots in AD 66 with the murder of the Jewish priests. Many popular Bibles translate the final Hebrew word "shomem" as the "desolator" implying that the one committing the desolation will receive something to be "poured out," i.e., a punishment in some form for his desolations. However, the word is more appropriately translated as "desolate" or "desolated" referring to the entities suffering the sanctioned destruction. In context, this would be the Jewish people. As they had provoked God's judgment, they would suffer these consequences at the hands of another foreign nation (Rome) until the war's end.

Such an analysis leaves 3½ years for which to account after the Messiah's death. The expiration of the 490-year period would, most likely, be an event that would indicate Israel's final rejection of what the

Messiah had initiated in saving them, since Jesus' ministry and the initial gospel spread was to the Jewish people. Scholar J. Barton Payne believes that "the 490 years conclude with the 3½ years that remained, during which period the testament was to be confirmed to Israel (Acts 2:38). It terminated in AD 33 which is the probable date for the conversion of Paul. At this point, the Jews, by their stoning of Stephen, in effect cut themselves off...."[128] Likewise, says Pastor Stephen Bohr, with this act, "God would no longer communicate with Israel through prophets and visions. When they stoned Stephen, as he was having a vision of Christ and was fulfilling his role as a prophet, God's communications came to a final end."[129] At this point, the gospel would be taken to Gentiles (Matt. 21:43), ending the exclusive nature of the message.

---

[128] J. Barton Payne, *The Imminent Appearing of Christ* (Grand Rapids, MI: Eerdmans, 1962), pp. 148-149.

[129] Stephen Bohr, *Studies on Daniel*, "Notes on Daniel 9," p. 333. https://secretsunsealed.org.

DANIEL CHAPTER 10

Verse 1

"In the third year of Cyrus king of Persia a message was revealed to Daniel, who was named Belteshazzar, and the message was true and one of great conflict, but he understood the message and had an understanding of the vision."

If Cyrus began his reign after the first year of the Medes under Darius (538 BC), then the present time should be Spring 535 BC. Daniel's Babylonian name still served as his identification within the kingdom. Here, it seems, was the beginning of Daniel's final vision that proceeds through the end of his book and provides some of the most accurate predictions that cause most modern scholars to wonder if predictive prophecy is truly possible. Their only recourse is to try to prove that the book was written at the time the following events took place – in the mid-second century BC.

In 538 BC, Cyrus issued the first decree that permitted the Jewish return to Israel from Babylonian captivity with a commission to rebuild the temple that Nebuchadnezzar had destroyed in 586 BC (Ezra 1:1-3). Within two years, construction had begun (Ezra 3:8). It might be safe to say that Daniel's infirmed state coupled with his position of influence in pagan government kept him from returning with his people.

Verses 2-3

"In those days, I, Daniel, had been mourning for three entire weeks. I did not eat any tasty food, nor did meat or wine enter my mouth, nor did I use any ointment at all until the entire three weeks were completed."

Rashi interprets the time frame as twenty-one years. But most Christian commentators analyze the time given as three weeks of abstaining from these things. The Hebrew language suggests "clean" food (Gen. 27:15) while anointing oneself with oil in the ancient world was considered a pleasure. Daniel must have restrained from these likings to express humility in a sorrowful situation. Though Israel had returned to its lands, there were no doubt obstacles to their future endeavors for national rehabilitation. Rebuilding the temple would face special difficulties. Daniel most likely engaged in intensive contemplation on behalf of his people as fasting usually produced divine revelations.

Verses 4-5

"On the twenty-fourth day of the first month, while I was by the bank of the great river, that is, the Tigris, I lifted my eyes and looked, and behold, there was a certain man dressed in linen, whose waist was girded with a belt of pure gold of Uphaz."

The Hebrew language suggests a "cluster of pearls" in the belt (Rashi). The first month was *Nisan*, when Passover and the feast of unleavened bread take place. The Tigris ran alongside the Euphrates through ancient Mesopotamia, or Western Asia (Turkey, Syria, Iraq). This man from Daniel's vision is clothed in fine linen, the garb of royalty or a high priest.

Verse 6

"His body also was like beryl, his face had the appearance of lightning, his eyes were like flaming torches, his arms and feet like the gleam of polished bronze, and the sound of his words like the sound of a tumult."

Jewish commentators draw parallels with the Sea of Tarshish (Tractate Hulin), which would symbolize the man's size. Beryl (sea color) is a variety of topaz. His voice is heard from far off. Daniel's descriptions are remarkably similar to those in the book Revelation of the man relaying the vision to John – Jesus Christ: "One like a son of man, clothed in a robe reaching to the feet, and girded across his chest with a golden sash. His head and His hair were white like white wool, like snow; and His eyes were like a flame of fire. His feet were like burnished bronze, when it has been made to glow in a furnace, and His voice was the sound of many waters….His face was like the sun shining in its strength" (Rev. 1:13-16).

Verses 7-8

"Now I, Daniel, alone saw the vision, while the men who were with me did not see the vision; nevertheless a great dread fell on them, and they ran away to hide themselves. So I was left alone and saw this great vision; yet no strength was left in me, for my natural color turned to a deathly pallor, and I retained no strength."

An interesting note from Rabbinic tradition states that the men referred to might have been Haggai, Zechariah, and Malachi (Rashi). They were shaken by the presence of the vision while Daniel himself was greatly terrified, a consistent theme in his revelations throughout the book. Such is a testimony to God's power over even our senses, as Daniel was completely disarmed by the grandeur of this vision.

Verses 9-12

"But I heard the sound of his words; and as soon as I heard the sound of his words, I fell into a deep sleep on my face, with my face to the ground. Then behold, a hand touched me and set me trembling on my hands and knees. He said to me, 'O Daniel, man of high esteem, understand the words that I am about to tell you and stand upright, for I have now been sent to you.' And when he had spoken this word to me, I stood up trembling. Then he said to me, 'Do not be afraid, Daniel, for from the first day that you set your heart

on understanding this and on humbling yourself before your God, your words were heard, and I have come in response to your words.'"

Daniel passed out but was touched by this man as if to waken him. Because of Daniel's righteousness, he was given insight into future things (Dan. 9:23). The knowledge of Israel's destiny was being given to him. He had dedicated himself to reconciling his people and nation with their covenant God, the One whom they had betrayed but by whom they were yet promised an everlasting relationship. Daniel's abandoned and prostrated character were laid at the feet of a God who desires a contrite heart (Psalm 51:17). Thus, he received a response.

Verse 13

"But the prince of the kingdom of Persia was withstanding me for twenty-one days; then behold, Michael, one of the chief princes, came to help me, for I had been left there with the kings of Persia.'"

The angel informed Daniel that he was delayed in coming for the entirety of his fast. The most reasonable assumption with the angelic nature of the encounter is to assume that some supernatural battle was occurring, especially with Michael's (prince of the Jewish people) intervention. This might have been an angel that headed over the Persian nation in the spiritual realm. It is almost as if the angel would not have been able to notify Daniel had Michael not interceded. This confirms the authority given to lesser beings over the nations of the world during the Judaic age, an authority Jesus assumed in His ascension that heralded the beginning of a global transition between epochs (Matthew 28:18). It was Satan who offered Jesus the kingdoms of the world during His temptations in the beginning of the gospels; for how can one offer something that does not, in some capacity, belong to them?

Verse 14

"Now I have come to give you an understanding of what will happen to your people in the latter days, for the vision pertains to the days yet future.'"

Here returns the phrase that generates great distinctions within the Christian and Jewish communities regarding the end of all things. Reading the details of the prophecy is the key to its interpretation rather than predetermining the time and applying the details. The common translation that best describes the "end of days" is "latter days" which denotes the time at which Daniel's prophecy will be fulfilled. The context of Daniel, therefore, is not conducive to some distant, future event at the consummation of all things, but rather the circumstances surrounding the time of Israel's troubles as described throughout the book. Previous references to such language were in Daniel 2:28 and 8:17. The vision Daniel received would indeed commence over the next half millennium.

Verses 15-17

"When he had spoken to me according to these words, I turned my face toward the ground and became speechless. And behold, one who resembled a human being was touching my lips; then I opened my mouth and spoke and said to him who was standing before, 'O Lord, as a result of the vision anguish has come upon me, and I have retained no strength. For how can such a servant of my lord talk with such as my lord? As for me, there remains just now no strength in me, nor has any breath been left in me.'"

Daniel might be referring to the angel as "lord" in the reverential sense. Anyone from the divine counsel would have held an esteemed position over men. Daniel stands in a place of humility recognizing his lowly position compared to the messenger of God. The power of the circumstance overcame him so that he could not maintain himself.

Verses 18-21

"Then this one with human appearance touched me again and strengthened me. He said, 'O man of high esteem, do not be afraid. Peace be with you; take courage and be courageous!' Now as soon as he spoke to me, I received strength and said, 'May the lord speak, for you have strengthened me.' Then he said, 'Do you understand why I came to you? But I shall now return to fight against the prince of Persia; so I am going forth, and behold, the prince of Greece is

about to come. However, I will tell you what is inscribed in the writing of truth. Yet there is no one who stands firmly with me against these forces except Michael your prince.'"

This angel comforts Daniel despite the prophet's weakness in the face of divine prophecy, and he is clearly in a state of obedience. The description provided in this verse call the reader's attention to the unseen happenings in the spiritual realm. There must be an angel or spirit ruling over Persia with whom this angel is wrestling, and he will continue to do so until the appearance of the Greeks. Beginning with Nebuchadnezzar, Daniel's narrative confirms the divine or angelic influence present in the executive leadership of earthly empires during the Judaic age.

According to Rashi's commentary, "Although Israel was subjugated by the kings of Persia in those days, they exacted a light tribute from them, and they did not burden them heavily because the Holy One, blessed be He, caused them to have mercy on them." However, the Greeks would not be so kind. Daniel would now be shown the future which had been decreed by God. The angel stipulated that in his struggles with Persia, he was on his own, with the exception of Michael, Israel's protector.

DANIEL CHAPTER 11

Verse 1

"In the first year of Darius the Mede, I arose to be an encouragement and protection for him."

If one considers these two chapters to be placed chronologically in the book, it is important to recognize what might appear to be a discrepancy in dating between Chapters 10 and 11. The former is recorded to have occurred in the third year of Cyrus (Persia), while the present chapter begins with "in the first year of Darius [Media]." At first glance, it would appear that these must indicate separate visions given three-four years apart and, therefore, are not chronological. However, beginning with the last verse of the previous chapter, the angel proceeds to relay the vision in which he describes that when the Medes took over Babylon ("in the first year of Darius"), the angel stepped up to help Michael ("him"), Israel's protector. With Israel's captor, Babylon, now removed, the Jews required support as they neared the end of their exile and prepared to return to Israel. This introductory verse, therefore, is not saying that what follows occurred during the Darius the Medes first year but that the angel went to aid Darius at that time.

He described his favorable conduct toward Darius which extended to the Medes treatment of the Jewish exiles. Darius was a great admirer of Daniel, as seen in Chapter 6, meaning that the angel was providing support to Daniel and the Jewish people by leading Darius to see him as a mighty contributor and great asset to his reign. Likewise, history demonstrates that the Persians who followed were, indeed, sympathetic to the Jewish institution over the course of their dominion as Cyrus permitted Israel to return to their homeland and rebuild their city and sanctuary, a result that was probably influenced by this angelic character.

Verse 2

"And now I will tell you the truth. Behold three more kings are going to arise in Persia. Then a fourth will gain far more riches than all of them; as soon as he becomes strong through his riches, he will arouse the whole empire against the realm of Greece."

If this vision was originally given during the third year of Cyrus (Chapter 10) then counting three "more" kings would begin with his first son, Cambyses II (529 – 522 BC), followed by Bardiya, otherwise known as Smerdis (522 BC) and Darius I (522 – 486 BC). This would make the "fourth" who would arouse "all against the kingdom of Greece," Xerxes I (485-465 BC). History demonstrates that Darius the Great (I) was the first Persian king who implemented the conquest of Grecian lands, commencing the Greco-Persian wars in 499 BC (449 BC).

However, Xerxes is renowned for his invasion in 480 BC with which he amassed an army of soldiers from countless nations. Xerxes was the "fourth" king. After 449 BC, Persia realized their inability to conquer the whole of Greece, though the latter was not yet a global dominion of power, such as it became under the leadership of Alexander the Great. It was also under the royal name of Darius (III) that the Persian Empire fell to Alexander's Greece (330 BC).

Verses 3-4

"And a mighty king will arise, and he will rule with great authority and do as he pleases. But as soon as he has arisen, his kingdom will be broken up and parceled out toward the four points of the compass, though not to his own descendants, nor according to his authority which he wielded, for his sovereignty will be uprooted and given to others besides them."

This is a model description of the historic Greek Empire. The "mighty king" was Alexander the Great (356 – 323 BC), who at the peak of his authority and greatness was killed. The phrase "not to his posterity" is yet another confirmation of history as the kingdom was given not to Alexander's sons but was divided into four parts to be ruled by his four generals (see commentary from Dan. 7:6). In Daniel's Hebrew language, the term for "posterity" was interpreted as "sons and daughters" meaning that one's lineage, pedigree, or direct descendants (Amos 4:2) determined how power and authority was passed on. Conversely, in pagan cultures, the most influential person was generally given the kingship.

These four kingdoms would comprise a Greek authority that would not match that of Alexander's. As there is little debate among biblical scholars from every corner regarding the Grecian references, the historicism that so accurately describes the rise and fall of the Greek Empire throughout the prophetic narrative in Daniel is astounding. If one considers the compositional dating of Daniel to be sixth century, this account might be sufficient to convince even the most ardent biblical skeptic of the entire book's authenticity and historical authority.

Verse 5

"Then the king of the South will grow strong, along with one of his princes who will gain ascendancy over him and obtain dominion; his domain will be a great dominion indeed."

The geographic locations are important to understand relative to Israel. Egypt is to the South (Ptolemaic kingdom). The King of the South "will grow strong" and asserts his dominance against the kingdom of the North, an insinuation from the following verse. Two of Alexander's generals are identified: Ptolemy Soter was the king of the south in Egypt, while Seleucus Nicolator was the king over the "North" which included Babylon, Asia Minor, and Syria. The geographical significance of these two kingdoms is what lies between them – Israel. As these two fought each other, Israel suffered.

Many commentaries suggest that "one of his princes" is a reference to another of the four generals that took over besides Ptolemy ("king of the south"). This would mean that though Ptolemy would grow strong, one of the others would indeed grow stronger. The consensus dictates that this was Seleucus, the northern king. Though he served under Ptolemy, his empire would grow to reach as far as India, a dominion that would exceed that of Egypt.

Regarding the progressive interpretation of this chapter, the "king of the north" will be the successive line of Seleucid kings, and "the king of the south" will be the successive live for the Ptolemaic kings.

Verse 6

"After some years they will form an alliance, and the daughter of the king of the South will come to the king of the North to carry out a peaceful arrangement. But she will not retain her position of power, nor will he remain with his power, but she will be given up, along with those who brought her in and the one who sired her as well as he who supported her in those times."

The north and south kingdoms of Seleucus and Ptolemy would war over total authority in the kingdom, struggles that proved costly. The verse suggests that time will pass between the events of the previous verse and the marriage described in the present verse that would secure an alliance to bring reprieve to both sides. This would come after the first two kings of the previous verse.

By the time of Antiochus II, the third king, the Seleucids had faced intense pressure with the Syrian Wars. This extended to their efforts to push Ptolemaic influence from the nearby territories. Antiochus had gained ground, but it had come at a price. Ptolemy II had been pushed back. As the war concluded, the two sides desired peace. So, when Ptolemy II (Philadelphus), king of Egypt ("south"), sent his daughter to the north to broker a peace agreement by striking a dynastic marriage, Antiochus II (Theos), king of the north, was open to cooperation. Ptolemy would give his daughter, Berenice Phernophorus, in marriage if King Antiochus II would divorce his first wife, Laodice, and the child to be produced would reign over both kingdoms.[130]

When Ptolemy died, however, Antiochus, who was not particularly fond of Berenice, brought back his first wife, meaning that Berenice would lose her "position" of power. Laodice understandably trusted no one and realized that her position in the lineage was compromised. She returned and had her son murder all players through poisoning; Berenice ("she"), and her attendants from Egypt ("those who brought her"), and her son ("whom she brought forth" transliterated from "he who begot her").[131] Before Berenice was killed, she had realized the threat and attempted to start a rebellion that was squashed by Laodice's son, who then assumed the throne.

Verses 7-10

"But one of the descendants of her line will arise in his place, and he will come against their army and enter the fortress of the king of the North, and he will deal with them and display great strength. Also their gods with their metal images and their precious vessels of silver and gold he will take into captivity to Egypt, and he on his part will refrain from attacking the king of the North for some years. Then the latter will enter the realm of the king of the South, but will return to his own land. His sons will mobilize and assemble a multitude of great forces; and one of them will keep on coming and overflow and pass through that he may again wage war up to his very fortress."

The angel said that someone from Berenice's family ("one of the descendants of her line") would rise to power and come against the north to avenge her death. Ptolemy III Euergetes, her brother, had succeeded his father and proceeded to invade the territory of Seleucus II Callinicus, Laodice's son. This initiated the Third Syrian War.

---

[130] Branko van Oppen. *Chronique d'Egypte*. "Notes on Arsinoe I: A Study of a Shadowy Queen." January, 1 2014. Vol. 89, p. 177. Nearly all Christian commentators are in agreement of the characters of the prophecy in light of events following the division of the Greek Empire.

[131] Marcus Junianus Justinus, translated by Rev. John Selby Watson. Epitome of the *Philippic History of Pomopeius Trogus*. Book XXVII, Sec. 1, (London, York Street, Convent Garden, 1853). www.forumromanum.org

Indeed, it seemed Ptolemy's ultimate purpose was to support his sister, Berenice, who had fallen out of favor. Euergetes did experience success, capturing some of the region, enriching Egypt with the spoils of war, and returning numerous relics that had belonged to Egypt when they had been conquered by Persia in the previous centuries.

Seleucus, it appears, would eventually respond by reclaiming territory, but would not achieve enough success to march against Egypt. Since the subject of the ninth verse appears to be the king of the north, his "sons" must be a reference to his immediate successor, Seleucus III Ceraunus and Antiochus III (the Great). However, the latter would find true military success as the former garnered little achievement and was removed after just two or three years. This also confirms the grammatical change to the singular reference in the verse ("he will enter the realm" rather than "they"). As Ptolemy had taken Syria in his revenge mission for Berenice, Antiochus III returned, and a history of wars between Antiochus III and Ptolemy IV Philopator commenced. The former was able to recapture Seleucia, take Ptolemais, Tyre, and even Gaza. Antiochus would also show fearlessness in going after the fortified areas of Egypt, notably besieging Raphia, which is widely held as one of the largest battles of the Hellenistic (Greek) world. He would, however, lose this skirmish.

Verses 11-13

"The king of the South will be enraged and go forth and fight with the king of the North. Then the latter will raise a great multitude, but that multitude will be given into the hand of the former. When the multitude is carried away, his heart will be lifted up, and he will cause tens of thousands to fall; yet he will not prevail. For the king of the North will again raise a greater multitude than the former, and after an interval of some years he will press on with a great army and much equipment."

The narrative of war between these two kingdoms continues as Ptolemy IV Philopater fought back. There is noticeable ambiguity with the continuous Hebrew references to "he" and "his," admittedly making the passages somewhat difficult to follow. However, history demonstrates that Ptolemy gathered a massive army of close to 75,000 units and marched from Egypt to engage, gaining a victory against Antiochus' army of around 65,000 units, not far from Raphia.[132] Antiochus reportedly suffered extensive casualties, and Ptolemy won the struggle.

Though the victory reinforced his confidence, Ptolemy had not won so decisively that he regained the total control that he hoped for ("he will not prevail"). Though a truce would be reached for a time, Antiochus III would see an opportunity after the death of his rival Ptolemy IV Philopater to reclaim some of his lost territory. Antiochus had conducted other successful military campaigns to the east (Persia and India), acquiring control over greater forces and wealth than he had previously, which he would muster and take with him in his conquest to exact vengeance upon Egypt for the previous losses.

Verse 14

"Now in those times many will rise up against the king of the South; the violent ones among your people will also lift themselves up in order to fulfill the vision, but they will fall down."

It is recorded that "before the end of the third century native unrest was a serious matter in Egypt" ("south") and these "revolts had plagued Egypt even…beginning with Ptolemy IV (221-203 BC)."[133] These uprisings lasted through the next two decades under Ptolemy's son, Ptolemy V Epiphanes, who assumed the throne at age five. Additionally, Philip of Macedon came into alliance with Antiochus after Ptolemy IV's death, and factions in Alexandria were also rising up. Even Israel got into the action as the Jewish factions loyal to Ptolemy were seceding and turning to Hellenistic paganism, thereby, coming under the good graces of the ruling kingdom to the north.

Up to this point, the nation had been divided into sections under

---

[132] Paul Johnstono. *The Army of Ptolemaic Egypt 323-204 BC: An Institutional and Operational History.* (Yorkshire: Pen & Sword Books Limited, 2020) xxiii.

[133] Joseph Ward Swain, "Antiochus Epiphanes and Egypt." *Classical Philology*, Vol. 38, No. 2 Apr., 1944. pp. 73-94. p. 74.

the rule of both the north and south kingdoms. However, sensing the growing softness of Egypt, the lawless ones were the Jews who had broken out of the true Torah position, away from the true Israel and the worship of God, turning to the north and the Antiochus line. However, such a turn would not see victory.

Verses 15-16

"Then the king of the North will come, cast up a siege ramp and capture a well-fortified city; and the forces of the South will not stand their ground, not even their choicest troops, for there will be no strength to make a stand. But he who comes against him will do as he pleases, and no one will be able to withstand him; he will also stay for a time in the Beautiful Land, with the destruction in his hand."

As stated, Ptolemy V Epiphanes would assume rulership at a very young age. Egypt's weakness under its immature leader would not withstand the barrage from the north kingdom, and Antiochus and Philip believed "they were bound by the ties of nature to have defended, they then egged each other on to adopt the policy of partitioning the boy's kingdom between themselves."[134] The specific historical references could, most likely, be at Paneas, followed by Sidon and Patara (198 BC). The "Beautiful Land" is Israel, alluding to the king from the north gaining complete control over Judea. Such was the circumstance for Israel as they endured the constant stream of armies passing through their nation as the north and south warred.

Though Antiochus III was not reported to have been responsible for destruction or sacrilege in the nation, Israel would now come under the power of Greece.

---

[134] Polybius, *The Histories*, Book XV, sec. 20. Evelyn S. Shuckburgh. translator. (London, New York. Macmillan. 1889. Reprint Bloomington 1962.) Book XV, Sec. 20. https://www.perseus.tufts.edu.

Verse 17

"He will set his face to come with the power of his whole kingdom, bringing with him a proposal of peace which he will put into effect; he will also give him the daughter of women to ruin it, But she will not take a stand for him or be on his side."

Jewish commentators understand this to be describing the period of oppression for the Jewish people during the time of the Antiochus line. The Greek king knew he must bear down all his military strength upon the Egyptian kingdom to subdue it, while expecting the support of the Jews. Israel, too, hoped for peace through the surrender of the Egyptian kingdom to the north. But Antiochus was experiencing military uprisings in other parts of the kingdom, most notably with the Romans. He, thus, attempted to acquire the Egyptian kingdom's capitulation or friendship through a marriage alliance. Antiochus offered his daughter Cleopatra to Ptolemy V to secure Egypt's loyalty as the Roman forces from the west posed an increasing threat. Egypt would have undoubtedly aligned with Rome should they be presented with the opportunity. The marriage took place in 193 BC. Antiochus probably hoped that his daughter would ultimately help bring the entire kingdom under his authority, however, Cleopatra exhibited greater fidelity to her Egyptian husband than her father ("not take a stand for him").

Verses 18-19

"Then he will turn his face to the coastlands and capture many. But a commander will put a stop to his scorn against him; moreover, he will repay him for his scorn. So he will turn his face toward the fortresses of his own land, but he will stumble and fall and be found no more."

Upon securing Egypt in his favor, Antiochus turned in preparation for combat with the approaching Roman military power. In doing so, he turned toward the islands of the Mediterranean, capturing numerous locales. However, one Roman consul, Lucius Cornelius Scipio, stopped his advances and turned the tables on Antiochus. This Roman commander had achieved a victory over Hannibal and the Carthaginians in Africa and had, thus, gained great notoriety in military circles. After taking some lands, thereby reproaching the Romans, Antiochus was initially pushed back by their forces after being defeated at Thermopylae in 191 BC. However, a decisive loss was sustained at Magnesia in the following year. Antiochus' army numbered around 60,000 infantries with more than 12,000 cavalries against a Roman army fielding less than half that total. [135]

The will, training, and composure of the Roman army combined with superior military tactics decimated Antiochus' army such that his entire kingdom was jeopardized. Such a loss to his military force can likely be seen as nothing less than divine providence in the course of human affairs. It is important to note that this was a turning point in world events between the transition of two world empires that Daniel had foreseen. Antiochus was forced into a peace agreement through which the burgeoning Romans forced him to abandon all of his lands to the west and pay such recompense that he did not have. As one scholar notes, "The victory established the Romans as the new, undisputed hegemon of the Mediterranean world." [136]

Often, history hopes to demonstrate the magnanimity of the human will in a "David vs. Goliath" military conquest, and any victory of such renown surely initiates a transition of leadership. Antiochus fled the land, returning to his own strongholds, to seek ways of acquiring the materials to make good on promises to the Roman consul in exchange for grace and was summarily killed by the inhabitants of his own kingdom as he attempted to loot the local temples. [137] Without question, he "stumble[d] and f[e]ll and [was] found no more" (187 BC).

---

[135] Livius (Livy), *The History of Rome*, books thirty-seven to the end, with the epitomes and fragments of the lost books. literally translated, with notes and illustrations, by. William A. McDevitte. (York Street, Covent Garden, London. Henry G. Bohn. John Child and son, printers, Bungay. 1850.) Book 37, Chapter 37. https:/www.perseus.tufts.edu.

[136] Nikolaus L. Overtoom, "Battle of Magnesia (Romans vs Seleucids)." *Conflict in Ancient Rome: The Definitive Political, Social, and Military Encyclopedia,* 2016, p. 1026.

[137] Justinus, *Philippic History,* 32.2.

Verse 20

"Then in his place one will arise who will send an oppressor through the Jewel of his kingdom; yet within a few days he will be shattered, though not in anger nor in battle."

This "one" who takes his place refers to Antiochus' successor, his second son Seleucus IV Philopator, described by some Christian commentators as a "covetous" man who loved only wealth, taxing his subjects beyond acceptability. According to 2 Maccabees 3:7, Philopator may have even sent his treasurer to Jerusalem to plunder the temple. The meaning of "a few days" could figuratively describe a comparatively short and uneventful reign. Often, a given number of units in scripture is rendered in proportional parts, especially when identifying a specific timeframe. This could be rendered as years, which was but twelve years, a far cry from the thirty-seven experienced by his father.

Philopater's death was not in a military conquest at the hands of a foreign enemy; rather he was poisoned by his own treasurer, Heliodorus.[138] This paved the way for Antiochus IV Epiphanes, whose legacy would leave a lasting offense to the Jewish people, to assume power. Though Philopater had a son, who would have been the rightful heir to power, he was being held captive in Rome as part of the peace agreement brokered by Antiochus III. And Antiochus IV took advantage.

Verse 21

"In his place a despicable person will arise, on whom the honor of kingship has not been conferred, but he will come in a time of tranquility and seize the kingdom by intrigue."

Enter the great villain of Jewish history – Antiochus IV Epiphanes, the "little horn" of Daniel 8. The Hebrew word for "despicable" most closely resembles "vile" and expresses extreme scorn (Is. 49:7, Psalm 22:6), one of exceptionally egregious character, or none at all. The

---

[138] Appian, *Syrian Wars*, Horace White, ed. (New York. THE MACMILLAN COMPANY. 1899.) Chapter 8, sec. 45.

phrase "seize the kingdom by intrigue" could be a reference to his acquisition of power by illegitimate means, which he did not through his lineage, because Seleucus Philopater's son would have been next in line for succession.

Therefore, the nation did not confer this position upon him through ceremony, but he obtained it through the chaos of his brother's murder. In doing so, he did not conduct a military campaign to usurp power ("time of tranquility") but quietly and underhandedly. The description for "intrigue" is flattery. It is reported that Antiochus IV gained the assistance of Eumenes, king of Pergamus, and his brother Attalus in exchange for his aid in their resistance against Romans, therefore making promises to people for their support in his acquisition of the throne.[139] Likewise, "he sedulously cultivated the friendship of the Greeks and devoted great care to convincing the Romans of his loyalty.[140]

Verses 22-23

"The overflowing forces will be flooded away before him and shattered, and also the prince of the covenant. After an alliance is made with him he will practice deception, and he will go up and gain power with a small force of people."

The "overflowing forces" is a reference to a force that would be overwhelmed by this king as Antiochus had developed a very strong army. For the sake of history, Antiochus IV is dealing with Ptolemy VI by this time. There is great diversity on the identity of the "king of the covenant." In 172 BC, conflict broke out with Egypt during which Epiphanes was the victor, and in 169 BC the latter invaded Egypt directly. Polybius, possibly Antiochus Epiphanes's' most prolific historian, described this time: "Antiochus went to war because the regents attacked him; he defeated them, got rid of them, and made peace with the lawful king...."[141] Peace was, thus, brokered between the two. However, the "prince" was not the one who made it, but rather the beneficiary, the king of Egypt – Ptolemy VI Philmetor.

---

[139] Ibid.
[140] Swain, p. 79.
[141] Ibid., p. 85.

Though Antiochus would call Philometer a "friend," he would invade Egypt a second time, presumably to retain political control.[142] Internal strife among political opponents in Egypt had become rebellious and unpredictable. And as Antiochus' appetite for growth increased, he realized that he could not advance with an erratic Egyptian leadership behind him. Thus, he invaded Egypt in 168 BC. It would seem by the language that Antiochus would work deceitfully to achieve his aims, despite the covenant, almost as if there were no covenant.

As a matter of interpretation, many Christian commentators have postulated that the "prince of the covenant" is the high priest of Israel, who at that time would have been Onias III. However, nowhere in scripture is Israel's high priest ever referred to with this Hebrew designation, leaving us to conclude that the verse continues its description of Greek history during the growth of Roman power.

Verses 24-25

"In a time of tranquility he will enter the richest parts of the realm, and he will accomplish what his fathers never did, nor his ancestors; he will distribute plunder, booty and possessions among them, and he will devise his schemes against strongholds, but only for a time. He will stir up his strength and courage against the king of the South with a large army; so the king of the South will mobilize an extremely large and mighty army for war; but he will not stand, for schemes will be devised against him. Those who eat his choice food will destroy him, and his army will overflow, but many will fall down slain."

In describing the conduct of Antiochus IV Epiphanes, he would distribute wealth and bribes to disguise friendship, while plotting their ultimate conquering ("peaceably"). Neither of his predecessors took Egypt for their own; Antiochus Epiphanes did. He attacked Egypt (169/168 BC), taking Pelusium and Memphis, laid siege to Alexandria, and attempted to take the kingdom for himself. Though Egyptian forces would muster resistance, they could not stand against this affront. The easy assumption is that those who call the king of the south (Ptolemy)

---

[142] Ibid., p. 81. From Polybius' *Histories* 28.23.

friend would betray him. The army will not be properly overseen and will be dispersed, falling quite easily.

Verses 27-29

"As for both kings, their hearts will be intent on evil, and they will speak lies to each other at the same table, but it will not succeed, for the end is still to come at the appointed time. Then he will return to his land with much plunder; but his heart will be set against the holy covenant, and he will take action and then return to his own land. At the appointed time he will return and come into the South, but this last time it will not turn out the way it did before."

The two kings, within this context, must be Antiochus and Ptolemy. No matter their plans for power over the great land that rested been them in Israel, despite their contrivances, God remained in control having appointed the right conclusion of all affairs. The "appointed time" is Jerusalem's eventual capitulation meaning that, regardless of the planning by these two kings, their actions would be limited since God had already decreed Israel's punishment at the hands of Antiochus.

Upon his return to the north kingdom from the Egyptian campaign, Antiochus' heart would turn against Israel, and he began contemplating the rumors he was hearing about their restlessness under his rule. Decrees were passed to suppress the local religious customs which had never been practiced by the previous kings of the Seleucid kingdom. However, Antiochus led a second attack on Egypt two years later in 168 BC ("he will return and come into the south"). This time, he was met by a Roman ambassador (Popilius Laenas) who threatened him with war should he proceed. He, thus, did not experience the same success as his previous campaign ("the way it did before").

Verses 30-32

"For ships of Kittim will come against him; therefore he will be disheartened and will return and become enraged at the holy covenant and take action; so he will come back and show regard for those who forsake the holy covenant.

Forces from him will arise, desecrate the sanctuary fortress, and do away with the regular sacrifice. And they will set up the abomination of desolation. By smooth words he will turn to godlessness those who act wickedly toward the covenant, but the people who know their God will display strength and take action."

The Kittites were from a town called Kittim in Cyprus, which by that time were Roman. The confrontation Antiochus experienced was a great blow to his ego. In addition, according to the Maccabees, while Antiochus IV was in Egypt, a rumor had started that he had been killed. He had received word that Israel had rejoiced upon hearing this news and had formulated plans to revolt from under the Greek thumb. Polybius stated that Antiochus left Egypt with his anger greatly aroused. Already spiteful from having been confronted by the Romans and humiliated in his concession to leave Egypt, his ire turned toward Israel and "the holy covenant." He mercilessly slaughtered many Jews ("he will succeed"), but retained some relationship with those willing to forsake the religion of their fathers and turn toward the Hellenization of the land.

The thirty-first verse begins the description of the true desecration of Israel. Among the great insults of Antiochus were the desecration of the temple by plundering its resources, installing idol worship ("silent abomination"), slaughtering unclean animals, and lawfully ending the daily sacrifice, possibly the greatest outrage to the Jewish religious customs. He ordered a statue of Jupiter Olympus erected on the temple grounds. Antiochus had convinced apostate Israel to fall under his authority, but those who remained true to the God of Israel would constitute His remnant.

The description of "the people who know their God" is, most likely, the Maccabean brethren who rose to defend Israel in the midst of this persecution.

Verses 33-34

"Those who have insight among the people will give understanding to the many; yet they will fall by the sword and by flame, by captivity and by

plunder for many days. Now when they fall they will be granted a little help, and many will join with them in hypocrisy."

This would seem to describe a martyrdom that occurred as the true remnant tried to convince the apostates of their error in following Antiochus Epiphanes. Josephus relates that true followers were persecuted in numerous ways and without pity. Despite the oppression of this time, those persecuted would receive small assistance from other Jews planning resistance; i.e., the Maccabeans.

Verse 35

"Some of those who have insight will fall, in order to refine, purge and make them pure until the end time; because it is still to come at the appointed time."

During this time, many of the devout would fall, and a spiritual purging of the people would commence; who would be truly faithful? This author is convinced that the majority of "end time" references, in the Bible, are speaking of the end of the Judaic age, which occurred at the destruction of Jerusalem in AD 70. This verse, thus, gives an overarching reminder that persecution will continue until the "time of the end, for there is yet until the appointed time" – which would be that event. Christian interpretation of the Old Testament must remember God's promises to curse Israel if they broke the covenant.

These curses are vividly described and exactly prophesied, which came to pass in AD 70, a defining moment in world history when the Old Covenant Judaic age closed and the kingdom of God, ushered in by the Messiah, Jesus of Nazareth, would begin its dominion throughout the earth (Dan. 2). The everlasting nature of the covenant, however, has been honored by God in that the Jewish people have not only been preserved to this day, but salvation has been brought to the rest of the world through them. And yet, he promised a new covenant would take its place (Jer. 31:31-34).

This verse's identification of the "end" fits neatly within the predominant context of the aforementioned destruction of Jerusalem as alluded to in 10:14 and concluded by 12:7. The events of Daniel have clearly been a narrative of first-century occurrences leading up this epoch changeover. Thus, the thirty-fifth verse produces anticipation of that event.

Verses 36-38

"Then the king will do as he pleases, and he will exalt and magnify himself above every god and will speak monstrous things against the God of gods; and he will prosper until the indignation is finished, for that which is decreed will be done. He will show no regard for the gods of his fathers or for the desire of women, nor will he show regard for any other god; for he will magnify himself above them all. But instead he will honor a god of fortresses, a god whom his fathers did not know; he will honor him with gold, silver, costly stones and treasures."

Antiochus was permitted to continue his brutality until his appointed time. He desired to compel the Greek gods upon the Jews, pressing their worship of these idols, and imposing his rage on enforcing such policies. He, no doubt, saw some level of spiritual elevation in his being as every temple he came across he plundered without clemency, asserting some psychological elements of being god-like. Antiochus would not be bound by the religion of his own land in his execution of conquest ("no regard for the gods of his fathers").

Some commentators infer a sexual orientation with this ambiguous reference; rather it should most likely be interpreted as supporting the notion that even the lust of women would not deter him from his objectives. He truly sought his own glorification, something that would not allow his rest until fully achieved. The "god of fortresses" would be a reference to the statue he erected in the temple of Jupiter Olympus as the Greeks did not previously worship him; Antiochus brought Jupiter back from Rome. It could also be Mars, the god of war, whom Antiochus favored for idol worship in the empire. According to Livy, Antiochus tried to build a temple to honor Jupiter in Antioch but died before witnessing its completion ("the god that his ancestors did not know he will honor").

The important element to consider is that while Antiochus is looked upon as the great villain of Jewish history (and rightfully so), he was God's instrument of punishment against the sin of His chosen people. They had not repented after their many chances.

Verse 39

"He will take action against the strongest of fortresses with the help of a foreign god; he will give great honor to those who acknowledge him and will cause them to rule over the many, and will parcel out land for a price."

Antiochus would use riches and art to promote his idol worship, giving out dominion over lands under his authority. According to the Maccabees, Antiochus did devise a plot to divide the land of Israel, giving the land to pagan or Jews who professed their allegiance. Historically, this practice is a grave error that results in calamity for the offending ruler and nation and spells out imminent doom for the offender.

Verse 40

"At the end time the king of the South will collide with him, and the king of the North will storm against him with chariots, with horsemen and with many ships; and he will enter countries, overflow them and pass through."

Thus comes a crucial point in the interpretation of this prophecy. The vast majority of Christian commentators understand this portion of verses to be a prediction of the close of Antiochus' reign up to his demise. This, they believe, most efficiently continues the progressive narrative of successive kings in the Seleucid and Ptolemaic Empires. Indeed, riding that wave would seem highly reasonable, and frankly, simpler.

This angel's extensive prophecy, which began in Daniel 10:20, finishes at Daniel 12:4 when he ordered the entire vision sealed. Let us assume that these commentators are correct and Chapter 11, indeed, culminates in Antiochus' death and proceeds directly into Chapter 12. The first verse of Chapter 12 opens with "Now at that time," a clear indication that what follows in the next three verses must describe events immediately following those listed in the previous verse (v. 45); in this case, what these commentators believe to be Antiochus' death. This poses a seemingly insurmountable interpretive problem because the next three verses that lead up to the prophecy's close illuminate events that did not occur at all under his rule, the Greek Empire's dominion, or even in the BC era.

Therefore, a transition from Israel's time under the authority of the Greek Empire to that of a different time must be present in this portion of the prophecy. Could "at the end time" of the present verse be that point? Consider the following:

The first two verses of Chapter 12, which are described just before its sealing and, therefore, plainly fall within the prophecy's framework, proceed to describe one of the cornerstones of modern church theology. The first pronounces an unparalleled tribulation that would occur against Israel which required Michael's assistance in mediating on behalf of God's faithful, while the second states that a resurrection and harvest would simultaneously transpire at which many would receive eternal life, the rest eternal contempt. These concepts define the modern church view of a future resurrection and judgment meaning that their doctrinal weight has been paramount for NT thought.

If the commentators are correct that the present chapter closes still describing affairs during the Greek Empire, this means that a concurrent tribulation, resurrection, and harvest of the Jewish people must have occurred at the time immediately following Antiochus' death (164 BC). This really cannot be. These pivotal events were scheduled to occur for Israel at a moment of synchronized judgment and salvation when even the Israelite dead would be resurrected to receive it. Such would be a consummating occasion for which Israel had longed when her truly righteous would finally be redeemed and would shine "like the brightness of the expanse of heaven" (Dan. 12:3). This would be at the arrival of God's messianic kingdom as heralded by – the Messiah. Daniel has already informed us that this kingdom would be established during the fourth kingdom of Daniel's visions – the Roman Empire. [143]

Thus, prior to Chapter 12, a transition must have occurred to mark

---

[143] One elementary reason for this conclusion is the harvest in Daniel 12 is a consummating event in Israel's history administered one harvester. This man is identified as Jesus of Nazareth who did not arrive until 150 years later.

the changeover between the Greek and Roman Empires, for God had promised that it would be during the latter that Israel would see "the time of the end" and the close of their Judaic age (Dan. 2:44). Though such a literary shift admittedly lacks an outward flawlessness, the "time of the end" might be the most applicable scriptural connection to a required transition in timing. This change in the prophecy, then, requires a new identity of the "kings" of the north and south though the geographic locations remain the same. Indeed, Daniel mentioned no names or dates throughout the prophecy, though these "kings'" identities changed throughout as the narrative progressed. Thankfully, history enables us to follow.

There are other reasons why Antiochus cannot be the "king" in this portion of the prophecy. One is that Jesus directly identified the tribulation of Daniel 12:1 in his Olivet Discourse as that which would befall Jerusalem within His generation (AD 70). If one takes Jesus at His word, then the events of Chapter 12 must fall into the first-century Roman Empire. Another is that there is no credible historical record of another clash for Antiochus with the Egyptians prior to his death like the one stated in this verse. There is one mention of a final campaign in the eleventh year of Antiochus IV in the writings of Jerome (fourth century), by way of Porphry.

However, all other historical accounts (Polybius, Livy, Josephus, etc.) do not verify it. Additionally, during this time period, Egypt was under Roman protection, meaning that with a military engagement, Antiochus would have immediately sparked war with the Roman Republic, something he had already intentionally avoided. Many of the accounts have Antiochus in the east securing funding for the Temple of Artemis in Elymais at that time. He was driven out from the area and died shortly after.

This author does not claim infallible knowledge regarding biblical prophecy. But a transition between empires must have occurred between the present verse and the closing of the prophecy (Dan. 12:4).

The traditional dating of the Roman Empire is 27 BC – AD 476, though the official kingdom, and eventual Republic, had existed many centuries before. The description of the battle between the king of the south and the king of the north must be interpreted as a conflict between the, then, ruling power of the Egyptian territories, and the corresponding leader in the north during the "time of the end" (period of the Roman rule up to the destruction of Jerusalem). The "king of the north" is, thus, now identified as Rome since 120 years after the death of Antiochus IV, Rome had overtaken the territories of the former Seleucid Empire. The rise of the Caesars began to take center stage. Likewise, the Ptolemys of Egypt had dwindled away as the last legitimate king of influence had passed and the former lands under Egyptian rule had been conquered.

According to biblical commentator Kurt Simmons' notes on Daniel 11, the southern leader is most likely a reference to the king of Pontus, Mithridates, who, with a massive army, had resisted Roman occupation of the southern regions and wrestled for control in the east. However, as known of Roman power, they swept through landscapes, crushing all in their path, nation by nation. This army was led by Pompey, the Roman general who defeated Mithridates, the only remaining combatant to clear the path to Egypt in the Mithridatic wars of 73 – 63 BC.

Verses 41-43

"He will also enter the Beautiful Land, and many countries will fall; but these will be rescued out of his hand: Edom, Moab, and the foremost of the sons of Ammon. Then he will stretch out his hand against other countries, and the land of Egypt will not escape. But he will gain control over the hidden treasures of gold and silver and over all the precious things of Egypt; and Libyans and Ethiopians will follow at his heels."

Pompey captured Jerusalem in 63 BC after deposing the last Antiochus figure from the Seleucid kingdom. The three nations listed, Edom, Moab, and Ammon (to the south and east of Palestine), were among the areas that did not get placed under Roman authority. The budding Julius Caesar - who entered Judea ("the Beautiful Land") in 47 BC - had a long history with Rome, a civil war and holding multiple positions with the government. After a long internal battle for power within the empire, he arrived in Egypt (47 BC) and placed it under Roman rule. He had an affair with Cleopatra (daughter of Ptolemy

XI), having a child, and formed an alliance with a potent ally. Multiple military opportunities in the Egyptian territories opened a path to the lands of Kush, located in the southern portions of present-day Sudan and Egypt, while his war with Mauritania paved a way into Libya.

However, it was Caesar Augustus who annexed Egypt (30 BC). As Rome expanded, he brought unprecedented growth to Libya and developed eventual peace with the Kushites (Ethiopian) by 21 BC. Augustus may not have set foot in Judea.

Verses 44-45

"But rumors from the East and from the North will disturb him, and he will go forth with great wrath to destroy and annihilate many. He will pitch the tents of his royal pavilion between the seas and the beautiful Holy Mountain; yet he will come to his end and no one will help him."

The closing verses indicate regional disturbances that required the attention of Rome's military forces. Eventually, they would establish themselves outside Jerusalem, between the city and the sea. The ruler in power during this event would come to his end in a rather undignified manner.

DANIEL CHAPTER 12

"Now at that time Michael, the great prince who stands guard over the sons of your people, will arise. And there will be a time of distress such has never occurred since there was a nation until that time; and at that time your people, everyone who is found written in the book, will be rescued."

As mentioned, the first three verses of this chapter belong with the body of Chapter 11. It may have been more appropriate to begin the chapter at the fourth verse. "Now at that time" keeps us placed in the narrative's present setting of the Roman Empire.

The Hebrew translation reads that Michael "will be silent," while the Greek says that he will "stand up." Either version can be understood in the context of the verse. If he were removed, it would indicate that during this period Israel's great protector would step aside and permit the Jews to endure a great tribulation. If he were empowered to "stand," it would be to protect the remnant during the persecution. Regardless, this suffering is precisely what Jesus prophesied in the Olivet Discourse about the impending temple destruction: "For then there will be a great tribulation, such as has not occurred since the beginning of the world

248

until now, nor ever will" (Matt. 24:21).[144] "The book" mentioned was also described in Chapter 7 when the judgment thrones were setup and "the books were opened" aligning these two passages at a consummating event for Israel (Dan. 7:10).

This verse provides encouragement that though many would perish, the true remnant of God would escape because of His great mercy. When Jesus gave the details of the Olivet prophecy, He prepared those listening for such an evacuation with the warning, "When you see the abomination of desolation...then those who are in Judea must flee to the mountains" (Matt 24: 15-16), and thereby guaranteed that God would ensure their survival in that "unless those days had been cut short, no life would have been saved, but for the sake of the elect those days will be cut short" (Matt. 24:22). Jesus gave the disciples numerous signs and warnings to ensure their knowledge of when God's followers needed to escape Jerusalem pending its destruction, which they would first witness at the arrival of the Roman armies (Luke 21:20).

It must be clear that this first verse of Chapter 12 introduced the destruction of Jerusalem in AD 70, as confirmed by its description as an unparalleled disaster for the Jewish people. What occurred was the recapitulation of Ezekiel's narrative of the first temple destruction, with the departure of God's spirit from His temple, allowing for its desecration and destruction by Nebuchadnezzar in 586 BC. Likewise, the effects of this tribulation were promised as part of the curse placed upon the covenant breakers (Deuteronomy 28), down to the minute details as confirmed by Jewish historian Flavius Josephus. The temple demolitions are the only two events in scripture which are classified as supporting a tribulation against Israel with no compare. Since one had

---

[144] Daniel's tribulation has many interpretations in commentaries from church history. This author's proposed connection with the Olivet Discourse is supported by commentators such as Ellicott, Gaebelein, and Benson. Others, such as Barnes and Jamieson-Fausset-Brown (JFB), believe the time spoken of referred to is the Jewish persecution under Antiochus Epiphanes in the 2nd century BC. All these listed understand the subject of the verse to be the Jewish people. Commentators like Matthew Henry and John Calvin believe this denotes all God's people, including the future church.

already occurred when Daniel was penned, the other must be described in this verse.

Though most Christian examinations of Daniel focus on more renowned passages such as Nebuchadnezzar's statue (Dan. 2), Shadrach, Meshach, and Abed-nego and the fiery furnace (Dan. 3), or the messianic implications of chapter nine (Dan. 9:24-27), this chapter carries immense weight in confirming the timetable of all things that would be fulfilled. It, therefore, is just as significant, if not more so, for our understanding of eschatology.

Verses 2-3

"Many of those who sleep in the dust of the ground will awake, these to everlasting life, but the others to disgrace and everlasting contempt. Those who have insight will shine brightly like the brightness of the expanse of heaven, and those who lead the many to righteousness, like the stars forever and ever."

After the tribulation period from the previous verse, a resurrection occurred. "Sleep" is death; "dust" is the grave. This resurrection would result in eternal life for the righteous and everlasting disgrace for the wicked. The latter phrase is repeated by Jesus in His parable of the wheat and tares (Matt. 13), where He described the fate of the good and bad seed at the harvest at the end of "this age." At that time, Jesus would remove "all stumbling blocks, and those who commit lawlessness, and will throw them into the furnace of fire," while the "righteous will shine forth as the sun in the kingdom of their father" (Matt. 13:41-43). The connection seems unmistakable. As preterist Dr. Don K. Preston has said of this connection, "This is a direct echo – [to use Richard Hays' term] of *Echoes of Scripture* – a direct echo of Daniel Chapter 12."[145] Daniel's prophecy is the description of a final reckoning for Israel ("your people") at end of their age – the Old Covenant age.

So, what about this resurrection? Make no mistake; this resurrection

---

[145] Heart of the Matter, "Don. K Preston Debates Jason Wallace on the validity of Preterism." *YouTube*. Uploaded on September 12, 2015. https: /youtu.be/ PjOMCLbPhvc. The debate centered on the topic of whether Jesus' Return occurred in AD 70 at the destruction of Jerusalem or is, yet, in the future.

in Daniel 12 is the source of the futurist belief in a final judgment day. This is not disputed in Christian theological circles. Jesus referred to this in John's Gospel: "For an hour is coming in which all who are in the tombs will hear His voice, and will come forth; those who did the good deeds to a resurrection of life, those who committed the evil deeds to a resurrection of judgment" (John 5:28-29). Indeed, Paul must have used this verse from Daniel to form his resurrection doctrine such as in Acts 24:15, "Having a hope in God, which these men cherish themselves, that there shall certainly be a resurrection of the both the righteous and the wicked" and reiterated in I Corinthians 15:51-57 when the "dead will be raised imperishable, and we will be changed."

According to Jewish tradition, the dead went to Sheol, which was not the Christian heaven or hell, but a place of waiting where the dead congregated (ex. Gen 37:35). It was distant from heaven, below the earth, in a realm of spiritual separation from God until those present were resurrected (Psalm 16:10, 17:15). Jacob went there (Gen. 37:35). David confirmed it (I Kings 2:6). Job lamented it (Job 14:13). According to Luke 16:22-25, however, there were at least two compartments in Sheol, one of blessing ("paradise") and one of torment where those present could see each other over a large chasm that separated the two. The righteous who had died awaited their resurrection in the paradise of "Abraham's bosom" (Luke 16:22) while the wicked in agony.

Jesus predicted that he would descend into Sheol for three days after His death (Matt. 12:40). He also told the thief who died next to Him on the cross that he would join Him in "paradise" the same day. Jesus' victory was acquiring the power over death through His own, which thus must have included going down into the "paradise" in Sheol where He gained authority over it. After three days, Jesus' body was resurrected, along with "many bodies of the saints who had fallen asleep…and coming out of the tombs after His resurrection they entered the holy city and appeared to many" (Matt. 27:52-53).

According to Paul's second letter to the Corinthians written two decades later, however, he knew a man that had been "caught up to the third heaven…into Paradise" (II Cor. 12:2-4). Jesus must have also initiated some form of a transfer of the Hadean "paradise" into the realm of heaven at His ascension. This might also be reiterated through a similar understanding of Ephesians 4:8 which states that "when He ascended on high, He led captive a host of captives, and He gave gifts to men," suggesting that when Jesus ascended from the lower parts of the earth, He brought back with Him the captives of the lower parts of the earth to which He had gone – the "paradise" in Sheol.

Before Jesus' death, the Old Covenant saints had no perfect sacrifice to cleanse them. Therefore, they remained separated from God in Sheol, awaiting redemption. Though the Gospels indicate a specific resurrection shortly after Jesus' own, the resurrection of the present verse would be at the long-awaited moment in time at which Israel's harvest would take place; a general resurrection of the just and unjust. This was the accumulation of martyred saints and Jews of antiquity awaiting their eternal reward who would reign with Christ over the kingdom or receive their judgment in Hades.

The process for awaiting eternal reconciliation with God was the old order of things which He promised would pass away (Rev. 21:4-5). The new order would be that saints no longer must retreat to the nothingness and separation of Sheol after their physical death; they were (and are) immediately resurrected to life in heaven to be united with Him (II Cor. 5:8, Philippians 1:23). It was at the destruction of Jerusalem that this consummation of judgment and salvation for Israel occurred and God's faithful were raised to eternal life with Him.

These two verses of the present chapter lay out an extraordinary prophecy. The first predicted that during the Roman Empire, Israel would experience a matchless tribulation. The language connections to Ezekiel and Jesus' Olivet Discourse in Matthew connect this time of extreme suffering to a calamity involving the Jewish temple. The next two verses explicitly describe a resurrection and harvest that follow the tribulation described in the first verse, meaning that these three events transpired concurrently. The question is, when?

Verse 4

"But as for you, Daniel, conceal these words and seal up the book until the end of time; many will go back and forth, and knowledge will increase."

There must be nothing more added to the prophecy at this point. This does not mean that the scriptures would not be further read or examined, but that its greater use would come at the time of its fulfillment. Unlike the book of Revelation which insisted that its prophecy be immediately sent out (Rev. 22:10) because its fulfillment was so close at hand, this angel ensures that his words would remain obscure until the designated time, which would be centuries into the future. As that time approached, its words became clear when Jesus began quoting and illuminating Daniel's book during his public ministry. And by the "time of the end" – Jerusalem's destruction – people would begin to understand its significance ("knowledge will increase").

Verses 5-6

"Then I, Daniel, looked and behold, two others were standing, one on this bank of the river and the other on that bank of the river. And one said to the man dressed in linen, who was above the waters of the river, 'How long will it be until the end of these wonders?'"

Daniel saw two heavenly beings, who are unidentified. The man clothed in linen could be from Daniel 10:5-6, whom many Christian commentators believe to be Jesus the Messiah. One of the angels was asked how long before all of these things listed come to fulfillment.

Verse 7

"I heard the man dressed in linen, who was above the waters of the river, as he raised his right hand and his left toward heaven, and swore by Him who lives forever that it would be for a time, times, and half a time; and as soon as they finish shattering the power of the holy people, all these events will be accomplished."

This is the definitive verse to understand when the tribulation, resurrection, and harvest of the first two verses would occur. They will be simultaneous with the moment at which the power of the "holy people" would be broken. This author is particularly persuaded that the "holy people" must be Israel given not only that they are the indisputable subject of the passage (with Michael's calling), but because identifying them as the future "church" seems untenable based on the scriptural markers. According to Dr. Don Preston:

> In order for Daniel 12 to be predictive of the resurrection at the end of the Christian age, Daniel's 'holy people' must be the church. This will not work. The power of the 'holy people' if the resurrection of [this verse] occurs at the end of the Christian age, must be the destruction of the gospel because the gospel is the power of God unto salvation to all of those who believe [according to] Romans 1.16...the kingdom of Christ has no end [according to] Daniel 7. The gospel which is the power of the Body of Christ will never be destroyed; Jesus, himself, affirmed that. Daniel's holy people was none other than Old Testament Israel and her power – and Israel's only power, the only power she ever possessed – was her covenant relationship with the Lord. Now, what that means is that the resurrection would be when Israel, and when her covenant relationship with YHWH, was completely shattered.[146]

Dr. Preston's argument is quite persuasive. Israel's power was never derived from a military might that would conquer the world. She never exerted controlling influence through economics, science, or philosophy. She was chosen from among the nations to act as a lens through which all could see the nature of the Creator of the universe. Indeed, Israel's story portrays who God is and what He wants in those He calls His own. No tale of such deep involvement of the divine is better chronicled. Israel's power – their covenant relationship with God – was not shared by anyone else on earth. It was their bond with Him. When Israel would carry the Ark of the Covenant into battle, her enemies knew that their efforts would result in inevitable defeat because God had arrived to protect His people (I Sam. 4:4-8). Dr. Preston implies that the question is whether this power was ever shattered. Since His people

---

[146] Ibid.

presently find salvation under a New Covenant, the answer would seem self-explanatory. And who brought a new covenant? Jesus the Messiah. When? In the first century.

Shattering Israel's power was to bring her people to helplessness by ending the Mosaic Law of the Old Covenant. It would break them into pieces, which also provides an accommodating visual of the dispersion that occurred when she was defeated. Indeed, this was warned in Deuteronomy – "For the Lord will vindicate His people, and will have compassion on His servants, when He sees that their strength is gone, and there is none remaining, bond or free" (Deut. 32:36) – and fulfilled within Jesus' Olivet prophecy that "they will fall by the edge of the sword and will be led captive into all the nations" (Luke 21:24). Leviticus promised the curse for Israel's defection: "I will make the land desolate so that your enemies who settle in it will be appalled over it. You, however, I will scatter among the nations and will draw out a sword after you, as your land becomes desolate and your cities become waste" (Lev. 26:32-33). There is only one event in all history in which this could have been accomplished – when God forsook his temple and city, thereby permitting their destruction.

The entire Jewish system, heritage, and institution completely collapsed within days following Jerusalem's demolition. And Luke's remembrance of the Olivet Discourse gives reliable confirmation that "these are days of vengeance so that all things which are written will be fulfilled...for there will be great distress upon the land and wrath to this people" (Luke 21:22-23). Indeed, the covenant breakers (Israel) were punished so severely at the destruction of the holy city that the New Covenant prophesied in Jeremiah made the Judaic age obsolete (Heb. 8:13). This does not break God's everlasting promises to Abraham, but rather the Old Covenant foundation was no more.

The defining element is that the events described leading up to the present verse – the tribulation, resurrection, and the harvest – would happen at the same time when the power of the holy people was shattered. The Old Covenant was not shattered at the cross, because the Jews continued its practices and ceremonies for the next forty years until the temple was burned to the ground by the Roman armies. Thus, the inevitable conclusion is that their power was shattered at the destruction of Jerusalem and its temple – meaning that these events must have simultaneously occurred.

It was John the Baptist who identified the identity of the harvester just prior to the start of Jesus' public ministry: "He who is coming after me is mightier than I, and I am not fit to remove His sandals; He will baptize you with the Holy Spirit and fire. His winnowing fork is in His hand, and He will thoroughly clear His threshing floor, and He will gather His wheat into the barn, but He will burn up the chaff with unquenchable fire" (Matt. 3:11-12). If the harvest happened in the first century, so must the harvester have come to separate the wheat from the chaff as promised (Matt. 13:30, John 5:28-29).

If the angel asked about the length of time that Israel would experience this "distress" during which Michael would stand aside, then the 3½ time frame fits perfectly in two ways. The first is the period from February/March AD 67 when Vespasian's forces arrived at Jerusalem to quell the rebellion to early September AD 70 when the city was sacked. During this time, the Jews lost numerous battles to the Romans but also experienced massive turmoil within their own walls, generating an endless stream of internal chaos as the people wondered how much longer they could stand. The second is the 3½ months during which Titus had complete access to the city from the time he breached its final wall to the day he departed the campaign (see **Daniel Chapter** 7: v. 23-25 commentary).

Verses 8-9

"And for me, I heard but could not understand; so I said, 'My lord, what will be the outcome of these events?' He said, 'Go your way, Daniel, for these words are concealed and sealed up and sealed until the end time."

Remaining in a state of confusion, Daniel continued his plea for wisdom, which was denied for the sake of the prophecy.

Verse 10

"Many will be purged, purified, and refined, but the wicked will act wickedly, and none of the wicked will understand, but those who have insight will understand."

Rashi had an interesting interpretation of this verse. He believed that this was a warning to those who miscalculate the timing of the prophecy. These calculations would be made clear and vindicated to identify those who understand them as pure in belief. However, there would be the "wicked" who offer miscalculations and deceive people into misunderstanding the timing of the end. When the time arrived, it would become clear to those who exercised wisdom. This author finds this a compelling commentary; however, one may also understand this reference to the fulfillment of the words. When this end arrived, it would produce the promised purification of redemption as stated in the third verse.

Verses 11-12

"From the time that the regular sacrifice is abolished and the abomination of desolation is setup, there will be 1,290 days. How blessed is he who keeps waiting and attains to the 1,335 days!"

Two final calculations are given: 1,290 days, followed by 1,335 days (an extra forty-five days).

This author understands the fallibility of human commentary. Thus, an important question when interpretating biblical calculations for establishing timelines: is the supposition reasonable? Our knowledge is finite, but as readers, we simply attempt to understand what the text is saying. If we can draw judicious conclusions about the two periods stated in the present verse, then the timing is interpreted to the best of our ability. If the reader disagrees with the calculations, then it should drive them further into the Word to find an answer themselves.

The first timeframe is a little more than 3½ years. The time of the daily sacrifice, however, must correspond with our current context – "the time of the end." Thus, the narrative refers to the "distress" of the Jewish people at the destruction of Jerusalem. As a matter of interpretation, the two events listed might provide the parameters within which to assess the calculation of 1,290 days. In other words, the countdown begins from the time that the sacrifices are stopped to the moment the prophesied abomination is set up. What were the sacrifices spoken of? Since the lawful, Old Covenant sacrifices for atonement performed by the priests continued until just a few months prior to the temple's destruction in August AD 70, it is reasonable to conclude that a different sacrifice is the intended subject of the present verse.

By mid-AD 66, the treatment of Jerusalem's citizens under their Roman procurator had become so deplorable that many Jewish zealots were prepared to retaliate in such a manner as to demonstrate a usurpation of Rome's authority. Most likely instituted by Caesar Augustus earlier in the first century, Israel had been committed to a sacrifice of two lambs and a bull, offered twice daily in the temple, in honor of the emperor. [147] It was, therefore, a Gentile sacrifice. That summer, a group of Jewish patriots, led by Eleazar ben Ananias, decided to send a message to Roman leadership about the current state of affairs in the city by abolishing this mandate. In forcing its complete rejection by temple administrators, the message was clear: the Jews wanted their independence. Though Josephus did not provide an exact date of this affair, he considered this cessation to be the "true beginning" of the Jewish-Roman wars that triggered the end-times for Jerusalem. [148]

Of the decision to end the sacrifices, Josephus conveyed that many of the leaders ("men of power") desired to make amends quickly with the Romans for what Eleazar had done so as to avoid a larger war and return to their own practices of sacrifice which would, thus, have been interrupted. [149] But their pleading fell on deaf ears. As they feared for their own safety should the Romans retaliate, they requested combat assistance from other Jewish leaders to come and quell what they perceived as seditious acts by these Jewish patriots. [150] One leader named Agrippa commissioned a militia of 3,000 horsemen to provide such aid.

---

[147] Josephus, *Wars*, 2.195.
[148] Ibid.
[149] Josephus, *Wars*, 2.17.3.
[150] Ibid., 2.17.4

Upon their arrival, great fighting between the two groups commenced and lasted for seven days within the city.[151]

Josephus identified the following eighth day as the festival of Xylophory, a timely tradition in which the Jews brought wood to their alter on the fourteenth day of the fifth Jewish month Av (26 August). The seditious members took advantage of this ritual observance that day and advanced on those who had come to suppress the rebellion, slaughtering many, burning buildings, and destroying important Jewish records.[152] The following day, they attacked local garrisons, slaying more men and wreaking havoc upon numerous defense capabilities.[153]

These dates provide a timeline from which to approximate the day the offerings ceased. The seven days of fighting within the city must be subtracted from the day of the festival (fourteenth day of Av). But one must also consider the time it would have taken for the militia to assemble and travel to the city. One commentator has suggested that a four-to-five-day turnaround on horseback is reasonable considering the remote location of the towns from which the militia came (Auranitis, Batanea, and Trachonitis).[154] Moving backward 11 days, it is reasonable to suggest that the zealots ended the Roman sacrifices around the third day of Av (15/16 August).

With the cessation of the daily sacrifices as the starting point, one might be able to calculate a 1,290-day progression to the placement of the "abomination of desolation." The "abomination of desolation" cited by Jesus in Matthew 24 is defined by Luke as the "armies" that surround Jerusalem to initiate its "desolation" (Luke 21:20). As noted, the Roman army was signified by its emblems and ensigns ("silent") as it came into view. It was no secret that these ensigns were so revered by the Roman soldiers that they would pay regular homage in their encampments, which made these images intolerable pieces of idol worship to the Jews: "For that the laws of their country would not permit them to overlook

---

[151] Ibid., 2.17.5

[152] Ibid., 2.17.6.

[153] Ibid., 2.17.7.

[154] Ibid., 2,17.4. The four-day approximation was suggested by a preterist commentary by Kurt Simmons, "Commentary on Daniel Chapter Twelve: The Great Tribulation and Time of Resurrection." www.preteristcentral.com.

those images which were brought into it, of which there were a great many in their ensigns."[155]

Note that Jesus' purpose in relaying the Olivet prophecy was to ensure that God's remnant had time to leave the city. Josephus stated that Titus' siege began fifteen days prior to his breaking through the outer walls (6 May), which placed it around 22 April, AD 70.[156] However, the "abomination of desolation" is not the *day* of the city's siege – during which it would have been impossible for any citizen to have evacuated – but when the Roman army was beginning to surround the city to prepare for its assault.

Jesus told the disciples (Matt. 24:15-20) that when this became visible, the siege was imminent. Such was the urgency in His instruction that they "not go down to get the things out that are in [their] house, whoever is in the field must not turn back to get his cloak" (Matt. 24:17-18). And this must have been heeded, as many did flee the city, since according to early church father Eusebius, "The people of the church in Jerusalem were commanded by an oracle given by revelation before the war to those in the city who were worthy of it to depart and dwell in one of the cities of Perea which they called Pella."[157]

The question becomes: when was Jerusalem surrounded in this manner for its complete desolation?

Nero had sent General Vespasian to quell the initial rebellion in Jerusalem by early AD 67 and for 2½ years, the latter maintained operational oversight, accumulating regional victories against Jewish upstarts. However, when Nero committed suicide in AD 68, the empire was thrown into chaos, stalling normal military functions, while the affairs of state at home became unstable as numerous men fought over the emperorship. By 21 December, AD 69, after much executive infighting at home, the Roman Senate declared Vespasian emperor.

---

[155] Flavius Josephus. *The Works of Flavius Josephus*. Translated by. William Whiston, A.M. (Auburn and Buffalo. John E. Beardsley. 1895). 18.5.3. https://perseus.tufts.edu.

[156] Ibid., 5.7.2.

[157] Eusebius, *History*, 201 (3.5.3). Eusebius wrote around AD 290, a little over two centuries after the flight. This account is also told by Epiphanius (AD 315-403) and Remigius (AD 437-533) as the centuries followed.

The general was in Alexandria when the news arrived, and with his reign confirmed and established, he finally "turned his thoughts to what remained unsubdued in Judea."[158] Realizing the need to prioritize order in the empire, he thought it best to return to Rome, leaving the objective for his son, Titus.

Josephus recorded the approximate timing of Vespasian's return as when "the winter was now almost over," a seasonal change marking the beginning of spring around mid-late March to early April in the Hebrew Calendar.[159] This would have corresponded with his passing the responsibility of destroying Jerusalem to Titus. Admittedly, the precise day on which Titus incurred this task is purely speculative; however, the spring equinox would have likely occurred by 1 April, AD 70. Titus, probably wasted little time in executing his father's orders against Jerusalem, so it is reasonable to assume that within a month of the end of the traditional "winter season" (late March), preparations were underway to proceed to the city.

To complete his new objective, he had "resolved to set his forces in order at [Caesarea], before he began the war," which was sixty miles west of Jerusalem.[160] But the path from Alexandria was arduous and required some time to depart the city efficiently, make multiple stops to gather supplies, and rest his army at certain intervals. Josephus defined Titus' journey as taking "days," clearly implying that the general was well-organized in the march from Alexandria to Caesarea, likely 400 miles with the short sailing stint he afforded his army during the trip. A well-trained Roman infantry machine marching on constructed roads could cover seventeen-twenty miles per day, probably having reached Caesarea in roughly three weeks around the first few days of April AD 70.

A basic march from Caesarea to Jerusalem would have taken three-four days. When Titus began his journey, he sent ahead auxiliaries who would clear the path for the facilitation of encampments – including baggage and measuring the required space – to ensure an efficient arrival of soldiers and provisions for the 40,000-50,000-unit force. Josephus also articulated a short period of encampment in the days and

---

[158] Ibid., 4.656.
[159] Ibid.
[160] Ibid., 5.1.

weeks prior to Passover AD 70 (14 April), confirming that the defenders of Jerusalem could see to their "astonishment the Romans pitching three separate camps."[161] During this preparation time, Titus placed his legions within a mile of Jerusalem, in locations like "Seopus; from whence the city began already to be seen, and a plain view might be taken of the great temple," also ordering encampments at the Mount of Olives, reinforcing them and fortifying his positions around the city to withstand any Jewish counteroffensives since the fighting had already begun.[162]

Sacrifices ceased –> 43 months, 21 days –> Titus' armies encamp around Jerusalem.

15 August, AD 66 –> 1,290 days –> 6 April, AD 70.[163]

There is an additional time period in this section of 1,335 days. The verse indicates the expectation of blessing for those who would reach whatever event occurred at the end of this stretch. This author believes these two time periods are distinct yet do not overlap. Any citizen of Jerusalem would certainly have been humbled to have survived what happened at the city, included Christians who had already escaped Jerusalem and relocated far enough from the combat. But even the Jews who were dispersed among the surrounding locales after the city was sacked counted their lives in accordance with God's promise that, as His chosen people, they would never be annihilated. To have survived this episode in human history – during which the God of heaven sanctioned the most powerful empire in antiquity to drop the weight of its notorious strength upon His own people – would have been astonishing and certainly considered a blessing.

After Jerusalem was sacked on 4/5 September, AD 70, the remaining Jewish rebels fled to a Jewish fortification in southern Israel

---

[161] Ibid., 5.2.4

[162] Ibid., 5.67.

[163] The Hebrew calendar was based on lunar calculation. There were 29.5 days in one calendar month. Thus, the calculation for 1,290 days: 42 months of 29.5 days = 1,239 days + 1 leap year month = 30 days for a total of 1,269 days arrives at 15 March, AD 70. The 21 remaining days to tally 1,290 with a half a day variance based on how the Hebrew calendar started and ended a "day" arrives at 6 April, AD 70. For the timeline of Titus' arrival to Caesarea in the first week of April, see also Thomas Lewin's *The Siege of Jerusalem*, p. 13.

called Masada. This included women and children in flight from the devastation of the city. Though Jerusalem's fall had finalized the defeat of the fiercest elements of the rebellion, Rome knew that this small number of insurgents had persisted. Hoping to bring the war to its conclusion, Roman forces tracked them down and eventually surrounded the Masada stronghold. Though Josephus did not provide the year of its collapse in his *Wars*, there is credible evidence to suggest that the assault occurred in AD 74.[164] He did note that it occurred on the day of the Passover, the fifteenth day of *Nisan* (11 April that year) and "when Masada was thus taken...there were now no enemies left in the country."[165] With this defeat, the war was over.

Counting 1,335 days backward from Masada's fall brings the reader to 6 August, AD 70. What might have been the event that occurred to mark this date? Titus' armies set fire to the temple. It was the destruction of the temple – Israel's exclusive method for fulfilling her covenant oath to God through physical atonement – that Jesus had made the center of His Olivet Discourse. At this moment, the system from which their only power was derived was no longer accessible, and the Jewish institution collapsed. Israel's hostility had brought an end to everything that defined its identity, and her citizens were left with no way to continue any remainder of the Covenant that they had already willingly broken. Thus, the Old Covenant became obsolete (Heb. 8:13), and the path to this completion was unlike anything the nation had ever experienced.

Temple is burned to the ground –> 45 months, 6 days –> Masada is destroyed, ending the war.

5/6 August, AD 70 –> 1,335 days –> 11/12 April, AD 74. [166]

---

[164] See Steve Mason's *A History of the Jewish War: AD 66-74*, (New York: Cambridge University Press, 2016) pp. 561-575.

[165] Josephus, *Wars*, 7.10.1.

[166] The calculation for 1,335 days: 43 months of 29.5 days = 1,268.5 days + 2 leap year months = 60 days for a total of 1,328.5 days arrives at 11/12 August, AD 70. The six remaining days to tally 1,334.5 – with a half a day variance based on how the Hebrew calendar started and ended a "day" – arrives at August 5/6 AD 70.

To have survived until the end of such an ordeal – reaching the end of the war with one's life intact – would have, certainly, been a blessing.

Verse 13

"'But as for you, go your way to the end; then you will enter into rest and rise again for your allotted portion at the end of the age.'"

At the time that the prophecy would be fulfilled, Daniel would be resurrected to receive his reward. This would be at Israel's future consummation event as the present chapter describes. Recall that the kingdom that God promised to be set up during the Roman Empire would have no end (Dan. 2 & 7), meaning the age explicitly prescribed to end was the Judaic age.

DANIEL CONCLUSION

Dr. Michael Heiser has noted that modern readers have "been trained to think that the History of Christianity is the true context of the Bible."[167] Many forget that Jesus of Nazareth never intended to start a new religion; His first ministry, as a Jew, was to Israel (Matt. 15:24). Christianity was an off-shoot of the Jewish faith, part of the original root. Yet Christians exhibit the tendency to give their dispositions supremacy by reading the Bible as though God intended every verse in both testaments to have some application exclusively for them and their present circumstances.

Reading the Bible within the appropriate context of each book – setting, author, and time – is essential to acquiring an accurate interpretation. One must consider how NT writers utilized OT terms and phrases within their contexts. Though the NT does break from Rabbinic orthodoxy, most of its theology is entrenched in the Hebrew Bible and if one diligently, and honestly, seeks to understand God's Word, one must reconcile such passages with their corresponding references in the OT. Indeed, the Bible is a primarily Jewish narrative.

The Old and New Testaments complement one another in God's story of redemption for all men, whom He used Israel to draw back to Himself. Israel was to be His "own possession" (Deut. 7:6) because of His promise to Abraham (Gen. 12:2) and through them "all the families of the earth will be blessed" (Gen. 12:3). As God prepared Moses to direct the Israelites after their departure from Egypt, He explained that they would become distinct within His grand purposes: "Now then, if

---

[167] Heiser, *The Unseen Realm.*

you will indeed obey My voice and keep My covenant, then you shall be My own possession among all the peoples, for all the earth is Mine; and you shall be to Me a kingdom of priests and a holy nation'" (Ex. 19:5-6). Israel would be God's "servant" (Is. 41:8-9) who should act as a "light to the nations" (Is. 42:7) so that "all the peoples of the earth may know [His] name" (I Kings 8:43), "all the ends of the earth will remember and turn to the Lord" (Ps. 22:27), and His "salvation may reach to the end of the earth" (Is. 49:6).

God made Israel an illustration for the rest of the world to understand what redemption, obedience, and covenant relationship with Him looked like. But a failure to properly uphold this responsibility would have devastating consequences, the like of which are prevalent throughout Israel's history. Their violation of Old Covenant mandates for honoring the Promised Land, for example, resulted in not only their exile but captivity under a pagan empire for seven decades. Despite this punishment, God promised their survival and restoration: "'For I know the plans that I have for you' declares the Lord, 'plans for welfare and not for calamity to give you a future and a hope'" (Jer. 29:11). In Israel's despair, God assured His people that their future was intact.

Did you catch the context of that verse, Christian? This promise in Jeremiah – engraved onto expensive plaques that adorn the entryway of countless Christian homes and is frequently interpreted as a universal promise of financial prosperity for all those who follow God – was for *Israel* at a time when they faced conceivable ethnic annihilation. He would not allow such a result.

Over the centuries, Israel floundered in its idolatry, spiritual fornication, and disregard of covenant laws despite God's mercy and renewal. Leadership murdered the prophets that God established among them, blood for which the nation would atone as part of the curse that Jesus laid upon His first-century generation: "upon you may fall the guilt of all the righteous blood shed on earth, from the blood of righteous Abel to the blood of Zechariah, the son of Berechiah, whom you murdered between the temple and the alter" (Matt. 23:35). Those who betrayed the covenant relationship would be held in contempt; those who had exhibited fidelity would be given glory at a culminating time of simultaneous judgment and salvation.

Indeed, the first century witnessed the arrival of Israel's harvester (Luke 3:17) who would oversee the process of Israel's purification. This promise had been laid out by Daniel: "Now at that time Michael, the great prince who stands guard over the sons of your people, will arise. And there will be a time of great distress such as never occurred since there was a nation until that time; and at that time your people, everyone who is written in the book will be rescued. Many of those who sleep in the dust of the ground will awake, these to everlasting life, but the other to disgrace and everlasting contempt" (Dan. 12:1-2). Read these two verses. Who is Daniel talking about? Israel.

The Archangel Michael was Israel's exclusive guardian. His interjection into the circumstance would be necessary because of an event that was transpiring against the people over whom He was responsible. Likewise, the angel assigned to give the vision in the book was also speaking *to* Daniel, a Jew. This means that "your people" is Daniel's brethren – Israel. Thus, the corporate tribulation, resurrection, and harvest listed are contextually linked to Israel at an appointed time in history; the same time when their "power" as God's people was shattered (Dan. 12:7).

With the arrival of Jesus of Nazareth, suddenly, warnings of Daniel's appointed time begin pouring out onto Israel's first-century generation. Jesus advised: "Do not marvel at this; for an hour is coming, in which all who are in the tombs will hear His voice, and will come forth; those who did the good deeds to a resurrection of life, those who committed the evil deeds to a resurrection of judgment" (John 5:28-29). Paul cautioned councils that "believing everything that is in accordance with the Law and that is written in the Prophets; having a hope in God, which these men cherish themselves, that there [is about to] be a resurrection of both the righteous and the wicked" (Acts 24:15). As the time drew closer, Peter addressed how the pagan world still beckoned for lusts and comparatively affirmed that "they are surprised that you do not run with them into the same excesses of dissipation, and they malign you; but they will give account to Him who is ready to judge the living and the dead" (I Peter 4:4-5).

Daniel's resurrection of the just and unjust – an event surrounding Israel – was being affirmed by the Savior and his disciples to prepare their nation for a final purification. This would be Israel's long-awaited fulfillments of atonement and blessing that must begin with them but, once completed, would establish a new system that extended to the nations of the world. But it had to occur in sequence as there would be "tribulation and distress for every soul of man who does evil, of the Jew first and also of the Greek, but glory and honor and peace to everyone who does good, to the Jew first and also to the Greek" (Rom. 2:9-10).

This was accomplished by Jesus of Nazareth as Paul declared: "Christ redeemed *us* from the curse of the Law, having become a curse for us – for it is written, 'Cursed is everyone who hangs on a tree' – in order that in Christ Jesus the blessing of Abraham might come to the *Gentiles*" (Gal. 3:13-14, emphasis mine). God's original promise had endured (Gen. 12:2-3) as, indeed, salvation came from the Jews (John 4:22).

The roots of Christianity are deeply embedded in Jewish history. After all, Jesus consistently called upon the ancient scriptures during His public ministry, Paul developed most of his teaching knowledge from ancient Jewish doctrine – having learned from Rabbi Gamaliel and "strictly according to the law of our fathers" (Acts 22:3) – and around half of John's Revelation is taken from OT language and imagery. Thus, the Christian student needs to examine the Hebrew Bible thoroughly, especially if making "end-times" hope an integral constituent of their faith. However, if we ignore appropriate parameters of hermeneutics, we risk creating our own narrative. And since the church considers Daniel's eschatological components to be the book's primary theological thrust, it must be read carefully. One of the most interesting trends in evangelical behavior is the propensity for linking contemporary events with perceived eschatological bible verses. Indeed, it does seem that every United States president is perceived as the possible Antichrist in fundamentalist circles, a designation inevitably accompanied by some form of public demonization.

Such a characterization goes back even to Franklin D. Roosevelt, whom due to his liberal spending agenda for strengthening social welfare, thereby increasing the federal government's role in American society, 1930's fundamentalists had labeled as the Antichrist based on the character's biblical classification as an authoritarian who would gain power through the false promise of security. As one scholar noted, "Roosevelt's efforts to expand the power of the federal government and his internationalist inclinations seemed to parallel fundamentalists' end-times fears about the rise of totalitarian states and world rule by a Satan-inspired dictator."[168] It did not help FDR that he received 666 votes on the first set of ballots at the 1932 Democratic Convention.[169] It was hardly difficult for evangelical leaders to convince church congregants that a vote for FDR was a vote for the Antichrist. And the frequency of such a condemnatory label has only increased with the rise of social media, as modern presidents like Barak Obama and Donald Trump have been similarly vilified.

But why should evangelicals limit their scope to US politics? In 1932, two prominent American missionaries, Ralph and Edith Norton, toured Europe to assess the religious state of several of its countries. They eventually arrived in Italy where they had the unique opportunity to interview Benito Mussolini, the nation's famous Prime Minister who fought alongside Hitler's and his Nazi party in Germany during World War II. In their evangelical religious studies, the Nortons came to believe that the books of Daniel and Revelation predicted a future ten-nation confederacy – through which the Antichrist would exert global authority – that would be led by a resurrected Roman Empire (Dan. 2:31-35, 7:7-8, Rev. 13:1-2). In this interview, within the decade before World War II commenced, they asked Mussolini, "Do you intend to reconstitute the Roman Empire?"

As they proceeded to explain their understanding of biblical prophecy, Mussolini displayed surprise at their assertion, inquiring as to where the Bible made such a prediction. And "in one of the great ironies of fundamentalist history, by the time the Nortons had finished with Mussolini, he apparently believed – and maybe even hoped – that he was the long-awaited world dictator, the antichrist, prophesied in the

---

[168] Matthew Avery Sutton, "Was FDR the Antichrist? The Birth of Fundamentalist Antiliberalism in a Global Age." The Journal of American History, Vol. 98, No. 4 March 2012, p. 1052.

[169] Sutton, p. 1061.

book of Daniel."[170] What long-term effects did this have on the prime minister? We do not know. What we do know is that in the coming years he allied his nation with a political entity that would become responsible for the largest Jewish genocide in world history.

What good did these Christian evangelists accomplish through their missionary work in so manipulating a world leader's phycological senses that by the end of their meeting he should hope to fulfill one man's destined role as God's last archenemy whose subsequent political decisions and actions could bring about the end of the world? After all, many in the contemporary evangelical church are convinced that the worse things become, the more imminent the end must be. Did the Nortons think they could speed up the eschatological clock by persuading a biblically ignorant Mussolini of his role in a demonic takeover of the world to initiate Jesus' Return?

The universe is not ours to command.

What about this figure known as the future Antichrist? Not once is that name mentioned in the book of Revelation, though evangelical scholars insist his presence as one of the "beasts" revealed therein. He cannot be the "abomination of desolation" of Jesus' Olivet Discourse because Luke told us that this was the first-century Roman army that surrounded Jerusalem to bring its destruction (Luke 21:22). And if Jesus confirmed this identification (Matthew 24:15), then the reference in Daniel to the one who makes a seven-year covenant is also ruled out (Dan. 9:26-27). Likewise, he cannot be Paul's "man of lawlessness" cited in the second letter to the Thessalonians (2:2-12) because the language clearly indicated that the person to whom he was referring was alive at the time the letter was penned (AD 51).

The only places in which the word "antichrist" is present are in John's first and second epistles. His first gives a corporate definition of the term: "Who is the liar who denies that Jesus is the Christ? This is the antichrist, the one who denies the Father and the Son" (I John 2:22), while clarifying that the designation belongs to "those who do not acknowledge Jesus Christ as coming in the flesh. This is the

---

[170] Sutton, p. 1059. The reference was from Ralph Norton and Edith Norton, "A Personal Interview with Benito Mussolini," *Sunday School Times*, Aug 13, 1932, p. 423.

deceiver and the antichrist" (II John 1:7). John also utilizes this label in the plural form, applied to anyone who would deny the incarnation of Jesus as the Messiah, not one individual figure who would embody all evil. He likewise reminded them that by the time of his writing "many antichrists have appeared" (I John 2:18), and are "already in the world" (I John 4:3).

It should be clear that there are no linguistic or contextual connections between John's explicit descriptions of an "antichrist" to the other titles listed in the scriptures previously referenced found throughout the Bible. These links have been created by a church obsessed with deciphering hidden codes for future events. And using prophecies from Daniel to convince an unbeliever, such as the Nortons did with Mussolini, that he might be the most frightening, hated, and doomed figure in existence – based on misconstrued eschatological hopes – is misguided and potentially dangerous.

Daniel offers an astonishing narrative of world history which stands as unparalleled proof of the Bible's authenticity and reliability. Its contents can affect any number of religious or secular disciplines. For the simple historian, the narrative of Chapter 11 is so precise that it has forced scholars to argue that such accuracy must be the result of eyewitness testimony. Daniel's history provided information that was omitted by official Babylonian documents but later revealed to be correct by additional archaeological discoveries, such as the truth about the character of Belshazzar, the last king of Babylon. Daniel provided figurative descriptions of kingdoms that matched their historical characteristics, successfully predicting the state of world dominion for over half a millennium. His ninth chapter gave an accurate forecast of the destruction of Jerusalem and its temple, which occurred in AD 70, a fact that critics of predictive prophecy cannot reconcile even in their attempt to disprove the book's validity by baselessly altering its date of composition.

For the Christian apologist, Daniel predicted the four empires that would maintain successive dominion over the Jews (Babylon, Medo-Persian, Greek, Roman), that God's kingdom would be setup sometime during the Roman Empire (which Jesus confirmed upon his arrival), the year that the Messiah would be introduced (AD 26), and that He would be killed after 3½ years into this messianic advent (AD 30). The prophetic discourse in Chapter 9 stands as the only explicit reference to the Jewish Messiah's death in the OT.

The invaluable lessons gleaned from the book are innumerable. All the earth's inhabitants are nothing when compared to the great God of Israel, and without Him no one is able to accomplish anything. No one can interfere with Him. He will humiliate those who choose pride. God will make examples of peoples and nations with the express purpose of making His name great and demonstrating His ultimate power and sovereignty. When man exhibits arrogance, he may experience the wrath of God. We worship Him for Who He is – the Creator of all things Who has no rival. Everything a man has is because of either God's gracious nature or His incomparable will, and to neglect bestowing honor upon Him for such mercy and compassion will surely garner just reprimand from His glorious character.

Even the story of Shadrach, Meshach, and Abed-nego, which is popular among children's ministries, carries great significance in the Christian's personal faith. These men demonstrated the defining characteristics of the true follower of God and stand as antithetical to modern Christian optimism that God is a genie in a bottle whose existence is based on serving and blessing the desires of the human race. They swore devotion to a God Who may – or may not – save them from death and epitomized the paragon of belief in the Old Covenant relationship. This should be an example for the Christian standard.

Did Daniel give us the most profound OT messianic prophecy? It was revealed to him that the progression for Israel's reconciliation with God was given 490 years for completion upon a decree to re-establish Jerusalem after the Babylonian captivity (Dan. 9:24-27). Since the Israelites could not accomplish salvation of their own accord, God was required to intervene. What He would make available had the power to "make an end to sin," usher in "everlasting righteousness," and fulfill Old Testament prophecy ("seal up vision and prophecy"). The only source of this redemption, which completely removed the power of sin and established universal righteousness – in both Jewish and Christian theology – is the promised Messiah (II Cor. 5:21). This 490-year time period began in 458/457 BC when Artaxerxes of Persia commanded ("issuing of a decree") the support and restoration of the structures and administration of Israel's promised holy site ("rebuild Jerusalem...with plaza and moat, even in times of distress").

Then, 483 years later ("seven weeks and sixty-two weeks"), in AD 26, Jesus of Nazareth was anointed to begin His public ministry decidedly, yet subtly, identifying as Israel's Messiah ("Messiah the Prince"). His advent initiated an agreement ("firm covenant") with the people to whom he was ministering ("the many"), refining an old covenant with a stronger version that promised the required compensation for iniquity and completing the process of redemption, the final forgiveness of sins. After 3½ years, the length of Jesus' public ministry ("middle of the week"), He endured a violent death ("cut-off"), gave Himself for His people ("have nothing"), and represented the final sacrifice that brought all others to end ("put a stop to sacrifice"). This violence of His death would signify a new covenant through the cutting of His flesh and shedding of His blood. Despite Jesus' ("Messiah") arrival, Israel ("people of the prince") rejected Him as the Redeemer and later desecrated its own Temple by slaughtering their Jewish priests in AD 66 ("wing of abomination"). This travesty invited repeated judgment as God permitted Jerusalem ("holy city and sanctuary") to be completely destroyed at the hands of a massive army of Roman mercenaries ("flood") led by a foreign ruler, Titus Vespansian ("one who makes desolate"), under whom the desolations would continue until fulfilled ("a complete destruction") against Israel ("desolate").

The most intriguing element about Daniel's prophetic account, however, is found in its culmination at the appointed time, a reality that the angel had commanded remain sealed until that moment (Dan. 12:4).

This feature in Daniel is a unique contradistinction to another significant and extensive biblical prophecy – Revelation. John's NT Revelation was his vision written to seven churches in Asia Minor as encouragement toward their welfare within the anticipation of a rapidly approaching fierce judgment. In closing the vision, Jesus commanded that John "not seal up the words of the prophecy of this book for the time is near" (Rev. 22:10). Futurist scholars have adjusted the meaning of words like "near," "soon," "shortly," "at hand," and "quickly" throughout the NT to justify the fact that 2,000 years have passed since the prophecy was given, leaving Christians in a state of waiting for yet future events.

These scholars apply biblical axioms like to "the Lord one day is like a thousand years, and a thousand years like one day" (II Pet. 3:8), creating a transcendent meaning outside of man's understanding and compounding the notion by reminding the eager listener that God's "thoughts are not [our] thoughts, nor are [our] ways [His] ways" (Is. 55:8). To these thinkers, such terms must coincide with intervals of divine measurement. As such, these words represent an unlimited breadth of time rather than their simple meaning as provided by the most respected Greek concordances as "without any delay."

One avid futurist scholar, John Walvoord, has given an interpretation that greatly stretches the meaning of these terms. For example, he posits that "the expression 'at hand' indicates nearness from the standpoint of prophetic revelation, not necessarily that the event will immediately occur."[171] Within such an interpretation, the emphasis is on the sudden nature of the events when they do occur rather than the specific time of their manifestation. However, as Gary Demar has pointed out, Walvoord's connotation does not hold up when applied to "passages that contain the same time indicators [ex. Matt. 24:32, 26:18, John 2:13 7:2]" in other verses.[172]

One of the major challenges in trying to confront an uncompromising futurist is that the future cannot be tested. This inability to verify makes all future theories pliable and modifiable to the diversity of Christian interpretation, in turn, making the simplest terms become elastic and transmutable. Regarding these terms in Revelation, however, Dr. Kenneth Gentry notes that "a cursory reading of the passages before us unavoidably leads even the casual reader to conclude that John expected the fulfillment of prophecies with a very short period of time following his writing."[173] With this basic understanding in mind, the

---

[171] John Walvoord, *The Revelation of Jesus Christ*, (Chicago, IL: Moody Press, [1966] 1987), p. 37.

[172] Gary DeMar, *Last Days Madness*, (Powder Springs, GA: American Vision, [1999] 2019), p. 383-384.

[173] Kenneth Gentry, *Before Jerusalem Fell: Dating the Book of Revelation*, (San Francisco, CA: Christian University Press [1989] 1997), p. 134.

reason that Jesus did not want the vision sealed was because the events foretold were going to happen in short order. The churches to whom John's letter were addressed, thus, needed to hear the message so they could be prepared.[174]

When the time for Israel's judgment was upon them – as Malachi had prophesied, John the Baptist had warned, and Jesus prepared to make manifest – thereby initiating the establishment of the kingdom of God (Dan. 2 & 7), Jesus began to make direct connections between His warning about Jerusalem in the Olivet Discourse and the book of Daniel, drawing directly from the latter's language, expression, and prophecy. And for the same purpose as the message in Revelation; because the time was near. The Jewish prophet has predicted judgment upon Israel and Jesus confirmed that its arrival was imminent. The tribulation (Dan. 12:1), the resurrection, and harvest (Dan. 12:2) were foretold for Israel at the moment that their "power" was shattered (Dan. 12:7). There is only one moment in history that could have accomplished this fulfillment – the destruction of Jerusalem in AD 70.

This prophecy on the Mount of Olives might be the most significant chapter in the NT for encapsulating the breadth of OT fulfillment, especially since Luke reminded his readers that this was the event when "all things which are written must be fulfilled" (Luke 21:22). If this prophecy is interpreted from a preterist position, then its fulfillment stands as one of the most important proofs of Jesus' Messiahship. As long as one's interpretation remains futuristic, atheists have grounds to call Him a liar and a false prophet.

One simply cannot deny the historical nature of Daniel's narrative. From the time of the first beast, the Babylonian Empire, through the centuries of pagan dominion under the Persians, Greeks, and

---

[174] The inevitable conclusion from my statement is that the book of Revelation is not describing a future series of events but is following a historical narrative in the first century. This chronicle is figuratively narrating the destruction of Jerusalem in AD 70. The hypothesis is fully supported by the fact there is more evidence that the book was written prior to AD 70 rather than the traditional date of AD 90-95 as established by the evangelical church-at-large. For further evidence, see Dr. Kenneth Gentry's *Before Jerusalem Fell: Dating the Book of Revelation.*

Romans, to the transitions between empires as depicted by the people, wars, and even marriages that would identify the eras, and into the appointed time of the end, the book tells God's narrative in unique and meticulous detail. Will any commentator be able to identify every character accurately without question? Never; we are but fallible people. However, the parameters of history allow believers to draw reasonable conclusions that aid in our search to make evident the truths of God's Word.

Indeed, even Jesus charged those listening to His instruction; "If I do not do the works of My Father, do not believe me" (John 10:37). This direction poses a clear inference that if what He promised did not come to pass – things verified through judicious evaluation – *they should not follow Him*. Because Christians are taught that "without faith, it is impossible to please Him" (Heb. 11:6), many feel like they are exhibiting fateful doubt in God's Word when they pose inquiries that outwardly challenge church creed. When digging deeply into questions that have complicated or unclear answers, many believe they are questioning God and thereby exhibiting a lack of trust. But God did not give His Word to sit idle, and it certainly does not come back void (Is. 55:11). He is telling the consummate story of redemption, and He desires that it be seen in its glory and perfection.

This is the testament upon which Daniel stands.

Why does the futurist – who holds a view that, by its nature, is unprovable – dismiss the preterist perspective with such fervor, when it is the latter who can verify the facts that the greatest objectors use to dismiss Christianity's truth? God's Word is proven in history in that what He promised came to pass, which should confirm the believer's hope that He is Who He said He is – the very notion that Jesus commanded people to deny if left unsubstantiated.

Such is part of the lifelong process of building one's faith. God's followers are to test themselves (II Cor. 13:5), test the scriptures (Acts 17:11), test the spirits (I John 4:1), and let iron sharpen iron (Prov. 27:17), thus preparing them to give an answer for that which they believe (I Peter 3:15). The ancient Israelites were expected to "listen to the statutes and the judgments...so that [they, the Israelites] may live"

(Deut. 4:1). Christians are likewise instructed to show love to God by "keep[ing] His commandments" (I John 5:3) and to use "the sacred writings which are able to give you the wisdom that leads to salvation through faith which is in Jesus Christ" (II Tim. 3:15).

Learn of them and your faith will be immovable.

CHRISTIAN ESCHATOLOGICAL TERMINOLOGY

―――――――――

<u>Abomination of Desolation</u> – a term cited three times in Daniel (9:27, 11:31, 12:31) to which Jesus referred in the Olivet Discourse (Matt. 24:15). Futurists interpret this phrase to be a reference to the defilement of a yet future rebuilt Jewish temple (Israel's third in history), which must occur before Jesus' Second Coming. However, its meaning is found in Luke 21.20, the corresponding narrative to Matthew's description of the Discourse, "But when you see Jerusalem surrounded by armies then recognize that her desolation is near." This term refers directly to the consequences of the Roman army's assault on the city and destruction of the temple in AD 70.

<u>Antichrist</u> – According to futurists the ultimate enemy of Jesus Christ who will reign over the earth during the last days of judgment prior to Jesus' Second Coming. He will be the embodiment of evil who will present peace to Israel, and the world, during time of trouble, but eventually issue tyrannical political and religious control to usurp God's plans for saving mankind. According to evangelicals, he will sit in the future, third temple and be responsible for its desecration. However, the term "Antichrist" is found only in I and II John described as a group that opposes Jesus Christ and is present during John's lifetime.

<u>Day of the Lord</u> – a historical Hebrew phrase describing a period of divinely inspired judgment that conclusively defeated rebellious nations or cities. The term does not refer to one singular event in the course

of human existence, but is a progressive model for demonstrating God's wrath against His enemies. It is consistently labeled in the New Testament as coming like a "thief:" Matt. 24:43, I Thess. 5:2, II Pet. 3:10, Rev. 16:15.

Dispensationalism – a system of theology emphasizing the notion that Israel and the Church are completely distinct entities, with separate purposes, each going on their own unique course through history into eternity. It provides the theological basis for the pre-tribulation rapture in that God cannot deal with Israel and the Church together on earth, therefore the latter must be removed for the Jews to be saved in the "last days." The basic theological error with this hermeneutic is the stipulation that there are separate peoples of God that have separate hopes. One will not find this teaching in the theological literature of church history because historic Christian theology understood the Church to be the continuation of God's one program of redemption that began with Israel.

Eschatology – is a study of the "last things," developed in Western theology to examine common elements relating to the end of history. This would include concepts such as the destination of the soul, resurrection, and the fate of the earth.

Great Tribulation – a phrase found in Matthew 24:21 and Revelation 7:14 that futurists believe will be a seven-year period of unprecedented earthly trial and devastation, primarily intended for the Jews, but ultimately reaching all the nations of the earth. Evangelicals believe that this will be God's final attempt to deal with Israel. It will occur after the rapture of the church, but prior to Jesus' Second Coming. In actuality, it is Jesus' warning to first-century Israel of the consequence of Rome's attack on Jerusalem in AD 70, when the temple was destroyed. God's divine judgment would come upon them, and the only recourse was for the remnant to flee the city before they experienced its horrors.

Preterism – a hermeneutic that teaches the past fulfillment of biblical prophecies. It is a plain method of understanding that employs a literal and figurative reading based on what the context requires. The primary foundation for its historical interpretation is the sequence of events surrounding the destruction of Jerusalem in AD 70.

<u>Rapture</u> – an eschatological triggering event in which all believers will be secretly and safely removed from earth prior to God's ordained "end times" tribulation and wrath, leaving all others behind, and taken to heaven where they will wait until Jesus Returns. The primary roots for its theology come from Paul's first letter to the Thessalonians where he describes that followers of Jesus will be "caught up" (Greek "harpazo") to meet Him someday.

Printed in the United States
by Baker & Taylor Publisher Services